MW00718812

Rural Migration
in Developing Nations

Westview Replica Editions

The concept of Westview Replica Editions is a response to the continuing crisis in academic and informational publishing. Library budgets for books have been severely curtailed. Ever larger portions of general library budgets are being diverted from the purchase of books and used for data banks, computers, micromedia, and other methods of information retrieval. Interlibrary loan structures further reduce the edition sizes required to satisfy the needs of the scholarly community. Economic pressures on the university presses and the few private scholarly publishing companies have severely limited the capacity of the industry to properly serve the academic and research communities. As a result, many manuscripts dealing with important subjects, often representing the highest level of scholarship, are no longer economically viable publishing projects--or, if accepted for publication, are typically subject to lead times ranging from one to three years.

Westview Replica Editions are our practical solution to the problem. We accept a manuscript in camera-ready form, typed according to our specifications, and move it immediately into the production process. As always, the selection criteria include the importance of the subject, the work's contribution to scholarship, and its insight, originality of thought, and excellence of exposition. The responsibility for editing and proofreading lies with the author or sponsoring institution. We prepare chapter headings and display pages, file for copyright, and obtain Library of Congress Cataloging in Publication Data. A detailed manual contains simple instructions for preparing the final typescript, and our editorial staff is always available to answer questions.

The end result is a book printed on acid-free paper and bound in sturdy library-quality soft covers. We manufacture these books ourselves using equipment that does not require a lengthy make-ready process and that allows us to publish first editions of 300 to 600 copies and to reprint even smaller quantities as needed. Thus, we can produce Replica Editions quickly and can keep even very specialized books in print as long as there is a demand for them.

About the Book and Editor

Rural Migration in Developing Nations:
Comparative Studies of Korea, Sri Lanka, and Mali
edited by Calvin Goldscheider

What is the relationship between migration and rural social structure? How does the selective movement out of rural areas affect the economic and social conditions of migrants, their families, and their places of origin? Addressing these and other questions, the contributors to this book consider rural migration patterns in the context of social change and economic development in three less developed nations: Korea, Sri Lanka, and Mali. Through comparative analysis the authors reveal both the diversity and the cross-national similarities of rural migration, offering theoretical bases for its interpretation and pointing to policy implications for developing areas.

Calvin Goldscheider is affiliated with the Population Studies and Training Center and is adjunct professor of sociology at Brown University. Dr. Goldscheider is the editor of *Rural Migrants in Developing Nations: Patterns and Problems of Adjustment* (Westview, 1983).

Published in cooperation with
The Population Studies and Training Center,
Brown University

Rural Migration in Developing Nations
Comparative Studies of Korea, Sri Lanka, and Mali

edited by Calvin Goldscheider

with contributions by
Dayalal S. D. J. Abeysekera
Jin Ho Choi
Calvin Goldscheider
Robert E. Mazur

and Foreword by
Sidney Goldstein

Routledge
Taylor & Francis Group

LONDON AND NEW YORK

First published 1984 by Westview Press

Published 2019 by Routledge
52 Vanderbilt Avenue, New York, NY 10017
2 Park Square, Milton Park, Abingdon, Oxon OX14 4RN

*Routledge is an imprint of the Taylor & Francis Group,
an informa business*

Library of Congress Cataloging in Publication Data
Main entry under title:
Rural migration in developing nations.
    (A Westview replica edition)
    1. Rural-urban migration--Developing countries. 2. Urban-rural
migration--Developing countries. 3. Developing countries--Rural conditions.
I. Goldscheider, Calvin
HB1955.R87   1984   304.8'09172'4   84-2269

ISBN 13: 978-0-367-28635-4 (hbk)

To
Robert G. Burnight
Kurt B. Mayer
Vincent H. Whitney

Contents

Tables

Foreword

Reflecting the major attention given by Brown University's Population Studies and Training Center to problems of population movement and urbanization in developing countries, the Center initiated a Comparative Urbanization Project in 1972-73. Funded by a Ford Foundation Grant to the Center, the first objective was to pursue research on questions associated with urbanization, migration, and development in less developed nations.

The program sponsored a non-credit seminar in which an average of 12 trainees participated each year. This seminar served several purposes. First, its discussions identified research interests common to both the faculty and the student seminar participants. Growing out of the interest in the adjustment of rural-to-urban migrants, the seminar developed a set of core questions and sampling designs for use in field surveys in developing countries. It was expected that a small number of the trainees participating in the seminar would, in fact, undertake such field studies, focusing on the adjustment of migrants to big cities in less developed nations. The studies were intended to give the individual trainee experience in field work and to provide the trainee with data for a dissertation. Moreover, a body of comparative data would be compiled whose analysis would allow better insights into what demographic characteristics distinguish migrants from non-migrants, whether these characteristics affect adjustment in the urban area, and what implications the adjustment process has for the urban areas in which the migrants take up residence.

Under the Ford Foundation Grant, the Center funded four trainees during 1973-1977 to undertake field surveys as the basis for their doctoral dissertations. The field operations, encompassing approximately 750 households in each location, were completed in Seoul, Korea; Surabaya, Indonesia; Bogota, Colombia; and Tehran, Iran. These four projects provided the core studies of the first monograph in this series, *Urban Migrants in Developing Nations: Patterns and Problems of Adjustment.*

Fuller understanding of the relations between migration and urbanization, however, requires attention to assessing migration from the perspective of the rural origins of migrants to cities, as well as an urban perspective. It is important to gain insights on who out-migrates and why, as well as on who stays; to study the large movement that occurs in many countries between rural places; and to assess the return migration from cities that is a common experience of many rural to urban migrants. Growing out of this recognition, the two field studies initiated during 1977-78 in the Comparative Urbanization Project focused on rural areas. One was conducted in southern Korea with independent support from the Ford-Rockefeller Program; it involved surveys in three rural locations covering the determinants and consequences of urban to rural return migration. The second study, undertaken in Sri Lanka, was an assessment of rural resettlement programs; sample surveys, conducted in both the dry zones of destination and the wet zones of origin, allowed assessment of the adjustment of migrants and the impact which their out-migration had on the place of origin. A third project, utilizing data collected in Mali by the Department of Agricultural Economics at Purdue University under sponsorship of USAID, focused on interrelations between rural socioeconomic structure and migration; particular attention was given to factors affecting labor allocation. Again, each of these studies constituted the investigator's doctoral dissertation. These three rural-focused studies now provide the basis for this second monograph emanating from the Comparative Urbanization Project.

The authors of the individual studies and I and my colleagues in the Population Studies and Training Center are grateful to Dr. Calvin Goldscheider for the efforts he has devoted in both the volume on urban migrants and in this monograph to summarizing the individual studies and especially to assessing them comparatively. The rich insights he has drawn from these studies about the relations among migration, urbanization, rural development, and modernization document the value of comparative analysis; moreover, they constitute important contributions to our understanding of the theoretical and policy issues associated with population redistribution.

Since completion of the three rural-focused studies, four studies have again been organized in urban locations. A study in Semerang, Indonesia, focuses on the determinants and patterns of occupational change in relation to migration, with special attention to circular migrants in the city. The study in Accra, Ghana, investigates the modernization of health attitudes and its effects on infant mortality and fertility. The third study, in Juba, Sudan, concentrates on interrelations between female migration and labor utilization. The latter two have been completed, and the first of this latest round of urban studies is near completion at the time this monograph is being submitted for publication. The fourth study, about to be undertaken, will focus on the impact of ethnicity on migrant adjustment through a comparative assessment of migrants from different ethnic areas to Port Harcourt, Nigeria.

In addition to these urban-oriented studies, a new rural-oriented study is being initiated in Indonesia--the third Indonesian study in the Brown series. This one will focus on household labor allocations and labor mobility. Further illustrating the growing range of interests encompassed by the Comparative Urbanization Project are two international migration studies--one on "The Impact of Partial Modernization on the Emigration of Sudanese Professionals and Skilled Workers," and a second on "The Effect of Return Migration on the Social Structure of Two Spanish Villages."

Several other trainees have completed research within the general framework of the Comparative Urbanization Project, but not as a direct result of their major sponsorship by or involvement in the Project. These include: 1) an investigation of migrant adjustment in Thailand, based on the material from the Longitudinal Study of Social, Economic, and Demographic Change in Thailand; 2) an evaluation of employment and earning patterns of cityward migrants to Taipei; 3) an assessment of the impact on migration and labor absorption of development efforts in the underdeveloped areas of Southern Italy; and 4) the exploitation of data from the Malaysian Family Life Survey to assess the effect of migration definitions on the observed prevalence of migration and on migrant/non-migrant socioeconomic differentials. A full list of completed and ongoing doctoral dissertations is presented in the Appendix.

Despite the diverse settings and conditions under which the field projects have been implemented, each project has been highly successful. In part, this success reflects the strong motivation and training of the students involved. In part, it results from our practice of assuring local sponsorship; no student is allowed to undertake a field study overseas unless there is assurance of a strong local sponsor, usually a local population institute, which can provide both technical advice and assistance in recruiting field staff. Such support was negotiated in advance of the trainee's arrival overseas, and in every instance served the intended purpose very well. In addition, the trainees became involved in the activities of the local institutes, thereby contributing in important ways to furthering the respective institution's population research activities and the competence of some of its staff members. Upon returning to campus, each of the trainees made use of the facilities of the Population Studies and Training Center and the Social Science Data Center for the processing and analysis of materials.

The Comparative Urbanization Project has thus served its multiple purposes very well. The trainees who have conducted the field studies have gained excellent experience both in organizing a full project and in doing research in a less developed country. Their research findings provide new insights into the various forms that population movement takes as part of the multiphasic response to changes in economic and social conditions at origin, into the migrant adjustment process, and into the effects of migration on places of origin and destination. Other participants in the Center's training program have benefited by helping to plan the research instruments and the sample design and by reacting to the analyses undertaken by the trainees who undertook the field work. The substantial involvement of faculty has fostered closer faculty-student relations, with all the benefits such interaction produces. The close ties developed between Brown's Population Center and the institutions overseas that have sponsored the individual studies have proved of mutual benefit in furthering the training and research programs of the respective centers. The experience gained on these projects has been shared with other institutions in the United States and overseas and with international agencies; as a result, our instruments and sampling procedures have been adopted in modified form for much wider use.

The Project remains ongoing. This monograph, as the one before it, *Urban Migrants in Developing Nations*, represents an attempt to pursue the Project's comparative aspect. In this respect, it must be recognized that the Project combines a training and a research function through reliance on research carried out as "independent" doctoral dissertations. As such, considerable flexibility is given to the investigators with respect to the specific focus, design, and execution of the individual projects. The attempt to meet concurrently some of the research interests of the local sponsors introduces still more variability into the contents and design of the surveys. Furthermore, during the decade during which the Project has been ongoing, successive research efforts have taken advantage of the experience of the earlier participants. For these and other reasons, the "comparative" character of the overall project is a very loose one; if anything, the initial goal of standardization has given way, by intent, to considerable variability in focus, design, and policy relevance. In so doing, the contributions of the overall project have been enriched rather than restricted.

The Comparative Urbanization Project has thus provided rich opportunities for its participants to become more expert on the problems of comparative research in less developed countries; concurrently, it has generated research findings that provide new insights about migrant adjustments in rural and urban places, both specific to individual locations and comparatively across nations. Both functions should prove of value to the scholarly and policy-making communities.

Sidney Goldstein
Providence, R.I.
July 1984

Preface

The population of nations of the Third World designated as less developed is predominately rural and will probably remain so for the next several decades. Yet, much is happening to transform the social, economic, and demographic structure of these places. Migration is among the many processes changing the rural areas of less developed nations. Some people are moving out of rural areas to urban places; others are moving from one rural area to another. Sometimes the move is permanent; often it is not. Some movement is based on the decision of individuals and their families in response to social and economic opportunities. Increasingly, governments have developed direct and indirect policies and programs to sponsor, subsidize, and direct migration. Movements within and between countries are an integral feature of the changing social structure of less developed nations.

The most conspicuous populations to be affected by these rural movements are the migrants themselves. Areas of destination are obviously influenced by the influx of migrants, as is the population residing there. Households and families who do not move out of rural places are also influenced by those who do. In short, migration has an impact on movers and non-movers in places of origin and destination. Research has emphasized the urban context of rural out-migration by focusing on the adjustment of migrants in places of destination and the impact of migration on cities. Here we analyze rural areas as a basis for understanding why some people move out and why others stay; we focus on changes in rural structure to identify the effects of out-migration.

The studies presented in this monograph address the relationship between rural migration and social structure in three less developed nations: Korea, Sri Lanka, and Mali. Each case study focuses on a specific theme: (1) return migration to rural areas of Korea; (2) government subsidized movement from the rural wet zone to the rural dry zone in Sri Lanka; and (3) out-migration and labor allocation in Mali. Together, these projects are part of the complex puzzle of rural migration in developing nations.

In addition to the detailed case studies, two chapters were written specifically for this volume. The first provides a broad overview on rural migration and outlines some hypotheses about the relationship between migration and rural social structure. The concluding chapter focuses on comparisons of the results of the three case studies to highlight commonalities of theme and emerging issues.

The materials were organized specifically for this volume and have not been published before in this form or in comparative perspective. Much longer versions of the three case studies were doctoral dissertations in the Department of Sociology, Brown University (1979-1982). Parts of Chapter 1 were first organized for the conference on Rural Development and Human Fertility, The Pennsylvania State University, April 1983. That presentation focused on migration and fertility in less developed countries and was thoroughly revised and broadened for this chapter. The comparative materials in Chapter 5 were first presented at the summer Wednesday Workshop organized by the Population Studies and Training Center, Brown University, in August 1983. Reactions to that presentation helped clarify several important qualifications which subsequently were incorporated in the final version.

Since the longer reports of the three case studies were doctoral dissertations, they were evaluated systematically and in detail by faculty members of the Sociology Department. I want to thank my colleagues for their work on these dissertations. Sidney Goldstein was Chairperson of all three dissertations. Each of the other committee members, Barbara Anderson, Dietrich Reuschemeyer, and Alden Speare, Jr., served on two dissertation committees.

The decisions about what and how to select, edit, and distill from the longer dissertations were mine. Having edited and reorganized the material for this monograph, each author was asked to review his material. Each responded with comments and corrections and these changes are reflected in the final version. I also had the benefit of the detailed and insightful comments from Sidney Goldstein on the entire volume. He went through every page, sparing no red ink. All of us who have received manuscripts returned with his comments know the care and devotion he invests in evaluating constructively the work of colleagues and students. I continue to be indebted to him, as are the authors of these three case studies, for the standards he sets.

I also received helpful comments and suggestions from Frances Kobrin Goldscheider and Sally Findley on the chapters I prepared. They were improved by their constructive criticisms.

Editing this volume and its predecessor on Urban Migrants in Developing Nations would not have been possible without the support and facilities of the Population Studies and Training Center. Sidney Goldstein as Director of the Center and Alden Speare, Jr. as Chair of the Sociology Department were supportive of me and the project. I am grateful to both for providing me the opportunity to work on these materials. Some of the editing and the preparation of Chapters 1 and 5 was carried out when I was visiting at the Rand Corporation in Santa Monica, California. Peter Morrison arranged for me to be there and I thank him for his hospitality and friendship.

Kathy Eckstrand served as the technical editor of this volume as she was on the previous book. She read through and edited my prose and corrected my editing of other people's work. I depended on her to coordinate the details and to see the final manuscript through to its published version. She did a masterful job and I am grateful. Communicating from Providence to Jerusalem, Israel; Seoul, Korea; Maiduguri, Nigeria; and Harare, Zimbabwe was not an easy or rewarding task. Kathy did it with grace and efficiency and always with a smile.

Most of the text was typed and retyped by Carol Walker who, as in the past, was efficient and helpful. Gayle Grossmann, Judy Quattrucci, and Kathy Eckstrand completed the typing tasks, including the tables, and prepared the manuscript in its final form. Alice Goldstein coordinated these efforts and facilitated the efficient processing of the entire project. Again, my thanks.

This volume is dedicated to three former professors of sociology at Brown University who helped shape its program in population. They established the foundations--in vision and in deed--for Brown's emergence as a center of excellence in the education of demographers and in the study of population. We at Brown are indebted to them for their contribution to our program. As demographers and sociologists, we are grateful to them for their scholarly, educational, and institutional contributions. I am honored to call them teachers, colleagues, and friends.

Calvin Goldscheider

1
Migration and Rural Social Structure: An Overview

Calvin Goldscheider

Research on the relationship between migration and social structure has often emphasized the urban context. Studies have focused on the links between development and urbanization, the growth of urban places, the adjustment of migrants in the cities, and the problems associated with movers to various neighborhoods of metropolitan areas. The impact of migration on rural areas, their population and social structure, has received far less attention. Yet, it is clear that to understand migration processes in their complexity requires a dynamic theoretical model and methodology which includes the rural component as an integral element. Investigating rural social structure and migration is fundamental to an analysis of the social, economic, and demographic sources of urbanward migration, the selectivity of migration, and the consequences of migration for rural families and communities.

The premise of the studies reported in this volume is that there are important connections between migration and rural social structure which are critical for understanding less developed regions of the world. These connections operate at macro- and micro-levels of analysis. They are most conspicuous at the level of household and community where relationships between population change and social structure are most salient.

To place the research on migration and rural social structure in a broader context, we outline in this chapter the rural context of less developed countries and categorize various linkages between rural out-migration and social change. A brief description of the social demographic characteristics of the three countries which were studied concludes this overview.

The Rural Context of Less Developed Societies

Urbanization has been a major process associated with the modernization of societies and rapid urban growth has been a conspicuous feature of less developed nations. Demographic research has focused on the relative contributions of natural increase and migration to urban growth in more and less developed societies and has analyzed the socioeconomic adjustments of rural migrants in cities. Migration has been viewed as a vehicle of change for those who move and as a factor in the redistribution of population from rural to urban areas. Seldom has the study of urbanization led to a systematic examination of the impact of migration on rural social structure. Rural populations have often been viewed as marginal and therefore uninteresting analytically in the processes associated with modernization and development.

The demographic reality of less developed nations suggests that such neglect is unwarranted. The population size and structure of countries defined as less developed reflect in large part the consequence of population patterns in rural areas. The analysis of the effects of migration on rural areas is at the core of the demography of less developed countries and of the social, economic, and political correlates of their population processes. In particular, the proportion rural in less developed countries is high and most of these nations will remain predominately rural for the next several decades. United Nations estimates indicate that more than half of the total population of the world will be located in the rural areas of less developed countries in 1985. About two-thirds of the population in less developed regions are likely to remain in rural areas until around the first decade of the twenty-first century (U.N., 1982).

Three additional demographic patterns provide a context for exploring rural migration patterns in less developed nations. First, the size of the rural population is increasing at the same time that the proportion living in rural areas is decreasing. This is an exceptional pattern when compared to the historical and contemporary experience of most industrial nations (Goldscheider, 1983a; Davis, 1965; Goldstein and Sly, 1977). Between 1960 and 1980, the percent rural in less developed countries decreased from 78 percent to 69 percent but the rural population of these same countries increased by 40 percent (from 1,632 million to 2,285 million). Between 1980 and 2000, the United Nations estimates that the proportion rural in less developed regions of the world will further decrease to 56 percent. Yet, at the same time, the

2

estimated numerical increase in these areas will be from 2,285 million to 2,725 million. Although the projected pace of rural population will be slower relative to previous decades (the increase will be "only" 19 percent), the numerical increase estimated at over 441 million persons is only slightly smaller than the combined population size of the United States and the Soviet Union in 1970.

These data reveal the continuing high proportions rural in less developed nations as well as the changing population distribution. There has been and will continue to be an increase in the level of urbanization, part of which reflects net out-migration from rural to urban areas, and part of which reflects differential natural increase. Nevertheless, the amount of rural-urban migration is substantially greater than these net residual movements indicate. Not all rural-urban migration is permanent; return, repeat, and temporary movements are not reflected in the net redistribution estimates nor are stream-counterstream migrants (i.e., gross migration flows) included. No less important is the fact that not all rural out-migration is toward places defined as urban; some (and often a substantial proportion, if not a majority) is toward other rural areas. Hence, rural-urban population transfers may represent only a small percent of all rural migration. Taken together, the variety of migration flows from rural areas is greater than the net rural-urban migration inferred from urbanization estimates. Recognizing this, the net rural-urban population redistribution implies high rates of migration and large numbers of rural persons on the move.

A third feature is the heterogeneity of nations included among the less developed regions of the world. For example, Africa as a whole is projected to remain mostly rural until after the year 2010. Within Africa, the variation in urbanization levels is considerable. Eastern Africa is projected to remain mostly rural (i.e., 50 percent) until sometime after 2025, western Africa until after 2015, central Africa until after 1995, and northern and southern Africa until after 1985. Individual countries within Africa display an even wider range. In contrast, the Latin American region is already mostly urban with only 31 percent estimated to be rural in 1985, but Bolivia will be 64 percent rural in 1985 and will remain rural until the turn of the twenty-first century.

Similar variations characterize the Asian countries categorized as less developed by the United Nations. Only about 20 percent of China was urban in 1982 and most of the population is projected to remain rural until around 2015. Some east Asian countries (e.g., Korea) are already predominately urban, while Indonesia, Thailand, Vietnam, Bangladesh, and India, with a combined population of 1,127 million in 1985 are at least 75 percent rural and will remain so until sometime after the second decade of the twenty-first century. The increasing size of the rural population, the amount of out-migration, and the enormous variation among countries defined as less developed require systematic comparative research focusing on rural social structure and migration. Yet neither the data nor the theoretical frameworks available allow for a systematic assessment of these processes.

Official sources of data usually contain limited information about the extent of migration. In part, this reflects the complex nature of migration. There is a wide range of migration types, including local, short distance, temporary, seasonal, and labor mobility, as well as internal and international migrations which involve greater distances for longer periods of absence, and tend to be more permanent. Other criteria for classifying types of migration relate to the composition of the migration stream (e.g., individuals, families, accompanying children, chain, mass) and directionality (e.g., rural-urban, urban-urban, rural-rural, urban-rural). These and other distinctions are based on the implicit assumption that types and intensities of changes (demographic, social, economic, political, and cultural) associated with migration vary by the type of movement. Since the social, economic, and demographic determinants of various types of migration may be different, there is a need to specify the particular type of migration before linking migration to other processes. Moreover, since migration is repeatable and reversible, it is necessary to separate out return and repeat migrants from first-time movers. Combining types of migration and its character involves a complex system of migration flows (see Goldscheider, 1971, 1983a). Most data sources do not comprehensively provide information on all these types of movement and their correlated social, economic, and demographic variables.

Migration involves consequences for places of origin, for places of destination, and for migrants and their families. The wide range of types of movement included among the definitions of migration and the diverse determinants and complex consequences of various migration types imply that it is not fruitful to search for general relationships between migration and social structure without specifying the type of migration or comparing the variety of migration flows involved in the migration system (Goldscheider, 1983a).

People move out of rural areas to take advantage of relatively better social and economic opportunities elsewhere. Yet, not everyone has access to or knowledge about opportunities nor does everyone respond to the opportunities known and accessible. In-migration to rural areas, return migration to rural areas of origin, decisions to extend permanent migration, or to become a circular, seasonal, or temporary migrant are complexities in understanding the relationship between opportunities and migration. A core analytic theme therefore is the specification of factors and the identification of the contexts which define and shape the relationship between opportunities and migration.

Rural Out-Migration and Social Change

The demographic importance of rural areas and the wide range of migration types leads to the central issues of the studies reported in this volume: In what ways does migration to and from rural areas affect rural social structure? Which aspects of rural social structure are more clearly linked to the determinants and selectivity of migration? Indeed, what are the mechanisms linking geographic movement to social change? Several major ways of examining the linkages between migration and changes in rural social structure may be identified.

Size and Composition Effects

The migration of people from one area to another changes the size of both populations, other things being equal. The rate of migration, relative to population size at origin and destination, will affect the social and economic institutions of both communities. Economic production, consumption patterns, labor markets, household and family networks, political power, and other aspects of social, political, and economic organization which are related to population size will be affected by migration.

Migration not only involves the movement of a specific number of people from one place to another but the selective movement of persons with particular characteristics. In turn, these characteristics are linked to social, economic, political, and cultural aspects of places of origin and destination. Selectivity based on these affects the structure of population at both areas of origin and destination.

It is well-established empirically that migration from rural areas is selective of younger persons (particularly those between

5

the ages of 15 and 29). From a demographic point of view this means an alteration in the age structure of the population remaining in places of origin (in our case the rural areas of less developed regions) as well as the population in places of destination (rural or urban). As a result, in-migration to cities may increase the urban population directly through the transfer of population and indirectly through the influx of higher fertility populations from rural areas. Moreover, since in-migrants tend to be in the prime reproductive ages, in the short run at least, there is a structural effect of in-migration on period fertility. Together with the natural increase of the urban population, high urban population growth rates result.

The pursuit of that line of argument tends to neglect the demographic compositional effects of out-migration on rural areas of origin. These effects depend in part on the extent of rural out-migration (relative to the size of the rural population) and the degree of age selectivity. They also depend on the type of out-migration (in particular its permanence) and the additional selectivity by sex and marital status.

Selectivity by age, sex, and marital status as well as migration type have an impact on rural social structure through compositional changes and through changes in marriage patterns. Selective out-migration of young males or females who are unmarried may result in a changing rural marriage market; in turn, the timing of marriage may be affected through imbalances in the sex-ratio (by age) of the remaining non-married rural population. It is of course difficult to assess this effect, in part, because migration is dynamic over time. For example, single women may migrate out of rural areas later than single men or men might return to places of origin to marry or raise their children, returning to urban areas with their spouses and children. The permutations are extensive. The important point to note is that the compositional effects of rural out-migration occur through the age structural selectivity of migration as well as through sex-ratio imbalances brought about by sex-marital status selectivity. Again, type of migration (its relative permanence and whether primarily of individuals or young families) plays an important role in the extent and direction of these compositional effects. Moreover, the extent of temporary or seasonal migration may have consequences for the separation of spouses and in turn for fertility patterns, particularly their tempo and timing. The absence of husbands from home for a particular season or for some period of time may affect delayed childbearing and completed family size.

The age and sex selectivity of rural out-migration have clear potential consequences for economic levels and patterns of productivity. Indeed, any social, economic, political, demographic, or cultural factor linked to age structure, sex composition, or marriage-family formation patterns will be affected by the selectivity of rural out-migration. These patterns will be related as well to movements into rural areas through selective return migration or rural to rural movements.

The relative selectivity of migration by age, sex, and marital status--and its effects on social structure--do not necessarily imply either modernization or changed attitudes or values in rural areas. Nor can we expect that rural out-migration will have the same compositional effects in all cases, since there is variation in the extent of selectivity and in the rate and type of migration.

The compositional effects of out-migration on rural socioeconomic structure relate in complex ways to migratory selectivity along socioeconomic dimensions. Some out-migration from the rural areas of less developed countries is selective of the relatively better educated, more ambitious, wealthier rural poor. Under those circumstances, we would expect that the remaining rural population would be the least educated, poorest, and least receptive to change. Again, depending on the rate, type, and selectivity of migration, the remaining rural non-migrants are likely to be characterized by greater resistance to changes in behavioral patterns. Other migration streams have been bimodal in their socioeconomic selectivity: those with more resources and those with the fewest resources are more likely to move out of rural areas. The effects of complex socioeconomic selectivity on rural social structure are more difficult to specify.

One methodological implication of these compositional effects is that the study of the impact of out-migration on rural social structure needs to relate the socioeconomic and demographic characteristics of migrants to the characteristics of rural places of origin. Another is the need for data over time since the characteristics of both rural migrants and rural places are likely to change. All other effects of out-migration must take these compositional consequences as the starting point for analysis.

Diffusion through Migration

A second category of effects of out-migration on rural social structure focuses specifically on the role of migration in bringing new ideas to rural areas. Unlike compositional effects, diffusion of modernity deals directly with real changes in attitudes,

7

motivations, and behavior.

Migration has often been viewed as a vehicle or mechanism of change but almost always in the context of moving "traditional" rural persons into contact with modernity in the city. In this regard, the debates and counterdebates revolve around four core questions: (1) How "traditional" are rural migrants, particularly since rural out-migrants are selective of those with particular social-demographic characteristics and are often the least traditional of the rural population? (2) How "modern" are city residents? (3) How much residential and occupational contact occurs between migrants and the urban native born population? (4) What are the social, economic, and cultural mechanisms which link migration to social changes through exposure of migrants to modernity in the city?

As long as the migration is viewed as one way from rural to urban areas, questions about the effects of migration on urban areas are critical. Issues of diffusion relate essentially to when the rural population will become "urban-like" in behavior and characteristics. However, when types of migration are specified, a broader set of questions emerges relating to the direct diffusion of modernity back to rural areas through rural migration. Return migrants to the rural areas, and temporary and seasonal migrants, have a direct effect on rural communities. Moreover, there are indirect effects through remittances from migrants to rural places of origin, visits to rural areras, and urban visits of rural persons and other forms of communication which influence rural social and economic structure. Diffusion may occur by way of the transferal of goods and money from out-migrants back to rural areas, thus raising standards of living and consumption aspirations. It may involve information flows about social and economic opportunities in other places, educational possibilities, and modern ideas about consumption and production.

The extent to which these diffusion processes operate and the specific links to migration need to be examined in the context of the four core questions noted earlier directed at diffusion in urban settings. Yet conceptualized in broad terms, it is clear that rural out-migration remains a potential mechanism for change in the rural area through diffusion processes. Such diffusion can operate by way of changed attitudes, values conveyed to the non-mobile rural population, or more indirectly through the diffusion of information about opportunities or transferal of goods and cash. These are complex processes that may occur over time, operating at the family, household, and community levels and through kinship-ethnic-occupational networks.

Clearly these diffusion effects do not operate mechanically or automatically and thus are different from the compositional effects of rural out-migration. As before, however, the type of migration is critical in analyzing diffusion as is the economic and demographic contexts of the broader society. For example, moves to primate (or the largest) cities, which are the centers of modern social and economic development, are likely to contrast with moves to towns and urban places of smaller size where modernity has been less extensive. Migration to rural areas of destination may involve moving from rural areas with smaller populations to ones with larger populations, to specific rural areas where relative economic opportunities are greater, to rural areas as a step closer to more distant urban places, or as return migration back to rural areas. Unlike return migration from urban to rural areas, rural-rural migration may impact on areas of origin and destination through compositional effects (in more complex ways since the rural effects are located in two populations) as well as through diffusion, although we would expect that the latter set of effects would be less.

Clearly, we cannot ignore the potential effects of rural to rural migration. Since rural-rural moves have not been related directly or simply to modernization processes, links to social and economic changes have been relatively neglected in previous research.

Demographic-Behavioral Responses

A third set of migration effects on rural social structure may be derived from the theory of multiphasic responses and its extensions (Davis, 1963; Friedlander, 1969, 1983; Mosher, 1980a; 1980b; Zelinsky, 1983). In broad outline, the general argument is that in the process of transition to low and controlled population growth, populations respond in a variety of ways and with every means to population pressure and relative socioeconomic deprivation. These multiphasic responses include the range of intermediate variables determining control over marital fertility (contraceptive usage and abortion) as well as delayed marriage or celibacy, and internal and external migrations. Multiphasic demographic response theory is a modified Malthusian argument that views migration, in addition to mortality and fertility "checks", as one of the many ways populations respond to the pressures on the economic well-being of families, often brought about by rapid, sustained mortality reduction. Internal and international migrations reduce the

9

pressures of demographic growth by transferring people out of places (or nations) just as fertility reductions reduce growth rates through natural increase.

In rural areas, in particular, migration responds to population growth and the lack of rural economic opportunities. Movement from rural to urban areas provides an outlet for "excess" natural increase and fits "the interests and structure of peasant families in the evolving economy" (Davis, 1963:355).

In the original formulation, rural out-migration was viewed as only one of the multiple responses of the rural population in industrializing nations. An extension of the argument emphasized that migration may be a substitute for fertility reduction in rural areas (and vice versa) or a delaying mechanism for alternative responses (see especially Friedlander, 1969, 1983). In this view, internal and external migrations are short-term safety valves relieving population pressures and delaying fertility reduction. Hence, there is an interaction of migration and fertility in the process of demographic transition.

In this context, rural out-migration may result in delayed fertility reduction of the non-mobile rural population. Hence, the absence of change (i.e., sustained high levels of rural fertility) may be maintained by out-migration from rural areas. This effect is not the result of compositional changes but rather is a behavioral response to the relief from population pressure. When migration is relatively permanent and rates are high, fertility reductions of the remaining rural population may be slower. Recent research on Puerto Rico and Sweden (Mosher, 1980a, 1980b) demonstrates the utility of this approach as a theoretical guideline for the analyses of demographic transitions. Nevertheless, there has been no clear specification of the socioeconomic and demographic conditions within which migration is a substitute or joint multiphasic response (Goldscheider, 1982; Friedlander, 1983).

Social Organizational and Uprooting Effects

Two key processes of modernization are related to migration--structural differentiation and the expansion of the opportunity structure. The process of moving may involve a break with kinship dominance over economic resources and with family control over status; it may also relate to changing opportunity structures in rural places of origin or relative opportunities (economic and non-economic) in places of destination.

The extent of the uprooting effect of migration--particularly the break with family, kin, and community of origin--depends in part on the type, permanence, and distance of migration and on the whole complex of ties retained by migrants with their places of origin. These, of course, take on a variety of forms, ranging from visiting and return migration to remittances and chain migration. Nevertheless, one of the key changes which migration brings about in some degree or another is the removal from the family in the place of origin of total control over resources and status. Often it is not clear whether migration is the consequence of structural differentiation processes or its determinant. Yet, over time, moving may facilitate the separation of economic from family structures and allow them to be realigned in new ways.

In this context, changes in the fertility of the rural population and of rural migrants may be one set of consequences of rural out-migration. This is particularly the case when rural migration involves the separation of family from economic, political, and social roles. This changes the control exercised by the family and kin groups over economic and political sources and alters the dominance of the broader family-community unit over the status and role of women (Goldscheider, 1982, 1984). Changing opportunities exacerbate social class and generation gaps between those who participate early in processes of change and the late-comers. Migration of select members of a household further increases tensions among members, even when some resources are returned to the household by the migrant. These emerging inequalities may facilitate the development of new acceptable modes of behavior.

One of the mechanisms linking migration to rural social structure is therefore the impact of migration on kin control over resources. When migration results in the decline of kin dominance over economic resources and over the status of women, then migration generates some of the fundamental conditions for modernization. Not all migration automatically and inevitably leads to "uprooting" effects; hence, we should not expect uniform relationships between out-migration and social change.

The argument that migration may reflect responses to differential economic opportunities and may foster the breakdown of kinship dominance does not imply that kinship groups do not facilitate migration or that all kinship bonds are ruptured in the migration process. To the contrary: kinship groups often play a key role in the migration of selected household members and in their integration in places of destination (see Hugo, 1981; Goldscheider, 1983b). There is a growing literature identifying the continuous and extensive ties between migrants and their places of origin (Findley, 1977, 1982; Goldscheider, 1983a;

11

Simmons et al., 1977; Goldstein and Goldstein, 1981). Yet, these continuing and new ties do not necessarily imply kin dominance and control which decline in the process of selected types of movement.

Migration may free the individual migrant, at least in part, from some of the obligations and constraints of traditional rural societies and from the ascriptive status of place and family of birth. It may, as well, weaken the control exercised by the rural extended family over the lives and opportunities of those who remain in the rural area. This may also characterize return migrants and other non-permanent movements, since migrants do not always fit neatly back into the social, economic, and political structure of rural areas. Once the dominance of family-kin groups is challenged by some, it weakens for others as well.

While compositional effects of migration are indeterminate in terms of the predicted direction of change (i.e., it depends on the selectivity and type of migration), the effects of diffusion following migration are more likely to modernize rural areas over time. Similarly, the social organizational effects of migration, particularly the changing dominance of extended families over resources and status, would result in major social and economic change. In contrast, the demographic-behavioral effects of migration are hypothesized to provide relief from population pressure and are, therefore, alternatives to other responses. It follows, then, that rural out-migration would reinforce the continuity of rural social structure. Clearly these theories will vary in their predictions depending on the type and rate of out-migration. They refer to different societal contexts, economic patterns, and political regions, or have different time referents.

These hypothesized relations between out-migration and social structure require systematic and detailed empirical testing. As in other social science examples, the contradiction may be more apparent than real, since we need greater specification about short- and long-term effects, and about the societal context within which the out-migration and rural social change operate. The structure of economic opportunity, the patterns of household-family formation, the political regime, as well as the cultural context are important specifications.

The different implications of these migration effects for rural social structure are not only of analytic importance. They are of critical significance for questions of policy and programs designed to influence migration and rural development. In general, policies associated with internal migration in less developed countries have ignored the potential uprooting effects of migration. Neither rural-agricultural or urban-industrial policies, nor regional decentralized urban programs or centralized urbanization policies (Simmons et al., 1977; Findley, 1977; Goldscheider, 1983a) have systematically taken into account ways in which selective migration may alter the social organization of rural communities.

The overwhelming concerns (and often with justification) over the enormous growth of urban places and populations in the largest cities of less developed nations have often led to the oversimplified conclusion that policies to stem the tide of rural out-migration would help alleviate the problems of excessive urban expansion. Yet, urban population size will grow even without rural-urban transfers. More importantly, from the point of view of the rural communities, the retention of rural residents in their places of origin compounds the already severe problems of some overcrowded agricultural areas. The costs of non-migration go beyond economic issues of productivity and development, the allocation of labor accompanying development, and even beyond the sheer multiplication of people (Davis, 1975). Non-migration may delay the separation of economic resources from family-kin dominance and may slow down the differentiation process critical for modernization. On the other hand, the costs of selective rural out-migration should not be minimized, particularly if migration drains off the more qualified and better educated.

We noted that the heterogeneity among less developed regions of the world is substantial in terms of levels of urbanization. Nor are all rural places within countries similar in terms of their economic and social structure, ethnic-class composition, and demographic pattern. In particular, the impact of migration on rural social structure varies with particular sectors of the rural population. Farmers, workers, owners, landless, service workers, or agriculturists among other economic and social categories may be affected differently by migration patterns. These more homogeneous units need to be examined systematically.

In addition, we must not fall into the theoretical trap of treating areas and sectors in isolation from the broader societal context of which they are a part. Often the focus on rural areas has viewed the rural sector only marginally, as a reservoir for an urban labor force and in economic relationship to cities. Rural development studies have often focused only on the rural areas. Emerging from recent theoretical literature is the need to focus on issues of social and economic dependencies and sectoral connections within (and between) countries. In interesting ways, the analysis of migration is one of the important mechanisms

13

linking areas and populations.

The outline of issues and specification of relationships should serve as a theoretical map for addressing some neglected patterns of rural migration. The studies reported in this volume are part of the detailed comparative research in rural areas needed to build a firmer analytic base for studies in other countries and for the evaluation of policies.

The Three Research Studies

We focus in this volume on various aspects of rural migration in three countries which are grouped within the category of "less developed nations." These countries are, however, not homogeneous. Selected data in Table 1.1 illustrate some of the heterogeneity. Korea (South) has the largest population size of the three with over 40 million people, Mali has the smallest with about 7 million, and Sri Lanka has an estimated 15 million people. Korea and Sri Lanka have relatively similar birth and death rates, with the level of natural increase in Korea lower than in Sri Lanka. Total fertility is one child higher in Sri Lanka than in Korea, with similar rates of infant mortality and life expectancy, and about the same proportion under age 15 and over age 65. Two characteristics sharply distinguish Korea from Sri Lanka. The urban population in Korea was estimated at 57 percent, twice the level of Sri Lanka; per capita gross national product in 1981 was five times higher in Korea than in Sri Lanka. Yet, the proportion of economically active males engaged in agriculture was identical in both countries.

Mali, a west African country, is much less developed economically or demographically than either Korea or Sri Lanka. Birth and death rates are higher in Mali as is the rate of natural increase. The potential for more rapid population increase is high, as total fertility is close to 7 children per woman, birth rates are 47 per 1,000, life expectancy is low at 43 years, and 15 percent of the children die before their first birthday. While population size is small, it will double in a quarter of a century at current growth rates. The proportion rural is high (83 percent) and the GNP is only $185 per capita, per year. Fully 87 percent of the males are engaged in agriculture.

The variation in these demographic and economic indicators is matched by cultural and social differences. These will be reviewed as part of the details of each case study. Comparatively, these differences point to the need to exercise appropriate caution in reaching broad generalizations about migration and

14

TABLE 1.1

SELECTED CHARACTERISTICS OF KOREA, SRI LANKA AND MALI, CIRCA 1980

	Korea	Sri Lanka	Mali
Population Estimate (Millions)	41.3	15.6	7.3
Crude			
Birth Rate	25	28	47
Death Rate	8	6	21
Natural Increase	17	22	26
Doubling Time (Years)	41	32	26
Infant Mortality	34	37	153
Total Fertility	2.6	3.6	6.7
% Population Under Age 15/Over Age 64	33/4	35/4	46/3
Life Expectancy at Birth	64	66	43
% Urban	57	24	17
Per Capita GNP, 1981 (US $)	1,720	302	185
% of Males in Agriculture *	40.1	40.1	87.2

Source: Population Reference Bureau, 1983 World Population
         Data Sheet

*   Calculated from ILO, Yearbook of Labour Statistics, 1981, 1977.

development in less developed nations. At the same time, commonalities which result from comparing such disparate countries strengthen the search for broader generalizations. The detailed analysis of these case studies provides the basis for specifying and qualifying the contexts within which types of migration and selected dimensions of social change are related. Comparative differences in migration provide insight into the extent of migration and the characteristics of migrants in different social and economic settings and at different levels of development.

To identify the links between development, rural migration, and social change, each case study focuses in depth on particular aspects of rural migration. In Korea, the major analytic issues revolve around return migration to rural areas, its determinants and consequences. Issues of government sponsored migration between rural areas are examined for Sri Lanka, with a particular focus on the impact of this migration for the migrants and their communities. The research on rural migration in Mali emphasizes the different levels of analysis--individuals, households, and villages--to address questions of labor allocation and short- and long-term movements.

To capture these specific features of rural migration, different methodological strategies characterize each of the three studies. The focus in Korea is on urban to rural return migration, using carefully designed rural sample surveys, comparisons with an urban sample obtained from Seoul several years earlier, and an analysis of selected 1970 census data. In Sri Lanka and Mali, few existing official data sources were useful for a detailed examination of rural migration. The analysis of migration from the rural wet zone to the rural dry zone in Sri Lanka was therefore based on rural samples in both zones. This allowed for the separation of migrants who were part of a government subsidized program of peasant agricultural development from those who voluntarily moved to the dry zone. These, in turn, were compared to the native populations of both zones (with those of the wet zone subdivided further by whether internal local moves had taken place). In Mali, secondary analysis of data collected for other purposes from three regions and eight villages focused particularly on the community and household contexts of rural out-migration.

Each of the three studies stands on its own as a view of the complexities of rural migration in a particular nation or area. Together, the studies point to commonalities and differences among less developed countries and raise critical questions for detailed future research on migration and rural social structure.

References

Dasgupta, Biplab. 1981. "Rural-Urban Migration and Rural Development." In *Why People Move: Comparative Perspectives on the Dynamics of Internal Migration.* Edited by J. Balan. Paris: UNESCO Press.

Davis, Kingsley. 1963. "The Theory of Change and Response in Modern Demographic History." *Population Index* (October):345-366.

_____. 1975. "Asia's Cities: Problems and Options." *Population and Development Review* (September):71-86.

Findley, Sally. 1977. *Planning for Internal Migration: A Review of Issues and Policies in Developing Countries.* U.S. Bureau of the Census, Washington, D.C.

_____. 1982. *Migration Survey Methodologies.* IUSSP Papers No. 20. Liege.

Friedlander, Dov. 1969. "Demographic Responses and Population Change." *Demography* (November):359-381.

_____. 1983. "Demographic Responses and Socioeconomic Structure." *Demography* (August):249-272.

Goldscheider, Calvin. 1971. *Population, Modernization, and Social Structure.* Boston: Little, Brown & Co.

_____. 1982. "Societal Change and Demographic Transitions: Selected Theoretical Issues and Research Strategies." In *Population et Structures Sociales, Chaire Quetelet 1981.* Louvain: Universite Catholique de Louvain, pp. 83-106.

_____. 1983a. "Modernization, Migration, and Urbanization." In *Population Movements: Their Forms and Functions in Urbanization and Development.* Edited by P. Morrison. Liege: Ordina Editions.

_____. ed. 1983b. *Urban Migrants in Developing Nations: Patterns and Problems of Adjustment.* Colorado: Westview Press.

_____. 1984. "Migration and Rural Fertility in Less Developed Countries." In *Rural Development and Human Fertility.* Edited by W. Schutjer and S. Stokes. New York: McGraw-Hill.

Goldstein, Sidney. 1981. "Some Comments on Migration and Development." In *Why People Move: Comparative Perspctives on the Dynamics of Internal Migration.* Edited by J. Balan. Paris: UNESCO Press.

Goldstein, Sidney and A. Goldstein. 1981. *Surveys of Migration in Less Developed Countries.* East-West Population Institute Paper No. 71.

Goldstein, Sidney and D. Sly, eds. 1977. *Patterns of Urbanization: Comparative Country Studies.* Belgium: Ordina Editions.

Hugo, Graeme. 1981. "Village-Community Ties, Village Norms and Ethnic and Social Networks: A Review of Evidence from the Third World." In *Migration Decision Making: Multidisciplinary Approaches to Microlevel Studies in Developed and Developing Countries.* Edited by G. DeJong and R. Gardner. New York: Pergamon Press, Chapter 7.

Mosher, W. 1980a. "The Theory of Change and Response: An Application to Puerto Rico, 1940-1970." *Population Studies* 34 (March):45-58.

_____. 1980b. "Demographic Responses and Demographic Transitions." *Demography* 17 (November):395-412.

Simmons, Alan, Sergio Diaz-Briquets, and Aprodicio A. Laquian. 1977. *Societal Change and Internal Migration.* Ottawa: International Development Research Centre.

United Nations. 1982. *Estimates and Projections of Urban, Rural and City Populations, 1950-2025: The 1980 Assessment.* New York: United Nations.

18

Zelinsky, Wilbur. 1983. "The Impasse in Migration Theory." In *Population Movements: Their Forms and Functions in Urbanization and Development.* Edited by P. Morrison. Liege: Ordina Editions.

2
Urban to Rural
Migration in Korea

Jin Ho Choi

Introduction

Until recently, there has been little theoretical or empirical interest in return migration. Migration research has concentrated on the causes and the process of the initial move to urban areas, migrant adjustment at places of destination, and the analysis of overall migration streams without any breakdown of different types of movement (see Bovenkerk, 1974; Chapman, 1982).

Ever since Ravenstein (1885) set forth the notion of 'counter-current,' which implies the existence of return migration, a number of studies have pointed to the need for the analysis of this type of migration separate from an assessment of other types of movement. For example, Goldstein (1954, 1964) emphasized the importance of the repeated moves of the same person, which may include some return movement. Goldscheider (1971) also acknowledged the importance of return movement as an integral element in the study of the various aspects of the migration system.

It was not until the 1960s that systematic empirical attention among scholars turned to the analysis of return migration. Earlier studies of return migration had mostly centered on international return movements (e.g., Appleyard, 1962; Cerase, 1967, 1974; Hernandez, 1967; Richmond, 1968; Myers and Masnick, 1968; Comay, 1971). Since the late 1960s, more attention has been paid to internal return movements within a nation (for example, Campbell et al., 1974; Long and Hansen, 1975, 1977a, 1977b; Chapman, 1982; Goldstein, 1978).

In developing countries, the study of return migration generally focused on temporary return moves of wage laborers, occurring in conjunction with repetitive, cyclic, and oscillating forms of movement. These forms of movements, called 'circulation' by Mitchell (1961), received considerable attention particularly in Africa and in the Pacific islands, and to a lesser extent in Southeast Asia (Mitchell, 1961, 1969; Chapman, 1974, 1976, 1977; Gould and Prothero, 1975; Chapman and Prothero, 1977; Goldstein, 1978). The concept of circulation first referred to the ebb and flow of wage laborers in South-central Africa, but it was extended later to embrace all movements that both began and terminated in the local community, on the grounds that tribesmen return to their homes no matter what the reasons for their departure or no matter how long they have been absent. Such constant mobility reflects the conflict between the centrifugal attractions of commercial, social and administrative services, and wage employment, and the centripetal power of village obligations, social relationships, and kinship ties (Chapman, 1977).

Overall, the study of return migration is therefore a relatively new field of inquiry; knowledge of return migration remains extremely poor, and empirical evidence is scarce and inconsistent. A large part of the lack of theoretical and empirical knowledge on return migration may be attributed to the difficulty in obtaining satisfactory data. It was not until the 1960s that census data were used to identify and distinguish return migrants from other types of migrants by relating place of birth and place of previous residence to place of residence at the time of the census. The major limitation of measures of return migration derived from census sources is that they neglect intervening moves. These data are also very much affected by the spatial units in terms of which migration is measured--the larger the unit (e.g., province compared to district), the less the volume of migration detected. The most reliable way to obtain information on return migration is through the inclusion of migration life histories in a sample survey. However, the use of sample survey data poses the problem of securing enough cases of return migrants among all those sampled. Unless a survey has a very large sample size or return migrants are pre-identified using other sources, such as civil registration data, the number of return migrants is likely to be small.

Despite the difficulties associated with research on return migration, its separation from other types of movement has great significance. First, many investigators have recognized that the causes and nature of movement of return migration may differ from other types of migration (Eldridge, 1965; Miller, 1977). Recent econometric studies have indicated that potential return and non-return migrants respond quite differently to factors conditioning migration decisions. Therefore, the economic model of migration needs to disaggregate population movement into types of migrants. Such separation corrects for possible differences by type of migration in the propensity to migrate and thus reduces specification (aggregate) bias (Vanderkamp, 1971, 1972; Miller, 1973; DaVanzo, 1976, 1978a; Kiker and Traynham, 1976; Kau and Sirmans, 1976, 1978).

Second, part of the lesser interest in return migration has been attributed to the assumption that the volume and rate of return migration may be small and negligible. A number of studies, however, have documented that return migration represents a substantial part of total migration streams. For example, in the United States during the 1955-1960 period, migrants returning to their state of birth constituted 17 percent of all interstate migrants among whites and 14 percent among blacks. By the 1965-1970 period those proportions had increased to about 20 percent (Lee, 1974). In Canada, return migration was estimated as 19.9 percent of the total migration flows in 1966-1967, and 22.0 percent in 1967-1968 (Vanderkamp, 1972). In Korea, 9.1 percent of the total interprovincial migrants returned to their province of birth in the 1965-1970 period (U.N., 1975). A survey in Mexico revealed that 23 percent of the sample men of a large city (Monterrey) and 30 percent of men in a rural community (Cedral) had been return migrants during their lifetime (Feindt and Browning, 1972).

The number and proportion of return migrants may continue to increase in the future since the population 'at risk' of returning will be further enlarged through the process of continuous cumulation of rural to urban migrants. This is particularly true in countries like Korea where more than half of the population growth in the urban areas has been attributed to migration (Kwon, 1975). The evidence suggests that return migration, therefore, is sufficiently prevalent to deserve more attention, and may become more significant as a component of population redistribution.

Third, a carefully designed study of the characteristics of return migrants may make a significant contribution to the general study of migration differentials and adjustment. One factor which may distort the analysis of migration differentials at the point of destination is the selective characteristics of those who returned to the place of their origin. If the return migrants are negatively selected at the place of destination, then the characteristics of the original migrants tend to be upwardly biased; if they are positively selected, the characteristics of those remaining will be downwardly biased. Nevertheless, there is little empirical evidence about the selectivity of return migrants.

Beyond these questions, the study of the consequences of urban to rural return migration on both the individual and societal levels may have important policy implications for developing countries. Most developing countries now are experiencing an extraordinarily high rate of urban growth. Migration has played an important role in that growth. Certainly, rapid urban growth, particularly when it is concentrated in the largest cities in a country, creates many problems (Hauser, 1965; Goldstein, 1973). To cope with these problems of rapid urban growth, many governments of developing countries have formulated and adopted various policies. In Korea, for example, in order to curb the massive influx of people from the countryside into large cities, and to encourage urban residents to move out of the large cities, the government has adopted several policies including an imposition of a residence tax in large cities, restrictions on the transfer of high school students into large cities unless their entire family moves, stimulation of movement of industries into small cities or the countryside from large cities, and construction of small scale labor intensive industries in rural areas.

It is also often argued that return migrants can act as agents of social and economic change. As diffusers of cultural values and norms, and through bringing and sending back some financial resources from the city to rural places which may be used for rural development, they may accelerate modernization processes in developing countries (Goldstein, 1976; Connell et al., 1976). Testing the above hypothesis through the study of the consequences of return migration can contribute directly to the formulation and evaluation of alternative population redistribution policies.

If return migrants are positively affected by their urban experience either through income earning potentials or in the acquisition of modern attitudes, then migration to an urban center followed by return migration is not a waste of resources. Efforts should be directed to policies which encourage earlier migrants to move out of the large cities both to reduce urban pressures and to facilitate rural development. On the other hand, if return migrants have not benefited by their migration experience, compared to those who have remained in the rural places of origin, then return migration may involve a heavy cost. In this case, policies which seek to retard the massive influx of people into large cities may be legitimate. By assessing the demographic and

24

socioeconomic characteristics of return migrants in Korea with attention to the determinants and consequences of their return move, research may provide a firmer basis for the potential use of migration in policies designed to alleviate the problems of rapid urban growth and to further rural development.

The major objectives of the study are: (1) to identify the demographic and socioeconomic characteristics of urban to rural return migrants in Korea in order to ascertain the nature and degree of selectivity of return migrants from urban to rural areas; (2) to examine factors which may influence the return migrants' decision to move back to their place of origin; (3) to investigate the consequences of return migration for the individual return migrants and for the community of origin and destination.

Data Sources

To address these objectives, three different sets of data were used: the 1978 Urban to Rural Return Migration Survey, the 1970 Korean Population Census, and the Seoul City Migration Survey. The 1978 Return Migration Survey was conducted in Gyeongsangbugdo province in Korea, which is located in the southeastern part of the country about two hundred miles from Seoul. It is one of the economically well-developed provinces, where industrialization began at an earlier period compared to other provinces in the country.

Within Gyeongsangbugdo province three study areas were selected in order to allow an assessment of the effect of government policies on population redistribution. The first was Gumi Shi, where newly established industrial sites were located. Since 1971, when the industrial sites were first established, the population more than tripled from 24,000 to 72,000 in 1977. This rapid population growth changed the area from town (Eub) to city (Shi) status on February 1978 after the annexation of an adjacent Myon in 1977.[1] The industrial sites, which are located about 4

----

[1] This changing status of Gumi from Eub to Shi does not alter the nature of this study. Since Gumi remained a rural town for most of the study period of 1970-78, and only the original Eub boundary was included in the survey, movement to Gumi is still considered as a return to a rural area.

miles from the city area, consist mostly of textile and electronic factories. Both a railroad and a highway pass through the city to Seoul and Daegu, the provincial capital city.

Jeomchon Eub is a mining and commercial town around which a number of coal mines and cement industries are located. The area shows relatively stable population growth since 1956 when this area was designated as an Eub. In 1977, the population was 43,221.

Hayang Eub is located very close to Daegu. It takes about 40 minutes by local bus to get to the central city area of Daegu, which is about 13 miles away. The area is an agricultural town and has a number of orchards. Among the three study areas, Hayang retains the most rural characteristics. It had a population size of 23,339 in 1977.

The survey was designed to interview a sample of males living in the study area, who were at least 23 years old at the time of the survey; the sample was to encompass return migrants, other migrants, and natives. The desired sample size was about 300 completed cases for each of the following groups:

Return Migrants: Those born in the rural areas of Gyeongsangbugdo province and (1) living in Seoul at the time of the 1970 census (October 1, 1970) for more than three months; and/or (2) living in Seoul in 1974; and/or (3) living in Daegu at the time of the 1970 census (October 1, 1970) for more than three months.

Other Migrants: Those born outside of each study area.

Natives: Those born in each study area who had never migrated to any location outside the area except for moves associated with compulsory military service.

The age of 23 for respondents at the time of the survey in 1978 was decided on since the respondent would have been 15 years old at the time of the 1970 census. At this age males usually finish middle school and enter the labor force for the first time. Fixing the time point when return migrants lived in cities was necessary to ensure the comparability of the survey data to other data; these include the 1970 Population Census of Korea conducted on October 1970, and the Seoul City Migration Survey which was conducted in 1974-75.

Seoul is the largest capital city of Korea, with a population of 6.9 million in 1975. Its distance from each study area is 174,

196, and 217 miles from Gumi, Jeomchon, and Hayang, respectively. Daegu is the third largest city of the country and a provincial capital city of Gyeongsangbugdo province. The population of Daegu was 1.3 million at the time of the 1975 census, and Daegu is 29, 81, and 13 miles away from Gumi, Jeomchon, and Hayang, respectively.

The sample selection took place in several stages (see the Appendix). The final rural sample consisted of 285 return migrants, 270 other migrants, and 300 natives. Only a very small number of respondents eligible for interview by the criteria noted above and still at the address obtained through the civilian registry or through the household enumeration conducted for this purpose refused to be interviewed (see Appendix Table A.2).

In addition to this special sample survey of rural areas, the 1970 Korean Census was used to examine the selectivity of return migration. In particular, the one percent sample tape of the 1970 census was designed to select male migrants in Seoul and Daegu who were born in rural areas of Gyeongsangbugdo province, and were aged 15 years and over at the time of the census. Their demographic and socioeconomic characteristics in 1970 will be compared to the 1970 characteristics of the return migrants identified in the Return Migration Survey who in 1970 were living in Seoul or Daegu.

A third data source was the Seoul City Migration Survey conducted by Sarah Clark Green in 1974-75 (Green, 1977; Green, 1983). It was used to analyze the determinants of return migration. Migrants from rural areas living in Seoul were compared to return migrants from Seoul identified in the Return Migration Survey.

Return Migration in Korea: 1965-1970

Data from the 1970 Korean Census allow us to examine types of migration for urban and rural populations and selected aspects of urban to rural return migration. They provide an empirical overview and descriptive context for the detailed analysis of the determinants and consequences of return migration derived from survey data.

The 1970 Korean Census collected information on place of birth, place of residence five years before the census, and current place of residence. Based on these data, the Korean population was classified into five migration status groups: (1) non-migrants (individuals who were living in their province of birth in both 1965

27

and 1970); (2) settled migrants (individuals whose province of residence in 1965 was different from their province of birth but who were living in the same province in 1970 as in 1965); (3) primary migrants (individuals who had moved to their 1970 province of residence since 1965 and whose previous province of residence was the same as their province of birth); (4) repeat migrants (persons whose province of birth was different from their 1970 province of residence, and who had moved to their 1970 province since 1965 from still a third province); and (5) return migrants (persons who since 1965 had moved back to their province of birth from a different province). This typology follows that developed for Thailand (Goldstein and Goldstein, 1979).

The distribution of these five migration types for the Korean population five years of age and over by urban and rural residence categories is presented in Table 2.1. About three-fourths of the total Korean population were classified as non-migrants. However, the stability of the population varies with residence types. The rural population is the most stable and the urban population is the least stable. Over 90 percent of the rural population were classified as non-migrants in contrast to 54.8 percent of the urban population. The level of mobility of the town population falls between the urban and rural, but it is closer to that of the rural population.

Settled migrants is the next largest segment among migration status groups. About 15 percent of the total population moved out of their province of birth before 1965 and did not change their province of residence during the 1965-70 period. The proportion of settled migrants is much higher in urban places than in towns and rural areas. More than one-fourth of the urban population were settled migrants, compared to 10.4 and 5.3 percent of the town and rural populations, respectively. The proportion of settled migrants in urban areas is more than five times greater than that in rural areas, suggesting that migration accounted for much of the total urban population growth in Korea. The size of the settled migrant group is significant since it affects the volume of repeat and return migration. Together with the repeat and return migrants, it forms the population 'at risk' of re-migration (repeat plus return migration). The characteristics of the settled migrants as a group are also important for studying the selectivity of repeat and return migrants in the destination area. Comparison of characteristics of the settled migrants with repeat or return migrants in the same destination reveals selectivity of repeat or return migration.

During the five year period 1965-70, 9.1 percent of the total

TABLE 2.1

DISTRIBUTION OF TOTAL KOREAN POPULATION AND RECENT
MIGRANTS BY TYPE OF MIGRATION, BY 1970
PLACE OF RESIDENCE AND MIGRATION STREAM

	Non-Migrants	Settled Migrants	Primary Migrants	Repeat Migrants	Return Migrants	Total Percent
Residence in 1970						
Urban	54.8	28.1	13.4	2.6	1.1	100.0
Town	83.3	10.4	4.0	1.4	0.9	100.0
Rural	91.7	5.3	1.8	0.6	0.6	100.0
Total	75.6	15.3	6.8	1.5	0.8	100.0

	Primary Migrants	Repeat Migrants	Return Migrants	Total Percent	Number (in 100s)	
Residence in 1970						
Urban	78.1	15.3	6.6	100.0	(19,339)	
Town	64.1	21.6	14.2	100.0	(1,539)	
Rural	60.3	20.1	19.6	100.0	(3,941)	
Total	74.4	16.4	9.2	100.0	(24,819)	
Migration Stream						%
Rural-Urban	87.5	8.3	4.2	100.0	(12,198)	51.4
Rural-Rural	78.9	9.3	11.8	100.0	(2,722)	11.5
Urban-Urban	67.3	21.2	11.5	100.0	(6,356)	26.8
Urban-Rural	46.8	27.3	25.9	100.0	(2,444)	10.3
Total	76.9	13.8	9.3	100.0	(23,720)	100.0

Korean population moved across a provincial boundary. In all, 6.8 percent of the population left their province of birth to move to other provinces, and 1.5 percent moved to a province other than their province of birth; only a very small proportion of the population returned to their province of birth. In all, return migrants constituted about one-half of the repeat migrants and one-eighth of the primary migrants. The proportion of primary, repeat, and return migrants is higher in urban areas than either in town or in rural areas, reflecting higher overall mobility of the urban population. Including moves within the province and moves which occurred within the migration interval would increase the extent of repeat and return migration than that observed with census data.

The distribution of recent migrants among primary, repeat, and return migrants is presented in the middle panel of Table 2.1. Among the individuals who moved across a provincial boundary during the five year period 1965-70, 74.4 percent were primary migrants and 16.4 percent were repeat migrants. Those who moved back to their province of birth constituted 9.2 percent of all interprovincial migrants during the period. Comparatively, the extent of return migration in Korea was lower than in the U.S., but almost the same as in Thailand. During the 1965-70 period, the proportion of return migrants to the total interstate migrants in the U.S. was 20 percent for whites and 21 percent for blacks (Lee, 1974); it was 9.5 percent of the total interprovincial migrants aged 15 years and over in Thailand (Goldstein and Goldstein, 1979).

The proportion of primary migrants is higher in urban areas than in towns and rural areas. Almost eight out of every ten migrants in urban areas were primary migrants. Repeat migrants in urban areas were more than twice as numerous as return migrants. However, the proportion of return migrants in rural areas was almost the same as repeat migrants. As expected, the proportion of return migrants was highest in rural areas and lowest in urban areas, reflecting the predominant rural to urban migration in the past.

Rural to urban migration was still dominant in Korea during the period of 1965-70, but moves between urban areas also constituted a large proportion of all moves. As shown in the lower panel of Table 2.1, 51.4 percent of the total interprovincial migrants moved from rural areas to urban areas in the five year period. Urban to urban migration constituted 26.8 percent, and rural to rural and urban to rural migration were 11.5 and 10.3 percent of the total interprovincial migration, respectively. In all, urban places absorbed 78.2 percent of the total migrants between 1965 and 1970, pointing to the important role of migration for urban population growth in Korea. During the same five year period, Park (1978) estimated that migration contributed 63.8 percent to the total urban population growth, while natural increase accounted for 36.2 percent of urban population growth. The contribution of migration to urban population growth in the 1965-70 period was nearly two times larger than the preceeding five year period. During 1960-65, migration contributed 33.3 percent to the urban population growth, while natural increase and annexation accounted for 44.9 and 21.9 percent, respectively. This indicates that for the later half of the decade, migration played the most important role in the urbanization of Korea.

Each of the rural/urban streams can, in turn, be decomposed by type of migration. The proportion of primary migration was higher in the streams which originated in rural areas and lower in those from urban areas. In contrast, the proportions of both repeat and return migration were higher in the streams which originated in urban places. This reflects the fact that the vast majority of the rural population were still living in their province of birth. Thus, the propensity to be a primary migrant was higher in rural areas. On the other hand, a large proportion of the urban population came originally from a different province of birth, thereby increasing the probability of repeat or return migration. Among the four streams, the proportion of return migration was highest in the urban to rural stream (25.9 percent), and lowest in the rural to urban stream (4.2 percent).

Patterns of migration in the urban to rural stream are particularly important in our context. More than half of these migrants were multiple movers who had experienced another move before. The extent of return migration was significant in this stream: Over one out of every four urban to rural migrants was a return migrant.

The 1970 census distinguished urban and rural places for province of birth and province of residence in 1965 and in 1970. Using this information, return migration is defined as the movement of those who were born in rural areas and were living in a city in 1965 (regardless of whetheirr the city was within or outside the province of birth) and were living in rural areas of the province of birth in 1970. Therefore, it includes both intra- and interprovincial moves but the return movement was from urban areas to rural areas of their province of birth. With this definition, we can determine the extent to which rural born urban migrants moved to cities within the province of birth and moved to cities in another province, and their propensity to return to the rural areas of their province of birth.

Approximately 3.3 million of the rural born population five years of age and over were living in urban areas in 1965. Among them, 33.8 percent were living in cities within their province of birth, and 66.2 percent were living in cities outside their province of birth. Thus, the majority of rural born urban migrants moved to cities outside their province of birth. However, this proportion varied by province. For example, in Gyunggido province only 18.6 percent moved to cities within the province, while the remaining 81.4 percent moved to cities outside the province. In contrast, more than half (55.3 percent) of the rural born urban migrants moved to cities within the province in Gyeonsangbugdo province. These varying proportions in each province reflect two factors: the relative degree of attractiveness of provincial cities and the distance to the nearby large metropolitan centers outside the province. Thus, the higher proportion of urban migrants who moved to outside cities in Gyunggido and Gyeongsangbugdo province is related to the fact that Seoul and Busan, which are the first and second largest cities in the country and treated as separate provinces, are encompassed by those provinces, respectively. In contrast, the low proportion in Gyeonsangbugdo province is due to the the fact that Daegu (the third largest city in Korea) is located within the province. Variation among other provinces relates to distance to major cities.

Overall, among those who moved to cities outside their province of birth, 60.6 percent moved to Seoul. This is equivalent to 40.1 percent of the total rural born urban migrants. It is evident that Seoul is the most attractive place to go for urban migrants. In fact, urbanization in Korea during the past decades has been dominated by the growth of Seoul. During the intercensal period of 1960-66 and 1966-70, Seoul absorbed 52.8 and 54.8 percent of the total urban population growth, respectively (Yu, 1972, 1974). During the same intercensal period, net migration accounted for 57.7 and 80.7 percent of the total population growth in Seoul.

The survey conducted for the in-depth analysis of return migration was confined to those who were born in rural areas of Gyeongsangbugdo province and moved to either Seoul and Daegu and returned later to one of the three rural towns in the same province. Therefore, examining the movement of those individuals who were born in rural areas of the province and who moved to and from Seoul and Daegu has special importance. It will give us some insight about the extent of population movement between the study areas. However, it should be noted that the time reference is different between the census and the survey. The data from the census represent return migration between 1965 and 1970, but the survey included return migration between 1970 and the time of the survey in 1978. Therefore, it is expected that the size of the universe covered by the study population should be larger than that found in census data.

Of the 1970 population enumerated by the Korean census, 129,400 persons who were born in rural areas of Gyeongsangbugdo province were living in Seoul in 1965. This constituted 3.1 percent of the total rural born population of the same province. During the five year period 1965-70, 4.4 percent of these migrants returned to the same province of birth, 7.3 percent moved to other provinces, and 88.3 percent remained in Seoul in 1970. Of the return migrants, 2.3 percent returned to Daegu and 2.1 percent returned to rural areas of the province. Compared to the return migration from the distant capital city of the country, Seoul, the propensity to return from the provincial capital city of Daegu is much higher. The probability of return to rural areas from Daegu is 4.1 percent, which is about two times larger than the rate from Seoul.

Selectivity of Return Migrants

This descriptive background of migration patterns based on the 1970 Korean Census places return migration in the context of the broader picture. Nevertheless, census data are limited for in-depth analysis. Combining them with survey data on return migration enhances our understanding of the selectivity of return migration. To assess selectivity we compared the characteristics of return migrants with those of all in-migrants who were living in the same destination city, at the same time.

Generally, it has been assumed that return migrants are less educated and less skilled and thus are less economically adjusted and socially suited for urban life than migrants who do not return (Kuznets, 1964; Sanders, 1969; Simmons and Cardona, 1972; DaVanzo, 1977). It is expected, therefore, that return migrants from large cities, on the whole, are negatively selected from the total group of in-migrants. Return migration serves to 'weed out' the less successful migrants; the more skilled and better suited for urban life remain in the city. In turn, this implies that return migration increases the positive selectivity of those who remain in cities (Browning, 1971; Weller, 1974).

The above assumption has been supported indirectly by findings showing no differences between the characteristics of migrants and urban natives surveyed. Regarding such findings, researchers frequently indicate the possibility that return migration may cause the overall socioeconomic characteristics of the remaining in-migrants to appear higher than they really are through the process of negative selection of return migrants (e.g., Weller, 1974; Green, 1983; McCutcheon, 1983).

In addition to these indirect inferences, several studies have tested the proposition directly. Using data on the United States, DaVanzo (1977) found that those least capable of processing information efficiently--the less educated, the less skilled, and the less careful planners--were more prone to return because their initial move was more likely to have been based on limited or faulty information. In contrast, three studies using Latin American data reached a different conclusion. Simmons and Cardona (1972) found that many return migrants were better educated and better skilled. Feindt and Browning (1972), in their Monterey study, concluded that return migrants had a better education, occupation, and income than those who did not return. Others noted that return migration was dominated by family reasons, while economic and adjustment failures were minor reasons for returning (Chi and Bogan, 1974).

These findings are limited because they are based on individual reasons for return and/or a comparison of the characteristics of return migrants in the place of rural origin with those of non-return migrants in cities or natives in rural areas after the return migrants have returned. Frequently, the reason cited by respondents may be compounded by many others. Sometimes the respondent himself may not be aware of the exact reasons. It is also easier to say one returned for family reasons than to admit failure in the city. Moreover, issues of selectivity are difficult to analyze by comparing the characteristics of those who live in different places. For example, one cannot compare the income of non-return migrants in cities and return migrants in rural areas since city income is generally higher than rural income, as are costs.

In order to examine selectivity, comparisons should be made between the characteristics of return migrants and non-return migrants at the same place of destination, at the same point in time, before migrants returned. This can be achieved ideally by using longitudinal time series data collected from the same group of people. As an alternative method, we combined information on in-migrants identified in the census and on return migrants identified in the sample survey in which individual life histories were obtained from respondents. The focus is on two large urban destinations, Seoul and Daegu city, and one province of rural origin, Gyeongsangbugdo province, from which return migrants originally moved out with other in-migrants to either Seoul or Daegu, and to which they returned later.

In-migrants and return migrants are defined as follows:

In-migrants: those who were born in any rural area of Gyeongsangbugdo province and moved either to Seoul or Daegu city and were living there for at least three months at the time of the 1970, census (October 1, 1970).

Return migrants: those who differed from the in-migrants defined above in that they returned to one of three study areas of Gyeongsangbugdo province after October 1, 1970.

For both groups, males at least 15 years old at the time of the 1970 census are included. Age 15 is the age at graduation from middle school and the approximate age to enter the labor market for those not continuing on to higher levels of education.

The characteristics of in-migrants were obtained from the one percent sample tape of the 1970 population census of Korea utilizing information of place of birth and place of current residence. A total of 917 in-migrants to Seoul and 1,545 in-migrants to Daegu were identified. We excluded those serving in the military service because their socioeconomic characteristics were not provided. The final number of in-migrants included in the comparison was 873 and 1,475 for Seoul and Daegu, respectively. The time point is around October 1, 1970, when the census was taken. At that time, both in-migrants and return migrants lived in the same place, either in Seoul or in Daegu. The characteristics of return migrants are from the retrospective questions about life history obtained in the survey. The number of return migrants included in the comparison is 112 for Seoul and 148 for Daegu. It should be noted that the groups (return migrants and in-migrants) are not mutually exclusive. The in-migrants include the return migrants, since they were resident in the respective cities at the time of the census according to their residence histories. In other words, comparisons will be made between the whole and one part. Selectivity will focus on the following characteristics: age, marital status, education, economic activity, and previous place of residence.

The data show that return migrants are younger compared

35

to the total in-migrants, and the difference is highly significant statistically (Table 2.2). The mean age of return migrants is 25.4 in Seoul and 29.0 in Daegu, and that of in-migrants is 29.7 and 30.1 in Seoul and Daegu, respectively. This indicates that return migrants from Seoul are younger than return migrants from Daegu, although there is almost no difference in age between in-migrants to Seoul and those to Daegu. Return migrants are concentrated in younger age groups: For Seoul, 29.6 percent of in-migrants are aged 20-29, whereas 62.5 percent of return migrants are in these ages; for Daegu, 37.8 percent of the in-migrants are between the ages of 20 and 34 compared to 71.6 percent of the return migrants.

The proportion of in-migrants aged 20-24 is smaller than return migrants for both Seoul and Daegu, although military service may affect that. The number of in-migrants from rural areas is reduced considerably since every young man of this age group is required to serve in the army for three years. In Korea, when men reach age 20, they are eligible to be drafted unless they are attending college or university. For college students, army service is postponed until after graduation. Military service may also influence return moves of young migrants. Everyone is drafted at the place of their domicile, which is the same as the place of origin. Therefore, many young migrants who moved to cities for better education or better jobs return to their place of origin and stay there one or more months before going to the army.

It is assumed that single migrants are more likely to return than those who are married. The rationale behind this assumption is that single migrants may be more attached to the place of origin (or family of origin) than are the married, and the cost of a return move is less for single persons.

The selectivity of return migrants with respect to marital status first appears to be different in Seoul and Daegu. For the total sample, single migrants are more likely to return from Seoul than are married migrants, whereas in Daegu married migrants are more likely to return (Table 2.3). However, this discrepancy disappears when age is controlled. For all age groups, more married in-migrants returned than single migrants, although the difference is not significant. The percent difference is larger in the younger age groups, but in the older age groups the difference is smaller and insignificant. Why are married in-migrants more likely to return than the single, contrary to expectation? Perhaps some married migrants moved to Seoul or Daegu by themselves, leaving their spouse and/or children behind at the place of origin.

TABLE 2.2

AGE DISTRIBUTION OF RETURN AND IN-MIGRANTS
BEFORE RETURNING TO PLACE OF ORIGIN:
SEOUL AND DAEGU

Age	Seoul		Daegu	
	Return Migrants	In-Migrants	Return Migrants	In-Migrants
15-19	8.0	18.4	3.4	23.8
20-24	36.6	11.0	20.9	10.7
25-29	25.9	18.6	27.7	14.1
30-34	16.1	18.0	23.0	13.0
35-39	4.5	11.6	8.1	11.1
40-44	3.6	8.4	4.7	8.5
45-49	3.6	4.2	6.8	6.6
50-54	0.9	4.0	5.4	3.7
55-59	0.9	3.1	-	3.7
60+	-	2.7	-	4.7
Total: Percent	100.0	100.0	100.0	100.0
Number	112	873	148	1475
Mean Age	25.4	29.7	29.0	30.1
Median Age	23.5	28.1	27.1	28.0

Significance Level of Differences of Means Test
for Age under 35   .000   .001

TABLE 2.3

SELECTED SOCIAL AND DEMOGRAPHIC CHARACTERISTICS OF RETURN
AND IN-MIGRANTS BEFORE RETURNING TO PLACE OF ORIGIN:
SEOUL AND DAEGU

	Seoul		Daegu	
	Return Migrants	In-Migrants	Return Migrants	In-Migrants
All Ages				
% Married	50.0	60.6	69.6	59.1
% High School+	63.4	51.5	44.6	39.5
% Employed	80.6	77.3	91.2	73.2
% Attending School	13.6	10.9	6.1	14.0
% White Collar	49.4	48.7	37.8	38.8
% Own Account	30.1	20.0	40.0	23.3
% Employee	66.3	74.3	56.3	70.4
% Duration >5 years	49.0	42.8	45.5	38.7
15-24				
% Married	10.0	2.3	11.1	3.3
% High School+	76.0	45.2	58.4	45.2
% Employed	63.6	51.8	74.3	52.3
% Attending School	31.8	32.7	22.9	38.9
% White Collar	46.4	29.9	42.3	19.0
% Own Account	14.3	2.2	23.1	3.7
% Employee	85.7	88.3	76.9	89.7
% Duration >5 years	61.7	58.4	38.9	53.0
25-34				
% Married	78.7	74.6	82.7	78.7
% High School+	59.6	59.6	45.3	47.0
% Employed	93.2	90.3	97.3	89.8
% Attending School	0.0	3.4	1.3	2.0
% White Collar	46.3	47.6	39.7	44.1
% Own Account	34.1	23.7	32.9	24.0
% Employee	61.0	72.5	63.0	69.5
% Duration <5 years	33.3	47.3	50.0	42.6
35+				
% Married	93.3	96.0	100.0	95.4
% High School+	33.3	48.4	29.7	29.2
% Employed	93.3	85.5	94.6	80.4
% Attending School	0.0	0.0	0.0	0.0
% White Collar	64.3	60.3	30.6	46.2
% Own Account	50.0	25.4	66.7	34.1
% Employee	42.9	68.8	27.8	59.8
% Duration >5 years	53.3	24.6	44.4	23.3

In such cases, they tend to return more easily once they complete the purpose of their original movement or they find their expectations can not be fulfilled. They may be returning to raise their families in their rural place of origin.

Many studies have assumed that migrants return to their place of origin because they are less adjusted in the city: The lower education level of return migrants has been associated with poorer adjustment (DaVanzo, 1977). In fact, studies of return migration in developing countries have documented that the level of education of return migrants is lower than that of out-migrants (Simmons and Cardona, 1972; Chi and Bogan, 1974). Based on this evidence, we hypothesized that migrants with less education are more likely to return than migrants with more education. The evidence, however, does not support the proposition (Table 2.3). Overall, return migrants are better educated than in-migrants. For Seoul, 63.4 percent of return migrants have at least a high school level of education, in contrast to only 51.5 percent of the in-migrants. Comparable figures for Daegu are 44.6 and 39.5 percent for return migrants and in-migrants, respectively.

When age is taken into account, a clear-cut positive selectivity by education of return migrants among those aged 15-24 is found. For the next older age group, 25-34, there are no differences in educational attainment of return migrants and in-migrants. For those aged 35 and older, fewer return migrants have at least a high school education in Seoul while no differences appear in Daegu.

The higher education level of return migrants among younger ages may reflect the fact that many may move into large cities for educational objectives. Once they achieve their desired level of education, a significant proportion return to their place of origin to take a job. It is reasonable to assume that if there are appropriate jobs available at origin for those with higher education, many would be willing to return there because of the desire to be near family and friends. In fact, the sample included one newly established industrial area in the origin province, where a large number of professional and technical jobs were available. In such an instance, it is easier for the young and newly graduated to take advantage of job opportunities compared to the older, more established in-migrants.

Type of economic activity was classified into employed, unemployed, attending school, and economically inactive. One of the interesting relationships between type of economic activity and return migration to be tested relates to whether unemployed migrants in the city are more likely to return. If expected employment does not materialize, many migrants may return to their place of origin because of the security offered by family. However, the evidence shows that the proportion employed is slightly greater for return migrants from Seoul and Daegu compared to in-migrants, but the differences are not statistically significant.

Another type of economic activity relates to attending school. In Seoul, more return migrants had been attending school in 1970 than in-migrants; the reverse is true in Daegu. This suggests that Seoul provides better education facilities than Daegu, and also that those migrants who move for higher education are more likely to return once they finish their desired level of education. Controlling for age does not change the pattern significantly. Among those aged 15-24, about one-third of return migrants and in-migrants were students in Seoul; in contrast, less return migrants were students in Daegu. This suggests that among migrants who moved to the city for education, the probability of return to take a job in the origin place is higher for those who moved to a remote than to a nearby city. In part, this is understandable because those who are in the nearby city can visit their place of origin more easily.

The data also show that there were relatively small differences in occupational type between return migrants and in-migrants. In both cities, the proportion white collar among return migrants and in-migrants was about the same. However, occupational selectivity varies with age groups. In the youngest age group, more white collar workers returned both from Seoul and Daegu. This coincides with the higher proportion of college educated return migrants in this age group. In the age group 25-34, the occupational differences between return and in-migrants are minimal. However, in the older age group, 35 and over, the proportion white collar among return migrants from Daegu was lower than for in-migrants. This is not the case for return migrants from Seoul.

The data show that workers of own account are more likely to return than workers in other status categories. For example, in Daegu 40 percent of return migrants are own account workers, compared to 23.3 percent of in-migrants (Table 2.3). When age is controlled, the same pattern persists in all age categories. By contrast, employees are less likely to be return migrants, and this is particularly so for old migrants. For example, 27.8 percent of return migrants aged 35 and over in Daegu were employees, while 59.8 percent of in-migrants were employees. This difference may reflect the greater ease with which own account workers could change their place of residence because they were less involved in organizational settings than employees. Perhaps own account workers include some who could not find paid employment and became self-employed.

Overall, the only consistent pattern of selectivity among the variables of economic activity was working status; own account workers are more likely to return than those belonging to other categories. The selectivity of type of economic activity and occupation in return migration is neither consistent nor significant. In short, with respect to type of economic activity and occupation, there is no clear-cut pattern of selectivity involved in return migration.

Did return migrants return within a short or long period after they moved to large cities? Many return migrants are assumed to return within a short period of time as a result of their failure to adjust to city life. Besides the duration of residence in the city, the place of residence of migrants prior to moving into large cities (urban or rural) may also have an important bearing on the propensity to return. Those who moved from rural areas may be more likely to return than those who migrated from other urban areas because of the easier adjustment to city life of urban in-migrants. In addition, whether migrants have been away for longer periods of time may also influence the propensity to return. It can be assumed that the longer the time period from when migrants left their place of origin, the less attached they are to the origin, and the less likely they are to return.

Our findings are more or less consistent with the above propositions, but not always strongly so. Those who migrated to their current residence within a five year period (recent migrants) are more likely to return than long-term migrants--those who moved in and have lived at least 5 years in the city (49.0 versus 42.8 percent in Seoul and 45.5 versus 38.7 percent in Daegu). This finding is statistically significant only for the older age group. For age groups under age 35, the relation of duration of residence to return migration is not statistically significant and is inconsistent for Seoul and Daegu, suggesting that factors other than length of residence affect the rate of return for young adults.

When recent migrants are subdivided into place of residence before the move (urban or rural), no significant effects on return migration were observed. This may be due to the fact that some of the migrants who moved for college education in Seoul received their high school education in the small provincial cities. And, as discussed before, the proportion of return migrants with a college level of education is much higher than in-migrants, particularly in this age group.

The proposition that those who have been gone from their province of origin for a long period of time are less likely to return holds only in Seoul. The proportion of those who left the origin province (Gyeongsangbugdo) more than five years ago is smaller among return migrants than among in-migrants in Seoul (7.8 versus 18.3 percent). This finding is consistent with the results of other research (e.g., DaVanzo, 1977) which suggests that once a migrant has departed a place, the propensity to return weakens with length of residence because most of the location-specific capital depreciates in value. Here, location-specific capital refers to any factor that tends to bind one to that place, for example, knowledge of an area, real estate one owns, and friendships that enhance one's feeling of belonging there. The absence of a difference in Daegu can be explained by the fact that Daegu's location is in the center of the province of origin and therefore it is easier for in-migrants to communicate with people in their origin place or visit them for maintaining connections. Thus the location-specific capital is less affected by intervals of absence in Daegu.

In sum, of nine variables examined, only two--age and working status--showed a consistent pattern of selectivity in return migration. For these two variables, the differences are large, and are in the same direction for all age groups, for different destinations. For the rest of the variables, differences are inconsistent, depending on age and destination. Most strikingly, however, the findings of this analysis contradict the prevailing proposition that return migrants are less educated and less skilled, and thus negatively selected from large cities. The return migrants of this analysis are, in contrast, more educated and more skilled, particularly among those in young ages. In part, this reflects the fact that the province included in this study is one of the economically well-developed regions of Korea and also includes a newly expanding industrial town. Therefore, return to this area may be more attractive and beneficial to those who are more educated and skilled.

Determinants of Return Migration

Why do migrants in urban areas return to their rural places of origin? What factors influence the return migration and which are relatively more important? We first compare a large number of demographic and socioeconomic variables for return and non-

42

return migrants at two different points in time--at the time of move and at the time of return. The relative effect of these variables on return migration will be assessed using multiple regression analysis. The variables included are: (1) background characteristics of migrants at the time of move--age, marital status, education, and prior urban exposure; (2) move related characteristics--knowledge of the destination, job information, prior job arrangement, unit of move, and reasons for move; (3) duration of residence in city; and (4) ties to hometown. The characteristics at the time of return include--education, occupation, personal income, possession of consumer objects, homeownership, and organizational affiliation.

The data for this analysis are derived from two different surveys. The data for non-return migrants are from the 1974 Seoul City Migration Survey; data for return migrants are from the 1978 Return Migration Survey. Throughout the analysis, non-return migrants are defined as males who were born in the rural areas of any province during in South Korea, and moved to and lived in Seoul at the time of the Seoul City Migration Survey, and who were aged 20-44 at the time of the Seoul survey. Return migrants are males who were born in rural areas of Gyeongsangbugdo province and moved to Seoul but later returned to that province during 1970-1978, and who were aged 20-44 at the time they left Seoul.

The Seoul City Migration Survey was conducted in Seoul as part of the Comparative Urbanization Project (Green, 1983; Goldscheider, 1983). The field interviews were carried out during the period from November 1974 to early 1975 for both male and female respondents aged 20-44 at the time of the survey. Among them, 163 respondents were selected for analysis here based on the definition of non-return migrants indicated above. From the Return Migration Survey, a total of 126 return migrants fit the definition specified for return migrants.

Since non-return migrants and return migrants were derived from different surveys conducted at different points in time for different purposes, some problems of comparability are inherent. The first relates to the fact that the birthplaces of non-return migrants include rural areas of the entire country. By contrast, return migrants were born in rural areas of only one province, Gyeongsangbugdo. Consequently, the analysis assumes that there are no differences in the major characteristics of migrants from Gyeongsangbugdo province and migrants from other provinces of the country. An examination of major demographic and socioeconomic characteristics of migrants included in the Seoul City Migration Survey by province of birth (including age, marital status, relation to head of household, education, economic activity, occupation, personal income, age, year moved to Seoul, and duration of residence in Seoul) showed that besides age at the time of move to Seoul, all other variables were not statistically significant at the 0.05 level. Thus, there appears to be no differences among migrants from different origins, and no known biases along these lines are associated with the analysis.

The second issue of comparability between non-return and return migrants relates to the differences in time when the information was collected: The survey for non-return migrants was conducted at the end of 1974, while return migrants left Seoul between 1970 and 1978. However, three-fourths of the return migrants fall within a two year time period around 1974 and, hence, the biases, if any, are minimal.

In order to identify factors affecting return migration, we compare a large number of characteristics of non-return and return migrants at two time points: (1) the time migrants entered Seoul and (2) the time of the survey for non-return migrants and at the time return migrants left Seoul.

Background Characteristics

On average, return migrants were slightly younger than non-return migrants at the time they initially moved to Seoul (Table 2.4). The median ages at move are 20.3 and 22.8 years for return migrants and non-return migrants, respectively. Return migrants moved to Seoul mostly at ages between 15 and 34. Only a few return migrants moved to Seoul at ages below 15 and over 35. Return migrants are significantly overrepresented at age 15-19: The proportion of return migrants in this age group is double that of non-return migrants. During these ages, migrants either enter the labor market for the first time or move to Seoul for higher education.

Cross-classification between age at move to Seoul and reasons for move shows that nearly half of the return migrants in this age group moved for reasons associated with education (45.3 percent), compared to only 18.2 percent of non-return migrants. More non-return migrants moved either for jobs (60.6 percent) or to follow the head of the household (21.2 percent) compared to return migrants with 39.6 percent and 3.8 percent, respectively. This suggests that migrants who moved to Seoul for educational

44

TABLE 2.4

SELECTED SOCIAL AND DEMOGRAPHIC CHARACTERISTICS AT THE TIME
OF THE MOVE: RETURN AND NON-RETURN MIGRANTS

	Non-Return Migrants	Return Migrants
Age*		
0-14	16.6	4.0
15-19	21.5	42.9
20-34	54.6	51.5
35+	7.4	1.6
Mean	21.9	21.6
Median	22.8	20.3
Percent Married		
Total*	39.3	23.8
<20*	3.2	1.7
20-29*	46.5	30.2
30+	96.7	92.9
Education (% High School+)		
Total*	36.8	51.9
<20	12.0	40.7
20-29	36.5	61.2
30+	61.5	38.5
Prior Urban Exposure	21.7	30.2
Visited Seoul*	49.0	30.1
Job Information	56.1	62.6
Individual Move		
Total*	50.0	73.8
Single*	62.6	84.4
Married	30.2	40.0
Reason for Move*		
Job Related	67.9	55.6
Education Related	10.9	27.4
Following Head	16.0	2.4
Duration of Residence in Seoul (years)*		
Mean	9.9	8.1
Median	7.8	7.5
Presence of Family or Kin in Hometown	95.0	97.6
Visit to Hometown*	75.2	95.2
Visit of Relative or Friend*	69.6	85.0

* = Chi Square significant at the .05 level

purposes are more likely to return. Another large difference is found for those under age 15. Only four percent of return migrants were under age 15 when they moved compared to 16.6 percent of non-return migrants. This suggests that those who moved in their early childhood are less prone to move back. Perhaps having spent most of their formative years in Seoul, their social ties to Seoul are much stronger than to the place of origin.

It can be expected that single migrants are more likely to return than married migrants. Single migrants tend to move individually to Seoul, leaving their families behind in the place of origin and retaining personal ties with them. Also, moving is in general easier for single migrants than for married migrants. Data in Table 2.4 show that more than three-fourths of return migrants were single at the time they moved to Seoul. However, the difference in marital status is not significant when age at move is controlled. Only for ages 20-29 are some differences observed, but they are not statistically significant. Therefore, the observed differences in marital status between non-return and return migrants are largely attributable to the differences in the age at move.

Level of education of migrants at the time of move to city may also be expected to influence return migration. However, the evidence does not support the hypothesis. Due to the small number of cases in each age category after removing those who had any education in Seoul after their move, we dichotomized education focusing on those with at least a high school education. Overall, return migrants had more education than non-return migrants when they entered Seoul, and the difference remained after age at move was controlled. Among migrants who moved at ages under 30, level of education is higher for return migrants than non-return migrants, and the difference is statistically significant. Only among those who moved when they were over age 30 did non-return migrants have higher levels of education than return migrants. One factor accounting for these findings is that the 'failure' stereotype of return migrants applies only to migrants who return after a short stay. Those who returned after several years resemble migrants generally and, like them, are positively selected. Therefore, duration of residence in the city may be a key factor which characterizes the nature of return migrants (cf. DaVanzo and Morrison, 1978). However, the small number of short-term return migrants in the sample prevents an empirical test of this.

Prior experience living in urban areas before moving to the urban destination has been found to have some effect on migrants' adjustment to city life (Rose and Warshay, 1957; Balan et al., 1973; Weller, 1974), and may affect return migration. Those who have prior urban exposure are expected to adjust better to city life than those with no prior urban exposure. Hence, they are less likely to return. The data show that a majority of both migrant groups did not have any experience of urban living before they moved to Seoul, implying that they moved to Seoul directly from rural areas. However, more return migrants had some experience living in urban areas before moving to Seoul than did non-return migrants. About 30 percent of return migrants lived in the city sometime before they moved to Seoul, compared to 21.7 percent of non-return migrants. The results therefore do not support our theoretical expectations. An alternative explanation relates to the fact that return migrants moved to Seoul stepwise, and thus seem to have more migration experience than non-return migrants. Perhaps student migrants who moved to Seoul for a college education obtained their high school education in the nearby provincial cities; those migrants who had a college level of education are more likely to return.

Move Related Characteristics

It can be assumed that migrants who planned their move carefully or prepared for the move well before they actually moved tend to adjust to the city life better than migrants who did not. In turn, this may affect the extent of return migration. Job information and general knowledge of the destination area are important to the prospective migrants when they plan to move.

The knowledge of the destination is measured by whether the migrant had visited Seoul during the year before his move. This included all visits for any purpose, including seeking a job; seeing family, relatives, or friends; business; and sightseeing. Less than half of both samples had visited Seoul before they actually moved, but the proportion who visited is higher for non-return migrants than for return migrants. Therefore, the results support the hypothesis that migrants who have less knowledge of the destination are more likely to return. Visiting family, relatives, and friends is the most dominant reason given for the visit to Seoul. This is suggestive of chain migration, pointing to an important role of previous migrants in providing necessary information to prospective migrants. In addition, the presence of families, relatives, and friends in the city may give substantial help to the new migrants in their early stage of settlement in the city and can be a continuing source of ties for migrants in the city. It is reasonable to expect that migrants who have more personal ties in the city will be less prone to return.

Among migrants who were eligible for work at the time of move, a large proportion had job information from different sources. The most important source of job information was relatives and friends. In contrast, very few obtained job information from newspapers and employment agencies. This indicates that information is mostly transmitted through personal contacts with previous migrants in the city rather than through public channels. Return migrants had more job information than non-return migrants (62.6 percent versus 56.1 percent), although the difference is not statistically significant. With respect to the accuracy of the job information, most migrants (82.5 percent) replied that their job information was accurate, and there was no difference in the reported accuracy of the job information between non-return and return migrants. While almost half of the migrants who were eligible for work had secured a job before they moved, no difference emerges between non-return and return migrants in the prior job arrangement. Therefore, the results suggest that amount and accuracy of job information, and securing a job before the move had no effects on return migration.

It is hypothesized that migrants who move alone tend to leave their families in the place of origin and thus are more frequently motivated to return. It is also easier for individual migrants to make another move to return home than it is for migrants who move with families. The results support the hypothesis. Nearly three-fourths of return migrants moved alone to Seoul compared to half of the non-return migrants (Table 2.4). When marital status at the time of move is controlled, the same pattern persists for never married migrants. However, for the married migrants, the same differential exists, although the difference is not statistically significant.

Stated reasons for the move to Seoul were classified into four broad categories: (1) job-related moves which include seeking a job, taking a job and transferring; (2) educational reasons which combine education for either the migrant himself or his children, but is mostly for the migrant; (3) following the head of household; and (4) the remainder. Although moving for a job is the most dominant reason for both non-return and return migrants, it characterizes the move of the return migrants to a lesser degree. More return migrants moved to Seoul for educational reasons compared to non-return migrants, and very few return migrants followed the head of the household. This indicates that migrants who move to the city for educational purpose are more likely to return after attaining their desired level of education in the city, particularly when there are some opportunities available in the hometown or somewhere close to their hometown. In contrast, migrants who moved to the city following the head in their early childhood tend to live in the city longer and form social ties in the city. They tend to find it less beneficial to move back to the place of origin even if attractive opportunities are available there. In fact, the proportion of child migrants (under age 15) is much higher for non-return migrants than for return migrants.

The length of time that migrants reside in the destination city may also affect return migration. Duration of residence of migrants in the city seems to influence decisions whether to stay or move again, and where to move. On the one hand, as many studies have indicated, a short period of residence increases the probability of moving again since migrants are less attached to the destination place (Goldstein, 1954, 1964; Morrison, 1971). On the other hand, it increases the probability of choosing the previous place of residence as the new destination because the previous residence is more familiar than other possible destinations.

Data on duration of residence in Seoul by migration status show that, on average, non-return migrants appear to live in Seoul longer than return migrants. The mean number of years lived by non-return migrants is 9.9 years, and it is 8.1 years for return migrants. About one-fourth of the return migrants returned within five years; another 40 percent returned after they stayed in the city 5-9 years. Less than 10 percent of return migrants lived in the city more than 15 years, whereas 24.6 percent of non-return migrants were in this category. Therefore, the data indicate that although return migrants stayed in the city quite a long time, their duration of residence is shorter than non-return migrants.

Previous studies on return migration suggested that any ties migrants maintained in the place of origin have an important bearing on return movement (Nelson, 1976; DaVanzo, 1977). This linkage may be personal and/or material. Here we focus on personal linkages to the hometown. The variables included are whether migrants had any family members in the origin place when they lived in Seoul, how often migrants visited their hometown, and how often people in the hometown visited the migrants in Seoul. The hometown refers to return migrants' home village instead of current town; since return migration in this study was defined based on province, the current town is not the hometown of many return migrants.

49

Almost all the migrants had families or relatives in their hometown when they were living in Seoul. Only 5.0 and 2.4 percent of non-return and return migrants, respectively, did not have families or relatives in the hometown. A large number of rural villages in Korea consist of a few clans of the same family origin resulting from a low mobility of villagers in the past. Often, a family clan has lived in the same village for hundreds of years.

Return migrants visited their hometown more frequently than non-return migrants. Only 5 percent of the return migrants did not visit their hometown when they were in the city. In contrast, almost 25 percent of non-return migrants made no visit. One or two visits a year is the most common. It is a custom in Korea that on a traditional national holiday, such as New Year Day and the full moon of August, all the family members get together in their home village and have a religious ritual for their ancestors.

Return migrants also had more frequent visits by relatives or friends from their hometown. Eighty-five percent of return migrants were visited by someone from their hometown at least once a year, while 70 percent of non-return migrants were visited by relatives or friends. Overall, the data indicate that return migrants maintained stronger ties to the hometown than did non-return migrants.

Socioeconomic Factors

Of prime interest in the study of the determinants of return migration is the differential socioeconomic status and other characteristics of return migrants and non-return migrants at the time migrants leave the city to return home. At the simplest level, the question is: are return migrants successes or failures in the city? The characteristics to be compared in the analysis are conventional measures of socioeconomic status--education, occupation, income, possession of consumer objects, homeownership, and organization membership. The first four represent socioeconomic and material aspects of adjustment to the city, and the latter two relate to housing and social aspects of adjustment.

It appears the the level of education of return migrants in the city is higher than non-return migrants (Table 2.5). The proportion of those having at least a high school level of education is 65.6 and 51.6 percent for return and non-return migrants, respectively. Return migrants are overrepresented in both high

50

TABLE 2.5

LEVEL OF EDUCATION AND MEAN YEARS OF SCHOOLING
AT THE CITY BY MIGRANT TYPE

Level of Education	Non-return Migrants	Return Migrants
None	3.1	1.6
Primary School	19.0	11.2
Middle School	26.4	21.6
High School	25.8	36.8
College or More	25.8	28.8
Total: Percent	100.0	100.0
Number	163	125

(Chi-square significance level = .1298)

(Significance level of differences of means test for high
  school or more = .0166)

	Unadjusted Mean	Mean Adjusted for		
		Age	Duration	Altogether
Non-return Migrants	10.46	10.44	10.38	10.38
Return Migrants	11.32	11.34	11.41	11.42
Eta (Beta)	.12	.12	.14	.14
Significance of F	.050	.044	.019	.021

51

school and college levels of education. To ascertain whether the observed difference in the level of education between non-return and return migrants is due to differences in age and duration of residence, results of a Multiple Classification Analysis (MCA) are presented. Control variables are entered as factors (categorical variables), and the table gives the mean value of each variable by migration type, (eta beta), and significance level of F, indicating the significance of the difference between return and non-return migrants after removing the effect of control variable(s). For MCA, level of education is converted into number of years of schooling. The first column in the table indicates the mean number of years of schooling. It is 11.3 years for return migrants and 10.5 years for non-return migrants. When the effects of age on level of education are removed, the mean value does not change much, indicating that the effect of age on level of education is not significant. However, when duration of residence is controlled, the difference between non-return and return migrants becomes slightly larger. Level of education is, therefore, higher for return migrants than for non-return migrants independent of age and duration of residence in the city.

Data in Table 2.6 show the occupational distribution of return and non-return migrants using a one-digit standard classification code and also dichotomized into white and non-white collar occupations. The white collar occupations include professional, administrative, clerical, and sales. Return migrants are overrepresented in clerical workers while non-return migrants are in production-related work. When the occupation category is dichotomized into white and non-white collar occupations, return migrants tend to have more white collar jobs than non-return migrants. In the MCA analysis, the proportion in white collar occupations changes as the effects of age, education, and duration of residence are taken into account. The difference in proportion of white collar workers between non-return and return migrants becomes larger when age and duration of residence are controlled. In contrast, controlling for education level reduces this difference. Since the effects of the control variables are in different directions, the net effects are almost insignificant. After removing the effects of these three variables on the proportion of white collar workers, the difference between non-return and return migrants persists and is little different from the unadjusted level.

Monthly personal income distributions of non-return and return migrants measured by Korean Won are presented in Table 2.7. Since income of return migrants refers to the time they left Seoul, and this varied between 1970 and 1978, their income was

TABLE 2.6

OCCUPATION DISTRIBUTION AND PERCENT OF WHITE
COLLAR WORKERS BY MIGRANT TYPE

Occupation	Non-return Migrants	Return Migrants
Professional	6.3	2.5
Administrative	—	3.4
Clerical	15.3	25.4
Sales	25.0	27.1
Service	10.4	11.9
Agricultural	0.7	—
Production	42.4	29.7
Total: Percent	100.0	100.0
Number	144	118

(Chi-square significance level = .0285)

	Non-return Migrants	Return Migrants
White Collar	46.5	58.5
Non-white Collar	53.5	41.5
Total: Percent	100.0	100.0
Number	144	118

(Chi-square significance level = .0716)

	Unadjusted Mean	Mean Adjusted for			
		Age	Education	Duration	Altogether
Non-return Migrants	.47	.45	.48	.46	.47
Return Migrants	.59	.60	.57	.60	.58
Eta (Beta)	.12	.15	.09	.14	.11
Significance of F	.046	.016	.106	.029	.070

TABLE 2.7

MONTHLY PERSONAL INCOME DISTRIBUTION AND MEAN
INCOME TRANSFORMED BY LOG BY MIGRANT TYPE

Income (Thousand Won)	Non-return Migrants	Return Migrants
0-24	11.6	13.0
25-49	45.7	19.4
50-74	26.8	25.0
75-99	5.1	12.0
100-149	8.7	15.7
150-199	1.4	5.6
200 and more	0.7	9.3
Total: Percent	100.0	100.0
Number	138	108
Median Income	40,300 Won	68,634 Won

(Chi-square significance level = .0000)

	Unadjusted Mean	Mean Adjusted for			
		Age	Education	Duration	Altogether
Non-return Migrants	1.63	1.62	1.64	1.62	1.63
Return Migrants	1.86	1.87	1.85	1.87	1.86
Eta (Beta)	.34	.35	.32	.36	.33
Significance of F	.000	.000	.000	.000	.000

54

adjusted using the consumer price index to make it comparable to income of non-return migrants (income around 1974).

Return migrants earned more income in Seoul than non-return migrants. Return migrants are consistently overrepresented in the higher income categories. The median monthly income of non-return migrants was 40,300 Won, while it was 68,634 Won for return migrants.

For the multivariate analysis, absolute income was transformed into log value because there were several cases having extremely high income which would affect the mean value. Age, level of education, and duration of residence have some effects on personal income. As was the case with occupation, when age and duration of residence are held constant, the difference between non-return and return migrants becomes slightly larger, but controlling for education reduces it. After removing the effects of these three control variables, the difference between return and non-return migrants in personal income remains large and statistically significant.

The three socioeconomic status variables--education, occupation, and personal income--are individual characteristics while possession of consumer objects represents the material well-being of the household. The index score of possession of consumer objects is based on fourteen items included in the questionnaire.[2] First, each item was weighted inversely to the proportion owned by the migrants. Weights were determined using a 5 percent cutting point between categories. These weights were summed for all the items owned and the index score range was between 0 and 72.[3]

----

[2] These include: radio, electric fan, TV, sewing machine, record player, rice cooker, camera, telephone, refrigerator, gas range, car, washing machine, piano, and air conditioner.

[3] There are alternative methods to construct an index of possession of consumer objects. One is simply to add the number of items owned; another is to give a different weight to each item based on the actual prices. Comparison of intercorrelations among these three indices indicated that the index based on the proportions owned is most correlated with the other two. The simple r of this index to the second and the third is .95 and .81, respectively, and between the second and

There is basically no difference in the consumer object index between non-return and return migrants; the mean is 10.86 and 10.31, respectively, being slightly higher for non-return migrants (Table 2.8). The eta, summary measure of overall relation, is very low. When age is introduced as a control variable, the pattern is reversed; the score is slightly higher for return migrants, but the difference is not significant. Education level has a strong effect on possession of consumer objects. The score increases consistently as education level goes up. When level of education is controlled, the difference becomes larger, reflecting the fact that return migrants had more education than non-return migrants. When duration of residence is held constant, almost no difference exists between non-return and return migrants. Overall, controlling for three variables does not alter the pattern, since no differences are statistically significant.

Social Ties and City Life

Previous migration studies documented that social and economic ties to the city are important factors distinguishing movers from stayers. One economic tie to the city is homeownership. Homeowners are in general less likely to move than renters because the process of buying and selling a house involves certain costs and financial risks; thus homeowners acquire an economic bond which ties them to a particular location (Rossi, 1955; Speare, 1970). Therefore, it was hypothesized that migrants who owned a house in the city would be less prone to return to places of origin.

There is a large difference in homeownership between non-return and return migrants: Almost half of the non-return migrants owned a house compared to only 22.6 percent of return migrants (Table 2.9). When age, education, and duration of residence are introduced for control separately, the difference between non-return and return migrants does not change much. Only a small proportion of return migrants owned a house in Seoul despite their higher overall socioeconomic status. This suggests that homeownership has a strong independent effect on

----

the third index is .73. Therefore, the index based on the proportions owned seems to be the most reliable measure.

TABLE 2.8

CONSUMER OBJECT INDEX SCORE BY MIGRANT TYPE

Index Score	Non-return Migrants	Return Migrants
0-4	42.9	40.5
5-9	14.7	18.3
10-14	12.3	12.7
15-19	9.2	11.1
20-29	12.3	10.3
30-49	6.1	6.3
50 and over	2.5	0.8
Total: Percent	100.0	100.0
Number	163	126

(Chi-square significance level = .8911)

	Unadjusted Mean	Mean Adjusted for			
		Age	Education	Duration	Altogether
Non-return Migrants	10.86	10.51	11.43	10.65	11.11
Return Migrants	10.31	10.76	9.56	10.57	9.98
Eta (Beta)	.02	.01	.08	.00	.05
Significance of F	.706	.699	.661	.706	.657

57

TABLE 2.9

HOMEOWNERSHIP AND NUMBER OF ORGANIZATIONS AFFILIATED WITH
BY MIGRATION TYPE (PERCENT AND MCA)

	Non-return Migrants	Return Migrants	Chi-Square Significance
Percent Homeowners	46.0	22.6	.0001
Number	163	115	
Organizational Affiliation			
None	59.5	81.7	
1	20.9	15.1	
2	12.3	3.2	
3	7.4	0.0	
Total %	100.0	100.0	.0000
Number	163	126	

Homeownership - MCA

	Unadjusted Mean	Mean Adjusted for			
		Age	Education	Duration	Altogether
Non-return Migrants	.46	.44	.47	.45	.45
Return Migrants	.23	.24	.21	.23	.23
Eta (Beta)	.24	.20	.26	.22	.23
Significance of F	.000	.001	.000	.000	.000

Organizational Affiliation - MCA

	Unadjusted Mean	Mean Adjusted for			
		Age	Education	Duration	Altogether
Non-return Migrants	.67	.67	.72	.64	.69
Return Migrants	.22	.24	.17	.25	.20
Eta (Beta)	.28	.26	.33	.25	.30
Significance of F	.000	.000	.000	.000	.000

return migration regardless of socioeconomic status of the migrants. It is probable that migrants who planned to stay in the city temporarily did not purchase a house.

Participation in formal and informal organizations in the city is another indication of social adjustment and attachment to the city (Zimmer, 1955; Freedman and Freedman, 1956; Omari, 1956; Germani, 1961; Kasarda and Janowitz, 1974). Migrants become better integrated into the urban social systems by participating in various kinds of formal and informal groups. Thus, the assumption is that migrants who are affiliated with any organization in the city are more fully integrated and are less likely to be return migrants.

As expected, the data show that more non-return migrants were affiliated with an organization than return migrants. About 40 percent of non-return migrants were members of one or more organizations in contrast to only 18.3 percent of return migrants. Of those affiliated with one or more organizations, half of the non-return migrants belonged to more than one compared to only 17.4 percent of the return migrants.

In the multi-variate analysis (lower panel, Table 2.9), the value indicates the mean number of organizations with which migrants were affiliated. The table shows a large difference between non-return and return migrants (eta is .28). Age, education, and duration of residence are positively related to organizational affiliation, and their effects are significant. Level of education has a particularly strong impact on participation in organizations. When the effects of all the control variables are removed, differences are slightly larger. Therefore, it is evident that return migrants participated less in urban social organizations and were less attached to urban social settings.

We have examined a number of characteristics of non-return and return migrants in order to assess whether there are any differences between them. Several distinguish return migrants from those remaining in the city. What are their relative effects on return migration? We organized those variables which had some statistical significance (at least less than 0.1 level) in a multiple regression equation. Categorical variables were dichotomized to make dummy variables and were assigned values of 0 or 1. Altogether twelve independent variables were entered stepwise in the multiple regression equation. Table 2.10 summarizes the results of the regression analysis. The table shows zero-order correlation coefficients (r), standardized beta coefficients, F values of each independent variable, coefficients of separate determination, and percent contributed by each

TABLE 2.10

RELATIVE EFFECTS OF INDEPENDENT VARIABLES ON
RETURN MIGRATION

Variable	r	Beta	F	S.D.	Percent	N
Marital Sta.	-.16	.0732	1.27	.0120	2.8	288
Prior U. Exp.	.10	.0714	1.66	.0069	1.6	263
Visit to Se.	-.19	-.2158	14.27**	.0413	9.7	279
Unit of Move	-.24	-.1397	5.46*	.0337	7.9	287
Reason	.14	.1678	8.40**	.0239	5.6	279
Duration	-.14	-.1488	5.46*	.0211	5.0	288
Ties	.19	.0979	3.02	.0182	4.3	285
Education	.12	.0748	1.18	.0092	2.2	288
Occupation	.12	.0664	1.25	.0079	1.9	261
Income	.35	.3649	41.66**	.1263	29.7	245
Homeownership	-.24	-.1679	8.13**	.0402	9.4	277
Organization	-.28	-.3024	24.54**	.0847	19.9	288
Total				.4254	100.0	

R^2 = .4254   F = 13.20**

Note: * significant at .05 level, ** significant at .01 level
      S.D. = separate determination

Dependent variable: 0 = non-return migrants
                    1 = return migrants

independent variable to the total variance explained by all independent variables (R^2).[4]

Overall, the twelve independent variables included in the regression equation explained 42.5 percent of the variance in return migration, and the equation is highly significant (at the 0.001 level). The most important variable for explaining return migration is personal income in the city. Migrants who earn more income are more likely to return, accounting for 29.7 percent of the total variance explained by all the independent variables. The next most important variable is organization affiliation in the city. Migrants affiliated with any organization are less likely to return. This accounts for 19.9 percent of the total variance explained. Visits to the city before the actual move and homeownership in the city also have significant effects on return migration. Both are negatively related to return migration. Those who did not make a visit to the city before the move and who did not own a house in the city are much more prone to return. Unit of move, reasons for move, and duration of residence in the city contribute some to explaining return migration. Other variables have very little effect on return migration and are not statistically significant. Characteristics related to city life have the most influence on return migration. Together they account for 63.1 percent of the

----

[4] For determining the relative importance of each independent variable on return migration, the coefficient of separate determination is useful (Ezekiel, 1941). Normally, one can compare standardized beta coefficients to assess the relative importance of independent variables in explaining variations in the dependent variable. Although the beta coefficient is useful and widely used, it takes into account only the direct effect. The coefficient of separate determination has several advantages over the standardized beta coefficient. It takes account of both the direct and indirect effects. Another advantage of using the coefficient of separate determination is that we can decompose variance explained by all the independent variables (R^2) into variance explained by each single independent variable. The sum of the coefficient of separate determination of each variable is the same as the total variance explained by all the independent variables. Thus, the coefficient of separate determination is directly comparable from one variable to another. The coefficient of separate

total variance explained. Background characteristics at the time of move and movement related characteristics are less important. They contribute only 14.1 percent and 13.5 percent of the total variance explained, respectively.

The most important finding of this analysis is that, on the whole, return migrants are not 'failures' in the city. In fact they seem to be a positively selected group of migrants. This contrasts with the common view of return migrants assumed by most of the literature. The stereotype of return migrants has been that they are less educated, less skilled, and less careful planners for the move, and that they are therefore less economically and socially adjusted to urban life.

How can we account for this discrepancy between our results and the expectation derived from the general literature? It seems that the characteristics of return migrants are largely dependent on the nature of the city of destination and the place of origin. The major determining factors are how easily migrants can survive in the city and the degree of opportunities available in the place of origin. Assuming that there is a great difference between urban and rural areas in terms of job opportunities and earnings, as in most developing countries, it is questionable how easily a migrant will return to a rural area if he should fail to adjust in the city. Unless he cannot survive in the city, he might find it beneficial to stay in the city rather than to return to the place of origin where very limited opportunities are available. In many ways, rural migrants in the city are able to manage their lives in the area of destination. Living in a squatter settlement and being absorbed in the traditional tertiary sector provide common examples. In fact, often they can earn more income in the city than in rural areas, even when they are not fully employed in the city. Therefore, it can be argued that those who are actually forced to become return migrants are small in number.

More important for return migration is whether any opportunities are available in the place of origin. If opportunities

---

determination of a variable is made up of the direct contribution of that variable plus a half of the joint contribution of that variable with each other independent variable. It is computed by simply multiplying the standardized beta coefficient by the zero-order correlation coefficient of each independent variable.

are available, migrants may be more inclined to return there. But there may be some selection process involved. It is likely that some migrants find it more beneficial to return to take advantage of opportunities in the place of origin than others. Migrants who are young, unmarried, more educated, and more job skilled are more likely to take advantage of the opportunities available. Therefore, migratory selectivity should be positive. The study area of this analysis is a relatively developed region in the country. Since one of the study towns has newly established industrial sites, economic opportunities have become available. This accounts for the positive selectivity of return migrants among migrants in the city.

Characteristics related to city life are more important in accounting for return migration than background and movement related characteristics. The effect of duration of residence and personal ties to hometown are not strong. While 'imperfect information' is not significant in explaining return migration, 'location-specific capital' has some effects. When we consider homeownership and organizational affiliation as the 'location-specific capital' in the destination city, and personal ties in the place of origin, the results indicate that the 'location-specific capital' in the destination city affects return migration more strongly than that in the place of origin; migrants who had more 'location-specific capital' in the destination city are less likely to return.

Consequences of Return Migration

What are the consequences of return migration? We focus on two types of effects: (1) The impact of urban living on individual return migrants. The emphasis will be on comparing the socioeconomic status of return migrants from Seoul, return migrants from Daegu, other migrants to the study area, and natives. (2) The effects of migration on the community of origin will be analyzed, particularly remittance flows and the extent of integration of return migrants in their communities.

Socioeconomic Status of Return Migrants

It is hypothesized that the migration experience of those returning to their community of origin may serve to raise their socioeconomic status after they return. Attaining a higher education in the city, acquiring some skills and urban work

63

experience, and bringing back money and goods from the city may raise their socioeconomic status (Simmons and Cardona, 1972; Nelson, 1976). In fact, the literature suggests that the socioeconomic status of return migrants is higher than that of natives (Campbell et al., 1974; Chi and Bogan, 1974). However, previous studies have not differentiated between the selectivity effects of the initial out-migration and the effects of living in an urban area. Simple comparisons of socioeconomic status between return migrants and natives do not reveal the extent to which differences in socioeconomic status are a consequence of their migration experience in the urban areas or to differences in their initial socioeconomic selectivity.

One way to address this problem is to control for socioeconomic status of return migrants at the time they moved out of the place of origin. However, this is often impossible since many migrants were very young when they migrated. Also, the point in time when return migrants left their origin place varies among migrants; thus it is unclear which time point should be used in comparison with natives. One procedure to overcome this problem is to control for father's education and occupation. It is assumed that father's socioeconomic status approximates the respondents' socioeconomic status at the time they left the place of origin. After controlling for father's education and occupation, the remaining differences in socioeconomic status between return migrants and natives can be attributed to the effects of migration.

A brief examination of respondent's age, father's education, and father's occupation background in the four groups reveals the necessity of taking into account selectivity. The return migrants from Seoul are the youngest (34.6) and the natives are the oldest (43.5). The difference in mean age is almost ten years between these two groups (Table 2.11). More than 80 percent of the return migrants from Seoul are under age 40, in contrast to only one-third of the natives. The mean age of the return migrants from Daegu and the other migrants shows only slight difference (mean ages are 39.0 and 40.7, respectively). More return migrants from Daegu are at ages 35-39, but more of the other migrants are at ages 30-34.

Father's education of the respondents is classified into seven categories from no education and illiterate to college level of education (Table 2.12). The third category, *Seodang,* is the traditional village school in which only Chinese letters and literatures are taught. As the data indicate, the level of father's education is generally low. *Seodang* is the most important level of education for the respondent's father. Some differences, however,

TABLE 2.11

AGE OF RESPONDENTS AT TIME OF SURVEY
BY MIGRATION STATUS

| | Return Migrants From | | Other | |
	Seoul	Daegu	Migrants	Natives
Under 30	24.8	12.2	12.8	14.3
30-34	32.8	18.2	21.8	9.3
35-39	23.4	31.1	16.3	8.6
40-44	8.8	18.9	17.9	19.7
45-49	3.6	5.4	8.2	17.9
50-54	2.9	2.7	7.8	15.1
55-64	3.6	11.5	15.2	15.1
Total:Percent	100.0	100.0	100.0	100.0
Number	137	148	257	279
Mean Age	34.6	39.0	40.7	43.5
Median Age	33.1	36.9	39.3	43.8

(Chi-square Significance Level .0000)

TABLE 2.12

FATHER'S LEVEL OF EDUCATION AND OCCUPATION
BY MIGRATION STATUS OF RESPONDENTS

Education	Return Migrants From		Other Migrants	Natives
	Seoul	Daegu		
None, illiterate	9.1	13.1	14.9	24.0
None, literate	16.7	11.0	17.3	24.0
Seodang	25.0	36.6	32.7	29.2
Primary	25.0	26.9	22.2	17.3
Middle	12.1	6.2	6.0	4.1
High	7.6	2.1	3.2	0.7
College	4.5	4.1	3.6	0.7
Total:Percent	100.0	100.0	100.0	100.0
Number	132	145	248	271

(Chi-square Significance Level .0000)

Occupation				
Professional-Administrative	7.0	2.1	5.6	2.5
Clerical-Sales-Service	26.4	13.9	15.2	4.8
Agricultural	62.8	79.9	71.6	88.0
Production	3.9	4.2	7.6	4.7
Total:Percent	100.0	100.0	100.0	100.0
% White Collar	32.6	14.6	20.8	6.9
Number	129	144	250	274

(Chi-square Significance Level .0000)

can be observed among the four groups of respondents. Father's level of education is generally higher for those who had experienced migration than for those who had not and highest for return migrants from Seoul and lowest for the natives. Father's education of the return migrants from Daegu and the other migrants is intermediate. Nearly half of the fathers of the return migrants from Seoul received a formal education compared to only 22.8 percent of fathers of the natives. The comparable figures for the return migrants from Daegu and the other migrants are 39.3 and 35.0 percent, respectively. About 12 percent of the fathers of return migrants from Seoul had at least a high school level of education, compared to about 6 percent for return migrants from Daegu and for the other migrants, and only 1.4 percent for the natives.

As expected, the usual occupation of a majority of fathers of the repondents is agricultural work (lower panel, Table 2.12). The proportions range from 62.8 percent for the return migrants from Seoul to 88.0 percent for the natives. Clerical and sales workers are more frequently found among fathers of the migrant groups than among fathers of the natives. When occupation is dichotomized into white and non-white collar jobs, more fathers of the return migrants from Seoul were engaged in white collar occupations than fathers of the other respondents.

In sum, the data indicate that there was a significant selectivity involved at the time return migrants initially moved out from the place of origin. Based on father's education and occupation, migrant groups in general have a higher socioeconomic family background than the natives, although the occupation of fathers does not necessarily refer to a fixed point in time and, therefore, is a very crude index of the socioeconomic status of migrants at the time of out-migration. Among the migrant groups, however, socioeconomic status is highest for the return migrants from Seoul, and little difference exists between the return migrants from Daegu and the other migrants. These findings confirm the general pattern that those who have higher socioeconomic status in rural areas are more likely to become migrants, and that among the migrants socioeconomic status was higher for those who move to the a larger than to a smaller city or to other rural areas.

As indicators of current socioeconomic status at the time of the survey, education, occupation, personal income, and possession of consumer objects will be compared separately among the four groups of respondents utilizing analysis of variance techniques. In these comparisons, father's education and occupation will be controlled in order to remove the effects of selectivity. Current age of the respondents will also be controlled.

Return migrants generally have a higher education level than both the other migrants and the natives (Table 2.13). It is highest for the return migrants from Seoul and lowest for the natives. Large differences are observed in college level education. Whereas 26.5 percent of the return migrants from Seoul attained a college level education, only 17.6 percent of the return migrants from Daegu and 10.9 percent of the other migrants reached that level; far fewer (2.5 percent) of the natives attended college. Similarly, about 37 percent of the return migrants from Seoul attained a high school level of education, compared to about 30 percent of the return migrants from Daegu and the other migrants. Only 15.5 percent of the natives had a high school level education. There are only a few return migrants who did not have a formal education, but one out of every five natives did not have any education and just under half had only primary schooling.

Results of the analysis of variance on level of education are shown in Table 2.14. Here, education is measured by number of years of schooling; migration status, age, father's education, and father's occupation are treated as independent variables. Among them, migration status, father's education, and father's occupation are included as factors (non-metric independent variable), and age as a covariate (metric independent variable). Interactions among factors were tested, and no significant interactions were found. However, interactions between factors and covariates are simply assumed not to be significant.

The first column in the table shows the mean years of education by different migration status groups, without taking into account the effects of other independent variables. The mean years of education is highest for the return migrants from Seoul and lowest for the natives, and it is higher for the return migrants from Daegu than the other migrants. The next three columns show mean years of education by migration status after controlling for age; age and father's education; and age, father's education, and father's occupation, respectively. In the last column, all the other independent variables are controlled. The overall relationship between years of education and migration status is shown by eta, and its significance level is indicated by P. In the first column the eta is .36 and it is highly significant, indicating that there are significant educational differences among different migration status groups when the effects of other independent variables are not taken into account. The relationship between years of education and migration status when other

TABLE 2.13

EDUCATION AND OCCUPATION AT THE TIME OF SURVEY
BY MIGRATION STATUS

Education	Return Migrants From		Other Migrants	Natives
	Seoul	Daegu		
None	0.7	7.4	12.8	20.5
Primary	15.4	26.4	28.0	43.5
Middle	20.6	18.9	19.5	18.0
High	36.8	29.7	28.8	15.5
College and More	26.5	17.6	10.9	2.5
Total:Percent	100.0	100.0	100.0	100.0
Number	136	148	257	278

(Chi-square Significance Level .0000)

Occupation				
Professional	5.5	11.6	4.2	1.1
Administrative	4.7	2.2	0.8	0.7
Clerical	22.0	9.4	16.5	4.5
Sales	21.3	12.3	16.5	10.8
Service	11.0	14.5	4.6	4.5
Agricultural	6.3	9.4	25.3	60.8
Production	29.1	40.6	32.1	17.5
Total:Percent	100.0	100.0	100.0	100.0
Number	127	138	237	268

(Chi-square Significance Level .0000)

TABLE 2.14

AVERAGE NUMBER OF YEARS OF EDUCATION AND PERCENT
WHITE COLLAR AT THE TIME OF SURVEY BY MIGRATION
STATUS (ANALYSIS OF VARIANCE)

	Unadjusted Mean	Age	Mean Adjusted for		N
			+Fa'Ed	+Fa'Occ	
Education					
RM-Seoul	11.08	9.71	9.57	9.43	123
RM-Daegu	9.40	9.14	8.98	9.03	141
Migrants	8.34	8.40	8.33	8.28	242
Natives	6.47	7.19	7.41	7.49	265
Eta (Beta)	.36	.21	.17	.16	
P	.000	.000	.000	.000	
R^2	.127	.382	.419	.429	

White Collar

	Unadjusted Mean	Ed.	+Age	Mean Adjusted for		N
				+Fa'Occ	+Fa'Ed	
RM-Seoul	.54	.42	.40	.40	.40	114
RM-Daegu	.36	.30	.31	.31	.31	131
Migrants	.38	.38	.37	.37	.37	223
Natives	.17	.26	.28	.27	.27	255
Eta (Beta)	.28	.13	.10	.11	.11	
P	.000	.002	.026	.021	.020	
R^2	.078	.260	.280	.281	.282	

70

independent variable(s) are held constant is shown by beta, and its significance level is also indicated by p below the beta. The R^2 in the first column shows the percent of variation in years of education explained by migration status alone. The R^2 for the next column indicates variations explained by migration status together with other independent variable(s) in that column. As can be seen in the table, migration status alone explains 12.7 percent of the variation in years of education.

As control variables are added one by one, the overall differences in years of education by migration status are reduced. Eta (beta) declined from .36 to .16. This means that each control variable has an independent effect on years of education. After eliminating all the effects of the control variables, differences among migration status groups still persist and remain highly significant. Thus, differences in years of education among migration status groups are not solely due to effects of other control variables. Altogether migration status, age, father's education, and father's occupation account for 42.9 percent of the variations in years of education. It may be concluded that differences in years of education among the respondents are partly attributable to their different socioeconomic origins, but migration status also has a significant, independent impact on educational level. Therefore, these findings support the hypothesis that experience in urban areas has an important effect in raising educational level.

As expected, few return migrants engage in agriculture after they return (lower panel, Table 2.13). Only 6.3 percent and 9.4 percent of the return migrants from Seoul and Daegu, respectively, return to an agricultural job, in contrast to 25.3 percent of the other migrants and 60.8 percent of the natives. A significant proportion of return migrants acquire a manufacturing job; in part this reflects the fact that one study area of this study is an industrial town (Gumi). But the proportion of production workers is higher for return migrants from Daegu and also for other migrants than for return migrants from Seoul. This suggests that the demand for less skilled jobs tends to be filled in local areas (see also Richmond, 1969). Return migrants, especially from Seoul, are much more represented in clerical, sales, and service occupations compared to the natives. More than 10 percent of return migrants are in professional or administrative jobs. However, the proportion of professional workers is higher for the return migrants from Daegu than the return migrants from Seoul. In part, this reflects the transfer of public school teachers, who are routinely moved within the province.

For the analysis of variance, the percent of white collar workers is used as a dependent variable. In the subsequent tables of analysis of variance, years of education of the respondents is included as another control variable together with age, father's education, and father's occupation. In the analysis of variance, years of education is entered as covariate. Again, no significant interaction was found among factors. Among different migration status groups, the proportion of white collar workers is highest for the return migrants from Seoul and lowest for the natives (lower panel, Table 2.14). More than half of the return migrants from Seoul are engaged in white collar occupations in contrast to only 17 percent of the natives. Slightly more of the other migrants have white collar jobs than the return migrants from Daegu. The overall differences in the proportion of white collar workers among migration status groups is significant (eta = .28). When the effects of control variables are removed, differences among migration status groups are reduced considerably. After removing the effects of all the control variables, differences among migration status groups are still significant at the 0.05 level. This suggests that the migration experience has an independent effect on occupation. All five explanatory variables (migration status and four control variables) explain 28.2 percent of the variations in occupation. Education of the respondents contributes most of the variation explained; both migration status and father's occupation also have some significant effects on occupation. Age of the respondents and father's education do not add much to the variation explained by education of the respondents and father's occupation, indicating that the effects of age and father's education have already been taken into account by other variables.

The third measure of socioeconomic status is personal income after return. Table 2.15 presents the monthly income distribution of the respondents. The unit in the category is 10,000 Korean Won. On the average, the return migrants from Seoul earn most and the natives earn least. The mean personal income is 162,900 Won for the return migrants from Seoul and 100,600 Won for the natives.

For analysis of variance, monthly personal income measured by Korean Won was transformed into log value because there are a few cases of very high income earners, and this may affect the mean income significantly. The bottom panel shows that there are significant differences in mean income among different migration status groups (eta is .26). However, the pattern is changed after education of the respondents is controlled.

72

TABLE 2.15

MONTHLY PERSONAL INCOME AND MEAN MONTHLY PERSONAL INCOME
LOG TRANSFORMED AT THE TIME OF SURVEY BY MIGRATION
STATUS (ANALYSIS OF VARIANCE)

| Income | Return Migrants From | | Other | |
(Thousand Won)	Seoul	Daegu	Migrants	Natives
0-49	3.4	7.6	19.1	33.2
50-74	14.4	16.8	13.9	19.8
75-99	8.5	6.9	12.6	12.6
100-149	31.4	32.8	25.7	14.9
150-199	14.4	16.8	13.9	6.5
200-299	16.9	9.9	7.4	9.2
300 and more	11.0	9.2	7.4	3.8
Total:Percent	100.0	100.0	100.0	100.0
Number	118	131	230	262
Mean Income	162.9	146.0	122.1	100.6
Median Income	120.3	100.4	99.8	70.0

(Chi-square Significance Level .0000)

Mean Monthly Personal Income (Log Transformed)

| | Unadjusted Mean | Ed | Mean Adjusted For | | | N |
			+Fa'Occ	+Fa'Ed	+Age	
RM-Seoul	2.09	1.99	1.98	1.98	1.98	105
RM-Daegu	2.06	2.01	2.01	2.01	2.01	124
Migrants	1.93	1.94	1.93	1.93	1.93	217
Natives	1.84	1.92	1.92	1.92	1.92	250
Eta(Beta)	.26	.10	.05	.05	.09	
P	.000	.049	.056	.072	.073	
R^2	.070	.257	.259	.261	.261	

As the second column shows, the relative position of the return migrants from Seoul and those from Daegu is reversed. This indicates that the higher income of return migrants from Seoul is due to their higher education level.

Adding other control variables together with education of the respondents does not alter the pattern. The effects of father's education and occupation, and age of the respondents on income are not significant when the effects of education of the respondents are removed. In all, the five explanatory variables account for 26.1 percent of the variation in income. The effect of migration status is only significant when education alone is controlled. When all the control variables are held constant, migration status is no longer significant. Therefore, the results suggest that the observed differences in mean personal income among different migration status groups are mostly due to differences in education level among them. As noted earlier, differences in education are significantly related to migration status.

The final indicator of socioeconomic status to be compared is possession of consumer objects. Each of the fourteen items included in the questionnaire was weighted inversely to the proportions of the item owned by the respondents. Then, the weight of each item was summed for all the items owned by the respondents to construct a single index.

As the data in Table 2.16 indicate, the mean score is highest for the return migrants from Seoul and lowest for the natives. The return migrants from Daegu and the other migrants are intermediate, but it is higher for the other migrants. The overall differences among migration status groups are significant at the .001 level. However, the mean score of each migration status group changes as education of the respondents is held constant: the mean score becomes highest for the natives and the mean score of the return migrants from Seoul becomes even lower than the other migrants. These changes suggest that education level has a strong effect on the possession of consumer objects; the high score of the return migrants from Seoul is largely due to their higher education level. When removing the effects of education, the overall differences among different migration status groups are reduced and are not statistically significant.

Adding other control variables--age and father's occupation--again changes the mean score of each group and alters the pattern further. Thus, in addition to education, age and father's occupation have significant independent effects on the possession of consumer objects. Only father's education does not have a significant effect. In all, 26.1 percent of the variation in

TABLE 2.16

INDEX SCORE OF POSSESSION OF CONSUMER OBJECTS
AND MEAN INDEX SCORE AT THE TIME OF SURVEY
BY MIGRATION STATUS (ANALYSIS OF VARIANCE)

Score	Return Migrants From		Other Migrants	Natives
	Seoul	Daegu		
0-4	23.4	31.1	29.6	32.6
5-9	28.5	29.7	31.1	37.6
10-14	19.0	17.6	15.6	15.1
15-19	10.9	8.1	7.8	7.2
20-29	7.3	10.1	11.7	6.1
30-39	6.6	2.7	3.9	0.7
40-49	1.5	0.7	0.4	-
50 and more	2.9	-	-	0.7
Total:Percent	100.0	100.0	100.0	100.0
Number	137	148	257	279

(Chi-square Significance Level .0046)

Mean Index Score

	Unadjusted		Mean Adjusted For			N
	Mean	Ed	+Age	+Fa'Occ	+Fa'Ed	
RM-Seoul	12.17	9.78	10.29	10.03	10.04	121
RM-Daegu	9.62	8.67	8.62	8.72	8.64	141
Migrants	9.98	9.95	9.90	9.79	9.76	242
Natives	8.49	10.13	9.97	10.14	10.19	265
Eta(Beta)	.14	.06	.06	.06	.06	
P	.001	.327	.253	.321	.244	
R^2	.020	.208	.247	.258	.261	

the index score of possession of consumer objects is explained by five variables. Among them, education of the respondents is most important, and age and father's occupation also have some effects. Therefore, the observed differences among migration status groups are mostly due to differences in educational level and partly due to age and father's occupation.

These results suggest that education of the respondents plays a key role in determining occupation, personal income, and possession of consumer objects. The differences observed for other socioeconomic status indicators are largely attributed to education. Education level of the respondents, in turn, was found to be affected significantly by migration status together with family background. Therefore, differences in socioeconomic status between return migrants and natives can be attributed to the initially high socioeconomic status of return migrants before they left their place of origin, and also to the education obtained as a result of their migration to the urban areas. In other words, the migration experience of return migrants had an independent effect in raising their socioeconomic status above that of natives and other migrants in the place of origin.

Multi-Variate Analyses

Not all the return migrants from the city benefited from their migration. Some of them may have gained more than others, and some may not have benefited at all. The question we address here is, what kinds of experiences in the city have an important effect in raising socioeconomic status, and what is the relative importance of the different factors?

Thirteen variables will be examined for the return migrants only, using multiple regression. The dependent variable is current socioeconomic status of the return migrants in place of origin after they return. A socioeconomic status index was constructed combining four indicators: education, occupation, personal income, and possession of consumer objects. The index was calculated by summing the standard score of the four indicators. The Spearman Brown coefficient of reliability of the index is .77.

The 13 independent variables consist of background characteristics and various aspects of city life and migration experience. Father's education and occupation, current age, and 'bring money' are also included in the same equation, although these variables are not the urban experience variable, in order to control for their effects on socioeconomic status. They may affect the current socioeconomic status of return migrants directly or indirectly through the urban experience variables. Industries in which return migrants were engaged in the city have been classified as being in the traditional or modern sectors. Following Moir's classification (Moir, 1975), the traditional sector includes construction, food, textile, and clothing manufacturing (consumer goods industries), retail trade, transport, and personal services. The modern sector consists of utilities, metal, machine, and miscellaneous manufacturing (producer goods industries), wholesale trade and banking, insurance and finance, storage, communications, and all community, business, and recreation services. Mass media contact score is the sum of the individual score of four media: newspaper, magazine, TV, and radio. Values ranged from zero to four assigned to each medium according to return migrants' degree of exposure, from not read, watch, or listen at all to read, watch, or listen every day. All the independent variables are entered in the equation stepwise.[5]

The summary results of the multiple regression analysis are presented in Table 2.17. A fairly large amount of the variations in socioeconomic status is explained by the equation. The thirteen independent variables altogether account for 65.6 percent of the variation in socioeconomic status of return migrants, and the whole equation is statistically significant at the .01 level. The analysis shows that obtaining a formal education of at least a high school level in the city is the most important variable accounting for the current socioeconomic status of return migrants. It alone accounts for 41 percent of the variation in socioeconomic status. In part, this reflcts the fact that most colleges and universities and also better high schools are located in the urban areas; the most beneficial gain of the return migrants from their migration experience is to attain more education in the city.

The next most important factor for socioeconomic status is the degree of mass media contact in the city. It explains 12 percent additional variation in socioeconomic status, above the variation explained by formal education attained in the city. The nature of economic activity in the city has some independent effect

----

[5] Hierarchial inclusion of the variables in the equation following the time sequence, i.e., first background variables and then the urban experience variable, produced almost the same results, although the variation explained by father's education and occupation increased a little more.

TABLE 2.17

SUMMARY RESULTS OF THE REGRESSION ANALYSIS:
SOCIOECONOMIC STATUS OF RETURN MIGRANTS

Variable	r	Beta	F	R^2	R^2 Change
Ed in city	.64	.3912	50.38*	.41212	.41212
Mass media	.58	.2538	23.41*	.53306	.12093
Occu in city	.47	.1995	17.93*	.57724	.04419
Indu in city	.40	.1753	12.89*	.61524	.03800
Bring money	.31	.1792	15.87*	.64937	.03412
Firm Size	.30	.0567	1.31	.65185	.00248
Organization	.27	.0546	1.44	.65444	.00259
Fa'occ	.24	.0302	0.41	.65498	.00054
Fa'education	.23	-.0249	0.27	.65541	.00043
Duration in city	.09	.0512	0.23	.65547	.00006
Age	-.28	-.0736	0.22	.65553	.00006
Age moved	-.25	.0713	0.18	.65584	.00031
Destination	.18	-.0057	0.01	.65587	.00003

F of whole equation 28.29*
* (significant at .01 level)

Note: Socioeconomic status is an index score. The other variables
are defined as follows: Ed. in city (0 = no, 1 = yes); mass
media contact in city (index score); occupation in city and
Father's occupation (0 = non-white collar, 1 = white collar);
industry in city (0 = traditional, 1=modern); money brought from
city (log of real amount); firm size (0-8 = self-employed to
largest);organization affiliation in the city (actual number);
father's education (1 = none, 2 = primary, 3 = secondary or more);
duration in city (single years); age (current single years of age);
age moved to the city (single years); destination (0 = Daegu,
1 = Seoul).

on socioeconomic status of the return migrants after they returned to the place of origin. The occupation and industry in which return migrants were engaged in the city contribute an additional 4.4 and 3.8 percentage points to the variation in socioeconomic status, respectively. Return migrants who had white collar jobs in the city and engaged in modern sector industries had a higher socioeconomic status after they returned. The amount of money return migrants brought with them when they returned also has some independent effects on socioeconomic status. However, the rest of the independent variables are not statistically significant, although their individual zero-order correlation with socioeconomic status is relatively high. This means that the effects of these variables are already accounted for by previously noted variables.

In sum, these findings support empirically the hypothesis that return migrants' experience in urban living contributes to raising their socioeconomic status by enabling them to attain more education, acquire better skills, and bring back some money from the city. In addition, mass media contact in the city is an important urban experience. In short, socioeconomic status can be increased when rural migrants attain formal higher education levels, are exposed to mass media frequently, and engage in modern economic systems.

Impact on Community of Origin

What influence do return migrants have on the community of origin? The literature suggests that return migrants may play a role as agents of social, economic, and cultural change in the rural community. They can contribute to these changes through accumulating and bringing back some capital from the outside, introducing new techniques and skills which they learned in the city, and spreading modern attitudes and values in the origin community (Miracle and Berry, 1970; Hayano, 1973; Connell et al., 1976). The high socioeconomic status of return migrants, would lead one to expect some effects of return migration on the community of origin.

We focus first on the flow of remittances from migrants in the city or elsewhere to the place of origin as well as any reverse flow of resources from the place of origin to migrants in the city and money brought back to the place of origin by migrants when they returned (Table 2.18).

Only a small proportion of return migrants sent remittances to their immediate families in the place of origin while they were in the city (about one in five). However, the proportion increased

TABLE 2.18

PERCENT OF RETURN MIGRANTS SENDING AND RECEIVING
REMITTANCES TO AND FROM FAMILIES IN THE ORIGIN

Remittances	Return Migrants From		
	Seoul	Daegu	Total
Sent remittances	19.0	18.2	18.6
Did not send	51.8	43.9	47.7
No families in the origin	27.7	37.2	32.6
NA	1.5	0.7	1.1
Total:Percent	100.0	100.0	100.0
Receiving money	21.2	7.4	14.0
Receiving goods	0.7	6.8	3.9
Did not receive	49.6	48.6	49.1
No families in the origin	27.7	37.2	32.6
NA	0.7	-	0.4
Total:Percent	100.0	100.0	100.0
Number	137	148	285

to 29 percent when one considers only those who had families in the origin, because one-third of the total respondents did not have immediate families in the place of origin when they lived in the city. There is basically no difference in the proportion sending remittances between return migrants from Seoul and Daegu.

The remittances were sent mostly three or four times a year. Only 25 percent of them were sent monthly. More important for remittance flows are the purpose and size of the remittances. Previous evidence suggests that most remittances are consumed in everyday household needs and are not large enough to invest in further improvement of the household economy (Connell et al., 1976). The data for Korea also indicate that the amount of remittances from the return migrants in the city was small, and the purpose was exclusively for living expenses for the household. The majority of remittances were less than 500,000 Korean Won (equivalent to 1,000 U.S. dollars) in a year. Only a small portion was used for business.

The flow of resources was not one-way. Almost an equal proportion of return migrants received remittances from families in the place of origin when they were living in the city. About 18 percent of the total return migrants, or 27 percent of those return migrants who had families in the area of origin, received remittances from their place of origin (lower panel, Table 2.18). The amount of remittances received was also small. Reverse remittances included a significant proportion of goods, mostly rice, particularly to return migrants from Daegu. Since Daegu is close to the place of origin, it is easier to transmit goods. Remittances were sent by families in the place of origin more regularly. Almost half of the remittances received by return migrants were sent every month. When we cross-classified remittances to and from the place of origin, about half of those return migrants who had families in the place of origin neither sent nor received remittances. Only 5.9 percent of return migrants both received and sent remittances, and 20.7 percent of them only received and 21.3 percent only sent it.

It is interesting to compare the results in this study to evidence from another country. In Indonesia, Hugo (1978) found that remission of money is almost universal among permanent as well as temporary migrants working in urban areas; 95.2 percent of all permanent migrants who were in the urban work force sent remittances. This indicates strong bonds of filial loyalty in Indonesia. However, with respect to amount and use of remittances, evidence in Indonesia is similar to that found in Korea. The amount of remittances sent by migrants in the city is not large; it consisted only of the 8 percent of the total household income in the village, and most of remittances were used for ordinary household expenses.

The last component of remittances concerns money brought back by the return migrants and their actual use of it. Almost three-fourths of return migrants brought some money with them (Table 2.19). However, it appears that the amount they brought was generally small. The median amount was 151,000 Won (U.S. $302), and 71.6 percent brought less than 1,000,000 Won ($2,000). Only 3.5 percent brought more than 5,000,000 Won ($10,000), and these amounts considerably affect the mean amount, which is 731,000 Won ($1,462). Return migrants from Seoul appear to bring slightly more money than return migrants from Daegu.

Together with the amount of money return migrants brought back to the community, the way return migrants spent the money is important for assessing the impact on the community of origin. The lower panel of Table 2.19 shows that a large proportion of return migrants spent their money for their household needs. Among those who brought some money, 58.8 percent used the money for buying a house, and 12.8 percent used it for living expenses. The most beneficial category to the community is spending the money for business use. About 24 percent of return migrants spent the money on their businesses.

These data point to the conclusion that the most important source of capital flow to the community of origin for developing the community economy is the money return migrants bring with them. Remittances to the place of origin when they were away in the city had almost no effect on the community economy. Most were small in amount and spent for daily household expenses. By contrast, the amount of money brought by return migrants was much larger, and also a part of that money was invested in the community.

Integration of Return Migrants

Another possible effect of return migration on the community of origin is through the role of return migrants in the process of social and cultural change. Since return migrants have higher socioeconomic status than natives and some exposure to the urban way of life, it is reasonable to expect them to play some role as agents of social and cultural change in the rural community.

However, empirical research has not clarified the pattern and extent of influence migrants exert over the community, since

TABLE 2.19

AMOUNT OF MONEY BROUGHT BACK BY RETURN MIGRANTS
TO THE ORIGIN PLACE AND THEIR ACTUAL USE

Amount	Return Migrants From		
(Ten Thousand Won)	Seoul	Daegu	Total
None	28.5	25.7	27.0
Less than 10	7.3	12.8	10.2
10-49	22.6	22.3	22.5
50-99	8.0	15.5	11.9
100-199	13.9	4.7	9.1
200-299	3.6	4.7	4.2
300-399	3.6	2.7	3.2
400-499	0.7	1.4	1.1
500 and more	4.4	2.7	3.5
NA	7.3	7.4	7.4
Total:Percent	100.0	100.0	100.0
Number	137	148	285
Mean Amount	79.9	66.8	73.1
Median Amount	15.3	14.8	15.1
Actual Use of Money			
For business	25.0	22.2	23.5
Buy house	54.5	62.6	58.8
Living Expenses	13.6	12.1	12.8
Saving	3.4	3.0	3.2
Other	1.1	-	0.5
NA	2.3	-	1.1
Total:Percent	100.0	100.0	100.0
Number	88	99	187

differences in socioeconomic status may lead to a lack of interaction between return migrants and natives in the community (Connell et al., 1976). To exert some influence over the community, return migrants should be well integrated into the community structure. In this sense, it is of particular interest to find out the extent to which return migrants are integrated in the community. One of the indirect indicators of that is intention to move out of the community of origin. However, it does not necessarily mean that those who intend to move out do not have any impact on community of origin. For instance, teachers and government officials are required to move out of the community because of the rotation policy of the government. Even if they are supposed to leave the community in the near future, they may still have some impact on the community of origin.

The data indicate that more return migrants intend to move out of the current place of residence than do natives (Table 2.20). About 43 percent of the return migrants from Seoul and 34.5 percent of the return migrants from Daegu intend to move out, while 30.7 percent of the other migrants and only 17.6 percent of the natives intend to do so. The relatively higher proportion of return migrants intending to move out suggests that return migrants are less bound to the community. A very large proportion of the return migrants who intend to move desire to go back to the city from which they returned. More than 70 percent of the return migrants from Seoul and 47.1 percent of the return migrants from Daegu want to move there again. The two cities, Seoul and Daegu, are selected by more than 80 percent of the return migrants from Seoul and 70 percent of those from Daegu. The natives seem to prefer the nearby provincial capital city to the remote capital city of the country, although a large proportion of them (32.7 percent) are still uncertain where they would go.

Reasons for the desired move indicate that economic reasons--for better job, to earn more income, and for better living--are dominant. This is particularly so for the natives compared to the other migrant groups. An interesting difference among migration status groups is that the return migrants from Seoul are more concerned about their children's education. More than a third of them want to move to provide educational opportunities for their children. This strong concern for the education of children can be explained by the fact that the return migrants from Seoul as a group are relatively better-off in the community and thus more of them can afford to provide a higher level of education for their children. Also from their own experience, they recognize that attaining higher education is most

84

TABLE 2.20

PERCENT OF RESPONDENTS WHO INTEND TO MOVE
OUT BY MIGRATION STATUS

Intention	Return Migrants From		Migrants	Natives
	Seoul	Daegu		
Want to stay	56.9	65.5	69.3	82.4
Want to move	43.1	34.5	30.7	17.6
Total:Percent	100.0	100.0	100.0	100.0
Number	137	148	257	279
Place to Move				
Seoul	71.2	23.5	26.6	18.4
Daegu	10.2	47.1	20.3	22.4
Other city	6.8	13.7	24.1	18.4
Rural area	6.8	3.9	13.9	8.2
Not decide	5.1	11.7	15.2	32.7
Total:Percent	100.0	100.0	100.0	100.0
Number	59	51	79	49
Reason for Move				
For education of children	33.9	17.6	25.3	16.3
For better job	27.1	33.3	27.8	36.7
For more income and better living	18.6	19.6	11.4	30.6
Other	18.6	21.6	29.1	10.2
NA	1.7	7.8	6.3	6.1
Total:Percent	100.0	100.0	100.0	100.0
Number	59	51	79	49

important for one's future career. Therefore, their concern for the education of their children may be equal to or more important than improving their own economic situation. The large proportion of other reasons for the other migrants reflects that a significant proportion of them want to move back to their place of origin. About 22 percent of the migrants intend to move because they have families there and it is their hometown.

Another indirect indication of integration of return migrants into the community comes from the natives' perception of the return migrants. Table 2.21 presents data showing that only 19.3 percent of the natives personally knew any return migrants. This low proportion seems to reflect the small number of return migrants compared to the total resident population and their general low visibility. It may also relate to the relative isolation of return migrants in the community.

Among the natives who knew someone who had returned from the city, there is a perception that the standard of living of return migrants is higher after they return compared to before they left the community. About 41 percent of the natives perceived that the standard of living of return migrants is higher than before they left, while 31 percent perceived it is lower.

Only 10 percent of the natives believed that return migrants had a negative influence on the community. About 35 percent of natives evaluated the influence of return migrants positively, and 41 percent responded that their influence was neither positive nor negative. Among the positive influences cited, the most frequent was that "return migrants offer good suggestions to the community." Very few return migrants were regarded as village leaders. Over 90 percent of the village leaders were natives.

Overall, the data suggest that although return migrants may have some potential for influencing the community positively, and there is some evidence that some of them did, their relative size is small and they tend not to participate actively in community affairs. Thus, there is no strong evidence to suggest that they have a significant infuence over the community, either through remittances or through their social roles.

Concluding Observations

This study's aim has been to assess the nature of return migration from urban to rural areas in Korea, to identify factors affecting the return migrants' decision to return, and to evaluate the consequences of return migration for the individual return

TABLE 2.21

STATUS OF RETURN MIGRANTS AS PERCEIVED BY NATIVES

	Percent	Number
Percent of Natives Who Know Return Migrant		
Know someone	19.3	58
Did not know any	80.3	241
NA	0.3	1
Total	100.0	300
Comparison of Return Migrants' Standard of Living		
Lower than before leave	31.0	18
The same as before	10.3	6
Better than before leave	41.4	24
Don't know	17.2	10
Total	100.0	58
Return Migrants'Influence to Community		
Positive	34.5	20
Indifferent	41.4	24
Negative	10.3	6
NA, DK	13.8	8
Total	100.0	58
Village Leader		
Return Migrant	0.7	2
Other Migrant	4.0	12
Native	90.3	271
NA	5.0	15
Total	100.0	300

migrants as well as for the community of origin.

In general we found that compared to non-return migrants, return migrants were relatively young, and thus more likely to be unmarried at the time they moved to the city. Return migrants had more education and had more experience of urban living, but had less knowledge of the destination when they entered the city. With respect to job information and prior job arrangements, they were not distinguishable from non-return migrants. Return migrants tended to move more as individuals, and more return migrants moved to the city for education. They lived in the city for a shorter period than non-return migrants, but they maintained strong personal ties to the place of origin while they lived in the city. The socioeconomic status of return migrants was higher than non-return migrants in the city, but return migrants were less likely to own a house and participate in organizations in the city. Overall, therefore, they were less integrated into the urban structure. The most striking finding was that, on the whole, return migrants were not 'failures' in the city as most of the literature has assumed.

We suggested that the nature of return migrants is largely determined by whether they are pushed from the city of destination or pulled by attractive conditions in the place of origin. If there are good job opportunities available in the place of origin, then many are willing to return because of the strong desire to be nearer family and friends. In such cases, it is more likely for the young and newly graduated to take advantage of job opportunities compared to the older, more well-established migrants.

Concerning the relative importance of various factors on return migration, we found that characteristics at the time they return, such as socioeconomic status, homeownership, and organization affiliation, are more important than background and movement related characteristics. The effect of duration of residence and personal ties to home town are not strong. In this sense, 'imperfect information' was not significant at all in explaining return migration, while 'location-specific capital' had some effects on return migration.

Finally, the consequences of return migration for both individual migrants and for the community of origin were assessed by comparing return migrants with natives. The findings indicated that, as a group, return migrants benefited from their experience of urban living. The socioeconomic status of return migrants was much higher than rural natives in the place of origin after return migrants moved back from the city. Although these differences were partly due to their initially higher socioeconomic status when they left the place of origin, these also resulted from their migration experience. Attaining a formal education in the city of at least high school level appeared to be of overwhelming importance for increasing socioeconomic status.

At the community level, however, the impact of return migrants seemed to be limited, although the direction of their impact was positive. Remittances from return migrants while they were in the city were small and most of the funds were spent for ordinary living expenses of the household. Only a small part of the money brought by the return migrants was invested for business in the community.

Return migrants were less integrated into the community structure. Possibly wide differences in socioeconomic status may lead to a lack of interaction between return migrants and natives. Many more return migrants intended to move out of the community compared to natives, and most of them wanted to move to the same city from which they returned. Education for their children was one of the most important reasons given for the expected move; for more than a third of them intended to move to the city again for the education of their children. However, there was an indication that return migrants may have a potential for contributing to rural development. A large proportion of natives who knew someone who had returned from the city reported that return migrants influenced the community positively.

The Korean government has adopted various population redistribution policies in order to curb the massive influx of people from the countryside into large metropolitan areas, particularly into Seoul. The results of this study clearly suggest that more emphasis should be placed on industrial decentralization. This policy measure could have a significant impact on redirecting out-migration to other than large metropolitan areas and could induce return moves of migrants from metropolitan areas. Further, return migrants from large metropolitan areas have great potential for making a contribution to rural development. Wherever the industrial sites are located within their province of origin--small city, town, or even rural area--return migrants may be able to gain social access to their home village more easily once they return to their province of birth. Frequent contact with their home village may increase their influence over the community of origin as diffusers of modern values and attitudes. Also, the proximity to their home village may increase their interest in the home village. This would, in turn, make it more likely that the frequency and amount of remittances would increase and the amount would be large enough to go beyond meeting daily needs, thereby allowing for longer term investments designed to improve living conditions of their families.

In pursuing this policy measure, however, great care must be taken in selecting a location, identifying the appropriate kind of industry, and also providing socioeconomic infrastructure and amenities. If the government fails to give full consideration to these, a large proportion of return migrants may move out again to the metropolitan areas. In fact, Kim and Donaldson (1979) pointed out that the program which located industrial estates in a small or medium sized city has not been successful in the past. They documented that despite government efforts, many of these industrial parks are still struggling to absorb industrial firms and labor from neighboring areas. Moreover, many of the people who came to these parts from the surrounding rural areas later moved to cities. One of the reasons for this may be a lack of sufficient investment by the government in the socioeconomic infrastructure in these industrial estates.

Second, 'closed city' policy measures may not be very effective. Indeed, these policies may have an opposite effect from their original goal. Most of the migrants moved to the city for either a job or an education. Particularly for the young migrants, the educational purpose of the move was important. The Korean government recognized this and therefore established new educational policy measures. For example, restrictions were placed on individual student transfers into Seoul unless the entire family moved. However, this policy measure may in turn induce movement of the whole family, considering the fact that most Koreans have a strong desire for their children to achieve a higher level of education, and most of the best universities are located in Seoul. Restricting job opportunities in the metropolitan area, for instance, by restricting new construction and expansion of facilities in Seoul and reducing semi-industrial zones within Seoul, may pressure or 'push' a large amount of return migration from the city. The 'pushed' return migrants are likely to be largely failures in the city, and thus their migration experience is neither beneficial to the individual migrants nor to the community of origin. Therefore, it can be argued that these 'closed city' policies may be useful and effective only after the other policy measures are sufficiently implemented.

Third, the effect of the New Community Movement on return migration appears to have been limited. The data indicate that among those who returned after the Movement started, only 12 percent replied that their decision to return was affected by the Movement. This low rate of influence on return migration is understandable because the major program was to increase agricultural incomes; thus the Movement might have been more influential in affecting movement to villages than to towns. It is less likely that return migrants from large cities are attracted by agricultural jobs after they return.

In sum, this study suggests that in order to relieve the acute problem of rapid population growth, particularly in large metropolitan areas and also to enhance balanced growth among regions, more effort should be put on the industrial decentralization policies. These policies could have an impact on redirecting potential migrants to the metropolitan area to move to other urban centers, but they also have an impact on inducing previous migrants to return from the large metropolitan area. In this respect, the industrial decentralization policy seems to be more important than policies designed to increase rural earnings. The impact of the latter policies may be largely confined to retaining rural people in their home village; they may have limited value in inducing return moves from the large metropolitan areas since it is less likely that migrants to large metropolitan areas will be attracted to return by agricultural job opportunities.

When return migration is induced by the attractive conditions of the place of origin, migrants who are young, more educated, and more skilled are more likely to take advantage of such opportunities and thus return. Once they have returned, they may contribute further to rural development. To the extent that they have a higher socioeconomic status, a higher level of formal education in the city, and also participate in the modern economic system in the city, they might be more modern than the average migrants in the metropolitan area. In turn, return migrants may act as agents of social and cultural change in the rural community of origin, and thus contribute to promote further rural development.

Appendix

Study Design of the Survey of Gyeongsangbugdo Province

The survey of Gyeongsangbugdo Province was carried out in several stages to maximize coverage of return migrants. These stages are detailed in this appendix along with an assessment of the reliability of the sample to study return migration.

Stage 1

The study was to have an equal number of completed interviews for each group of respondents regardless of their actual proportion in the total population. The first stage of sampling was designed to screen potential respondents as the basis for identifying and classifying each group of persons. The study planned to utilize the Civil Registration Record (CRR) for classifying and sampling. The CRR is kept at Dong (precinct) or Eub (town) offices and includes information on place of domicile of the household; a residence history for each household member; and age, sex, and relationship to the head of household of every household member. Based on this information, each group of persons can be identified. Before the field work was initiated, it was learned that the coverage and accuracy of the CRR was extremely unreliable. Consequently, it was necessary to conduct an independent household enumeration survey (HS). Because of the low probability of securing a sufficient number of return migrants, it was necessary to canvass all of the households in each study area.

A simple single page questionnaire was used for screening. It included questions on age, relationship to the head of household, place of birth, and residence history for every male member in the household aged 23 years old and over. Screening interviews were carried out by high school senior students from the given study area. About 15 to 20 households which comprise a Ban (neighborhood administrative unit) were allocated to each interviewer. Almost 13,000 households were visited by the interviewer, which is about 56 percent of the total number of households based on the annual population count (October 1977). Several factors explain the low coverage. First, mapping the entire area was impossible within the limits of the available budget. Instead, each Ban was allocated to an interviewer.

However, the boundary of many Bans was unclear to the interviewer, particularly at the central part of the area where houses are densely and irregularly located. Second, it was very common that multiple households were living together in one dwelling unit due to the housing shortage. This may have led to the omission of a number of households. Third, the household enumeration survey was carried out in one and a half days due to the limited resources available.

Based on the screening survey, however, a total of 630 potential return migrants from Seoul and Daegu were found. After a small team of interviewers revisited them and ascertained the dates lived in cities, a total of 241 possible return migrants were identified.

Stage 2

The results of the household enumeration survey were unsatisfactory due to its low coverage, and fewer than the expected number of return migrants were found. Although we did not know the characteristics of the omitted households, it seemed that those renting a room or two in a house were more likely to be omitted. These households were expected to consist mostly of young couples or single individuals. Thus, it seemed advisable to search further for return migrants to supplement the household enumeration survey.

The Civil Registration Record was used to locate more return migrants. The coverage of the CRR was improved before the field interview started, since in May 1978, a national election was held. In preparation for the election, the CRR was updated through a Dong officer's visit to every household to verify information in the Record. Examining the CRR, 471 additional potential return migrants were found after excluding 20 cases which overlapped with the household enumeration survey. Therefore, a total of 712 possible return migrants were identified from both the household enumeration survey and the Civil Registration Record.

Stage 3

Altogether 600 completed interviews with other migrants and natives were desired from three areas. The desired number of completed interviews in each area was first determined by allocating 600 to each area proportional to size of the male population. For example, in Gumi the percent of male population to the total male population of three study areas was 49.7. Thus, a total of 298 completed interviews with both other migrants and natives was desired for Gumi (600 x .497). Within a given area, the desired number of other migrants and natives were determined proportionate to their percent in each area based on the household enumeration survey. However, the results of the household enumeration survey indicated that in Gumi and Jeomchon the proportion of natives was smaller than the proportion of other migrants. The proportion of natives to the total resident population was 38 percent in both Gumi and Jeomchon, and it was 55 percent in Hayang. In order to secure a sufficient number of natives, a weight was given to natives so that the probability of natives being included in the sample was twice that of other migrants.

Stage 4

Since the household enumeration survey covered about half of the total households of the study areas, and the characteristics of households omitted from the survey were known, it was desirable to sample other migrants and natives both from the household enumeration survey and the Civil Registration Record (CRR) in order to reduce sampling biases and increase the representativeness of the sample. The proportion of the sample drawn from each source of sampling was calculated using the following formula.

Proportion from the HS: A+B/A+B+C
Proportion from the CRR: B+C/A+B+C
where A is the number of households enumerated in the HS, but not registered in the CRR; B is the number of households enumerated in the HS and also registered in the CRR; C is the number of households not enumerated in the HS, but registered in the CRR.

In order to determine the proportion of households included in A, B, and C, several Dongs were randomly selected in each area and efforts were made to match all households which were covered in the HS to all households which were registered in the CRR in these sampled Dongs. Based on this, a sampling fraction in each source was calculated using the above formula. For example, the number of desired interviews to be drawn from the HS in Gumi was calculated by 1,394/3,886 (A+B/A+B+C) x total desired number of interviews for other migrants and natives in Gumi. Through the same procedure, the desired number of completed interviews for other migrants and natives to be sampled from the HS and the CRR in each area were calculated.

Stage 5

In order to sample, one should ideally have a separate list of other migrants and natives, and then sample from each list. However, to make such lists required considerable work in reviewing information for all the households in the CRR, and this was not possible within the limits of available resources. Therefore, the needed number of both other migrants and natives were selected randomly from the HS and the CRR. Every effort was made to achieve the desired number of interviews for other migrants and natives from each source. If there were more than one male eligible for interview in the same household, only one was selected randomly.

The final size of the sample included in the survey for the varied migration status groups from each source in each study area is presented in Table A.1. In all, 2,204 individuals were sampled for interview. Almost an equal number, around 700 of each migration status group, was selected for interview. The number of return migrants, however, indicates the total we identified as possible return migrants.

The Interview and Completion Rate

Three different sets of questionnaires were used to interview each group of respondents. The sections common to all three groups were: screening questions which ascertained whether the respondent was eligible for interview according to the definitions being used; lifetime migration and occupation history; household roster; current conditions of social, economic, and cultural life; marital status and fertility of spouse of a respondent if he was ever married; some attitudinal questions for measuring respondent's degree of modernism; and interviewer's subjective evaluation of respondent's attitude toward the interview. In addition to these, the questionnaire for other migrants and return migrants added more sections, including detailed questions about

TABLE A.1

COMPLETION RATE BY MIGRATION STATUS OF RESPONDENT AND SOURCE OF SAMPLE

Migration Status and Sample Source	Number of Sample (1)	Number of Sample Used* (2)	Completed Interview (3)	Not Completed Interview (4)	Completion Rate** (5)
Return Migrants	712	690	285	405	41.3
HS	241	234	131	103	56.0
CRR	471	456	154	302	33.8
Other Migrants	776	575	270	305	47.0
HS	268	200	96	104	48.0
CRR	508	375	174	201	46.4
Natives	716	648	300	348	46.3
HS	295	276	141	135	51.1
CRR	421	372	159	213	42.7
Total	2,204	1,913	855	1,058	44.7
HS	804	710	368	342	51.8
CRR	1,400	1,203	487	716	40.5

Note: *The difference between (1) and (2) is number of sample not used, since we sampled twice the number desired.

**The rate was calculated by (3)/(2) x 100.

socioeconomic conditions of life at the time before and after moving to Seoul or Daegu and to the study area, linkage to the origin, and general information on migration and return migration. The field interviews were carried out from mid-July to mid-August 1978.

In all, 285 return migrants, 270 other migrants, and 300 natives were interviewed. The number of completed interviews for both return migrants and natives was less than desired, but it was higher for other migrants; because the definition of return migrant and native was more stringent, a large number of possible return migrants and natives were not qualified as a respondent (Table A.2). Overall, the final outcome of the number of completed interviews is satisfactory considering the limits of the available resources as well as the strict definition of return migrant.

Out of a total of 2,204 persons in the original sample, 86.8 percent were visited by the interviewers. Almost 97 percent of potential return migrants in the sample were visited, while 74.1 and 90.5 percent of other migrants and natives in the sample, respectively, were used. Considering the fact that the number of sample cases selected was more than twice the number of desired interviews for each group of respondents, the large number of ineligibles becomes obvious.

The overall completion rate was 44.7 percent based on the number of sample used. However, the rate varied by migration status of respondents. It was highest for other migrants and lowest for return migrants, although the variation was only between 41 and 47 percent. Consistently for all groups, the completion rate was higher for the HS sample than the CRR sample, but especially so for return migrants. This difference can be explained by the fact that those who were no longer living at the address given were more likely to be from the CRR sample. This means that many people who moved out did not report to the office. Moreover, our definition of all migration status groups was based on the place of birth. However, the information included in the CRR is place of domicile of the household instead of place of birth of each household member. Therefore, we actually selected samples based on place of domicile assuming that the place of birth and place of domicile were the same. Consequently, there were many cases which turned out to be not eligible for interview due to discrepancies between their place of birth and place of domicile.

The most frequently cited reason for incompletion is that respondents were no longer living at the given address (41 percent). This is particularly so for the CRR sample, reflecting the failure to report the move. The second reason for incomplete

TABLE A.2

REASONS FOR INCOMPLETE INTERVIEWS BY MIGRATION
STATUS OF RESPONDENT

Reasons for Incomplete	Return Migrant	Other Migrant	Native	Total
Not eligible for interview due to violating definition	35.8	8.2	45.1	30.9
R no longer living at that address	39.0	58.0	28.4	41.0
Unable to meet R	18.0	30.2	20.1	22.2
Unable to interview due to illness, physical handicap, etc.	2.7	1.6	2.6	2.4
Refused interview	4.4	2.0	3.7	3.5
Total: Percent	100.0	100.0	100.0	100.0
Number	405	305	348	1,058

interviews is failure to fulfill the specific definition criteria. About 36 and 45 percent of return migrants and natives, respectively, were not interviewed for this reason. For return migrants, most of those who were not eligible for interview lived in Seoul or Daegu before or after the 1970 census. While for natives, most of them turned out to have some migration experience, but they were not defined here as other migrants since they were born in the study area. Although there were some who did not qualify as a native but qualified as an other migrant since their place of birth was outside the study area, they were not interviewed because the original sampling plan was followed.

Slightly more than one-fifth of the incomplete interviews were attributable to interviewers being unable to meet the respondent; this was expected because the respondents were adult males and thus they were mostly outside home during the daytime. As compared to the above three reasons, very few were not interviewed because of the physical condition the respondents or because they refused to be interviewed. Considering the fact that the interview schedule for return migrants and other migrants was quite long, the mean length of time for interview was 70 and 47 minutes for return migrants and other migrants, respectively, there was a low rate of refusal.

Coverage of the Sample

In order to obtain some basis for evaluating the coverage of the sample, an independent survey for testing coverage of the CRR was conducted during the interview operation in Gumi. It was expected that the coverage of the CRR in Gumi would be the lowest among the three study areas since Gumi was growing rapidly at the time of the survey. Thus, the result in Gumi can be seen as a minimal estimate for the coverage of the CRR of the study areas.

For testing the coverage of the CRR, one Ban (smallest neighborhood unit) was selected from 13 Dongs, and interviewers copied the names of the household head for all the households registered in the CRR for each Ban. Then, they went to the Ban which was selected and checked with the Ban leader whether the households on the list were actually living in that Ban. In addition, a separate list of those households which were living in that Ban but not found on the list from the CRR was made based on the information given by the Ban leader.

In all, 497 households were listed in the CRR. Among them,

350 households lived in the registered Ban, 147 households were not living there, and 161 households were actually living in the Ban but not registered in the CRR. Therefore, 70.4 percent (350 out of 497) of the registered households in the CRR were actually living there and 68.5 percent (350 out of 511) of the resident households were registered in the CRR. This means that the CRR covered about two-thirds of the total resident households in Gumi. The sample therefore covers more than 68.5 percent of the population, since the coverage of the CRR was higher in the two other areas than in Gumi. Moreover, part of the sample was drawn from the HS which covered about half of the total households in the study areas. This suggests that the overall coverage of the sample in this study is relatively high.

References

Appleyard, R.T. 1962. "The Return Movement of U.K. Migrants from Australia." *Population Studies* 15(3): 214-225.

Balan, Jorge, Harley L. Browning, and Elizabeth Jelin. 1973. *Men in a Developing Society: Geographic and Social Mobility in Monterrey, Mexico.* Latin American Monographs, No. 30. Institute of Latin American Studies. Austin, Texas: The University of Texas at Austin.

Bovenkerk, Frank. 1974. *The Study of Return Migration: A Bibliographical Essay.* The Hague, Netherlands: Martinus Nijhoff.

Browning, Harley L. 1971. "Migrant Selectivity and the Growth of Large Cities in Developing Societies." In *Rapid Population Growth.* Ed. Roger Revelle et al. Baltimore: Johns Hopkins University Press, pp. 273-314.

Campbell, Rex R., Daniel M. Johnson, and Gary Stangler. 1974. "Return Migration of Black People to the South." *Rural Sociology* 39(4) (Winter): 514-527.

Cerase, Francesco P. 1967. "A Study of Italian Migrants Returning from the U.S.A." *International Migration Review* 1(3) (Summer): 67-74.

_____. 1974. "Expectations and Reality: A Case Study of Return Migration from the United States to Southern Italy." *International Migration Review* 8(2) (Summer): 245-262.

Chapman, Murray. 1974. "Mobility in a Non-literate Society: Method and Analysis for Two Guadalcanal Communities." In *People on the Move: Studies on Internal Migration.* Eds. Kosinski and Mansell. London: Methuen and Co., pp. 129-145.

_____. 1976. "Tribal Mobility as Circulation: A Solomon Island Example of Micro/Macro Linkages." In *Population at Microscale.* Eds. Kosinski and Webb. Christchurch: New Zealand Geographical Society, pp. 127-142.

_____. 1977. "On the Cross-cultural Study of Circulation." *International Migration Review* 12(4): 559-569.

Chapman, Murray and R. Mansell Prothero. 1977. "Circulation Between Home Places and Towns: A Village Approach to Urbanization." Paper presented at Working Session on Urbanization in the Pacific, Association for Social Anthropology in Oceania, Monterrey, California, March.

_____. 1982. "Themes on Circulation in the Third World." Working Paper No. 26. Honolulu: East-West Population Institute, East-West Center.

Chi, Peter S.K. and Mark. W. Bogan. 1974. "A Study of Migrants and Return-Migrants in Peru." Paper presented at the Annual Meeting of the PAA in New York City, 42 pp.

Comay, Yochanan. 1971. "Determinants of Return Migration: Canadian Professionals in the U.S." *Southern Economic Journal* (3)7:3: 318-322.

Connell, John et al. 1976. *Migration from Rural Areas*. Delhi, India: Oxford University Press.

DaVanzo, Julie. 1976. "Differences between Return and Nonreturn Migrants: An Econometric Analysis." *International Migration Review* 10 (1) (Spring): 13-27.

_____. 1977. "Migrants Who Return: Preliminary Findings from a Longitudinal Study." The Rand Paper Series P-5851. Santa Monica: The Rand Corporation.

_____. 1978. "Repeat Migration in the U.S.: Who Moves Back and Who Moves On?" The Rand Paper Series P-5961, Santa Monica: The Rand Corporation.

_____. 1978a. "New, Repeat, and Return Migration: Comment." *Southern Economic Journal* (October): 680-684.

DaVanzo, Julie and Peter A. Morrison. 1978. "Dynamics of

102

Return Migration: Descriptive Findings from a Longitudinal Study." The Rand Paper Series P-5913, Santa Monica: The Rand Corporation.

Eldridge, Hope T. 1965. "Primary, Secondary, and Return Migration in the United States, 1955-60." *Demography* 2: 444-455.

Ezekiel, Mordecai. 1941. Method of Correlation Analysis, Note 11 (Chapter 13), Separate Determination, pp. 498-500. New York: John Wiley.

Feindt, Waltraut and Harley L. Browning. 1972. "Return Migration: Its Significance in an Industrial Metropolis and an Agricultural Town in Mexico." *International Migration Review* 6(2): 158-165.

Freedman, Ronald and Deborah Freedman. 1956. "Farm-reared Elements in the Non-farm Population." *Rural Sociology* 21 (March): 50-61.

Germani, Gino. 1961. "Inquiry into the Social Effects of Urbanization in a Working Class Sector of Greater Buenos Aires." In *Urbanization in Latin America*. Ed. Philip M. Hauser. New York: UNESCO, pp. 206-233.

Goldscheider, Calvin. 1971. "An Outline of the Migration System." Proceedings of the International Population Conference, London, 1969, Liege: IUSSP, pp. 2746-2754.

_____. ed. 1983. *Urban Migrants in Developing Nations: Patterns and Problems of Adjustment.* Colorado: Westview Press.

Goldstein, Sidney. 1954. "Repeated Migration as a Factor in High Mobility Rates." *American Sociological Review* 19(5): 536-541.

_____. 1964. "The Extent of Repeated Migration: An Analysis Based on the Danish Population Register." *Journal of the American Statistical Association* 59: 1121-1132.

_____. 1973. "Interrelations between Migration

and Fertility in Thailand." *Demography* 10(2): 225-241.

_____. 1976. "Facets of Redistribution: Research Challenge and Opportunities." *Demography* 13: 423-434.

_____. 1978. Circulation in the Context of Total Mobility in Southeast Asia. Paper of the East-West Population Institute, No. 53, Honolulu, Hawaii: East-West Center.

Goldstein, Sidney and Alice Goldstein. 1979. "Types of Migration in Thailand in Relation to Urban-Rural Residence." Proceedings of the Conference on "Economic and Demographic Change: Issues for the 1980s." Vol 1. Liege: IUSSP, pp. 351-374.

Gould, W.T.S. and R. Mansell Prothero. 1975. "Space and Time in African Population." In *People on the Move*. Eds. Kosinski and Mansell. London: Methuen and Co., pp 39-49.

Green, Sarah Clark. 1977. "Dimensions of Migrant Adjustment in Seoul, Korea." Unpublished Ph.D. Dissertation, Brown University.

_____. 1983. "Migrant Adjustment in Seoul, Korea." In *Urban Migrants in Developing Nations*. Ed. Calvin Goldscheider. Colorado: Westview Press.

Hauser, Philip M. 1965. "Urbanization: An Overview." In *The Study of Urbanization*. Eds. Hauser and Schnore. New York: John Wiley and Sons, Inc., pp. 1-47.

Hayano, David M. 1973. "Individual Correlates of Coffee Adoption in the New Guinea Highlands." *Human Organization* 32(3): 305-314.

Hernandez-Alvarez, Jose. 1967. *Return Migration to Puerto Rico*. Berkeley: University of California, Institute of International Studies.

Hugo, Graeme J. 1978. *Population Mobility in West Java*. Indonesia: Gadjah Mada University Press.

Kasarda, John D. and Morris Janowitz. 1974. "Community Attachment in Mass Society." *American Sociolgical Review* 39 (June): 328-339.

Kau, James and C.F. Sirmans. 1976. "New, Repeat, and Return Migration: A Study of Migrants Types." *Southern Economic Journal* (October): 1144-1148.

_____. 1978. "New, Repeat, and Return Migration: Reply." *Southern Economic Journal* (January): 680-684.

Kiker, B.F. and Earle C. Traynham, Jr. 1976. "A Comment on Research on Internal Migration in the United States: A Survey." *Journal of Economic Literature* 14(3) (September): 885-888.

Kim, Son-Ung and Peter J. Donaldson. 1979. "Dealing with Seoul's Population Growth: Government Plans and Their Implementation." *Asian Survey* 19(7) (July): 661-673.

Kuznets, Simon. 1964. "Introduction: Population Redistribution, Migration and Economic Growth." In *Population Redistribution and Economic Growth, United States 1850-1950*. Eds. Eldridge and Thomas. Vol. III. Philadelphia: The Amerian Philosophical Society, pp. xxiii-xxxv.

Kwon, Tai Hwan et al. 1975. *The Population of Korea*. Seoul, Korea: Population and Development Studies Center, Seoul National University.

Lee, Anne S. 1974. "Return Migration in the United States." *International Migration Review* 8(2): 283-300.

Long, Larry and Kristin A. Hansen. 1975. "Trends in Return Migration to the South." *Demography* 12(4): 601-614.

_____. 1977a. "Interdivisional Primary, Return and Repeat Migration." *Review of Public Data Use* 5(2): 3-10.

_____. 1977b. "Selectivity of Black Return Migration to the South." *Rural Sociology* 42(3): 317-331.

McCutcheon, Laurie. 1983. "Migrant Adjustment in Surabaya, Indonesia." In *Urban Migrants in Developing Nations.* Ed. Calvin Goldscheider. Colorado: Westview Press.

Miller, Ann R. 1977. "Interstate Migrants in the United States: Some Social-economic Differences by Type of Move." *Demography 14(1):1-17.*

Miller, Edward. 1973. "Return and Nonreturn In-migration." *Growth and Change* 4(1) (January): 3-9.

Miracle, Marvin P. and Sara S. Berry. 1970. "Migrant Labor and Economic Development." *Oxford Economic Papers* 22(1): 86-108.

Mitchell, J. Clyde. 1961. "The Causes of Labour Migration." In *Migrant Labour in Africa South of the Sahara.* Publication No. 79. London: Commission for Technical Cooperation in Africa South of the Sahara, pp. 259-286.

_____. 1969. "Structural Plurality, Urbanization and Labour Circulation in Southern Rhodesia." In *Migration.* Ed. Jackson. Cambridge: Cambridge University Press, pp. 158-180.

Moir, Hazel V.J. 1975. "Relationships between Urbanization Levels and Labor Force Structure: A Cross National Analysis." Unpublished Ph.D. Thesis, Brown University.

Morrison, Peter A. 1971. "Chronic Movers and the Future Redistribution of Population: A Longitudinal Analysis." *Demography* 8(2): 171-184.

Myers, George C. and George Masnick. 1968. "The Migration Experience of New York Puerto Ricans: A Perspective on Return." *International Migration Review* 2(2): 80-90.

Nelson, Joan M. 1976. "Sojourners versus New Urbanities: Causes and Consequences of Tempoary Versus Permanent Cityward Migration in Developing Countries." *Economic Development and Cultural Change* 24(4): 721-757.

Omari, Thompson Peterk. 1956. "Factors Associated with Urban

Adjustment of Rural Southern Migrants." *Social Forces* 25: 47-56.

Park, Sang Tae. 1978. *Urbanization and Fertility in Korea 1960-70.* Seoul: The Population and Development Studies Center, Seoul National University.

Ravenstein, E.G. 1885. "The Laws of Migration." *Journal of the Royal Statistical Society* 48: 167-227.

Richmond, A.H. 1968. "Return Migration from Canada to Britain." *Population Studies* 22(2): 263-271.

_____. 1969. "Sociology of Migration in Industrial and Post-industrial Societies." In *Migration Change.* Ed. Jackson. Cambridge: Cambridge University Press, pp. 238-282.

Rose, Arnold and Leon Warshay. 1957. "The Adjustment of Migrants to Cities." *Social Forces* 36: 72-76.

Rossi, Peter. 1955. *Why Families Move.* Glencoe, Illinois: The Free Press.

Sanders, John. 1969. "The Depressed Area and Labor Mobility: The Eastern Kentucky Case." *Journal of Human Resources* 4(4): 437-450.

Simmons, Alan B. and Ramiro G. Cardona. 1972. "Rural-Urban Migration: Who Comes, Who Stays, Who Returns? The Case of Bogota, Columbia, 1929-1968." *International Migration Review* 6(2): 166-181.

Speare, Alden Jr. 1970. "Homeownership, Life Cycle Stage, and Residential Mobility." *Demography* 7(4) (November): 449-458.

United Nations. 1975. "Population of the Republic of Korea." ESCAP Country Monograph Series, No. 2. Bangkok, Thailand: Economic and Social Commission for Asia and the Pacific.

VanderKamp, John. 1971. "Migration Flows, Their Determinants and the Effects of Return Migration."

Journal of Political Economy (September):1012-1031.

_____. 1972. "Return Migration: Its Significance and Behavior." *Western Economic Journal* (December): 460-465.

Weller, Robert H. 1974. "The Structural Assimilation of Inmigrants to Lima, Peru." *International Migration Review* 8(4): 521-542.

Yu, Eui-Young. 1972. "Component of Population Growth in Seoul: 1960-1966." *Bulletin of the Population and Development Studies Center* 1: 1-15. Seoul: The Population and Development Studies Center, Seoul National University.

_____. 1974. "Seoul Metropolitan Development." Paper presented at the Organization of Demographic Associates Workshop, Manila, January.

Zimmer, Basil G. 1955. "Participation of Migrants in Urban Structures." *American Sociological Review* 20: 218-224.

3
Rural to Rural
Migration in Sri Lanka

Dayalal S. D. J. Abeysekera

Introduction

Sri Lanka is no exception to the general pattern of rural to urban migration found in most developing countries. Since the census of 1946, when place of birth and place of residence data were published, an unmistakable stream of migration to the Colombo District, containing the primate city of the country, has been documented.

There is, however, another aspect of population movement in Sri Lanka. Successive governments of independent Sri Lanka (as had legislatures before independence), consistently gave top priority to public investment in peasant agriculture. As a result, massive irrigation schemes which had fallen into disrepair over the centuries were resuscitated and new land brought under cultivation (mainly rice). Between 1952/53 and 1970/71, over 300,000 hectares of new land were brought under paddy (rice) cultivation and almost two-thirds of this was concentrated in the districts of the dry zone. The newly developed land was to be colonized by the landless peasantry concentrated in the wet zone districts of the country, which contained approximately 23 percent of the land area and over 60 percent of the population. As a consequence, the sparsely populated dry zone districts had unprecedented rates of net in-migration, far in excess of the Colombo District, which was the only district in the wet zone to have positive net migration during the three intercensal periods, 1946-1953, 1953-1963, and 1963-1971 (ESCAP, 1975:30-32). This constitutes the second dominant stream of migrants.

Apart from the inherent interest generated by the observation of a dominant rural to rural migration stream in the context of a less developed country, the study of this movement has value in the comparative analysis of urbanization. The level of urbanization in Sri Lanka has been low, a pattern which is somewhat characteristic of the South Asian region in general: 11.6 percent in 1901, 15.4 percent in 1946, and 22.4 percent in 1971. The more interesting observation is the decline in the growth rate of the City of Colombo, as well as of metropolitan Colombo, over the last three intercensal periods. During 1946-1953, the City of Colombo grew at 2.4 percent per annum but this dropped to 1.1 percent by 1963-1971; a similar drop occurred in metropolitan Colombo from 3.2 percent to 2.1 percent during the same periods (Department of Town and Country Planning, n.d.). Such observations in the context of burgeoning primacy and increasing metropolitanization in the majority of developing countries direct attention to the government's continued investment in peasant agriculture and direct and indirect income transfer programs from urban to rural areas as sources of the unusual pattern of urbanization in Sri Lanka.

This research addresses three basic questions: Who migrated to the dry zone? Why did they migrate to the dry zone? What changes in selected socioeconomic conditions, if any, have taken place among migrants since the move? The first two questions pertain to the place of origin (the wet zone) and concern the determinants of wet zone to dry zone migration. The last question relates to the place of destination (the dry zone) and is addressed to examining the consequences of migration.

One major expectation, inferred from public policy goals, guided the analysis of the determinants of migration. The government policy was to resettle the sparsely populated dry zone with the marginal peasantry of the wet zone. It was expected, therefore, that the migrants to the dry zone would be selected from among the landless or the minimally landowning peasant cultivators resident in the wet zone. Furthermore, since peasant societies are characterized by high levels of social integration, it was also expected that the propensity to migrate would be higher among those whose level of integration into the community was minimal.

Since a large stream of migrants to the dry zone had characterized the last three intercensal periods, it was inferred that the dry zone was a relatively attractive destination for the migrants. Accordingly, we expected that the migrants who settled in the dry zone would have improved their socioeconomic conditions since migration.

Theoretical Background

Substantial proportions of the population of most developing countries live at subsistence levels. Unemployment, underemployment, landlessness, illiteracy, and malnutrition are experienced on a large scale. Most countries have concentrated investments in the primate center and a few satellites of the center, while the rest of the country has been neglected. The net result of this development strategy has been to extend an invitation to the rural masses for an unqualified exodus. Sprawling shanty and tenement clusters along with high rates of growth are the conspicuous features of most cities of the developing world.

The development strategy employed by Sri Lanka has emphasized the creation of an attractive rural destination for potential migrants in which the explicit accent on agricultural work would result in the socioeconomic development of the nation as well as of the individuals and families concerned. Indicators of socioeconomic change over the last three decades substantiate the view that at the macro-level, Sri Lanka took massive strides towards development. This development took place concomitantly with the investment in peasant agriculture.

What has been the volume of internal migration in Sri Lanka and what has been its direction? Data from the 10 percent sample census tape of the 1971 census of Sri Lanka provide some insight into lifetime migration patterns.[1] These data show that

----

[1] *Non-migrants* are those who live in their district of birth; *primary migrants* are those whose district of birth is the same as their previous residence but whose current residence is different from district of previous residence; *repeat migrants* are those who have moved across district boundaries at least twice; *return migrants* are those whose current district and district of birth are similar but whose district of previous residence is different; *within district migrants* are those who live in different villages or towns but within the same district of birth; *uncertain migrants* are those who have moved out of at least one district but cannot be classified in one of the above categories; *foreign born* are those who were not born in Sri Lanka but lived there in 1971. Those lacking sufficient information to be classified in any of the above accounted for 9 percent of the sample.

almost two-thirds of the population reside in their district of birth and are non-migrants (Table 3.1). Of the migrants, equal numbers are primary and within district migrants. Only 4 percent of the migrants are repeat migrants and even fewer are return migrants.

In terms of attraction, Colombo is the most popular location with 32.8 percent of the migrants settling there. The dry zone is the next most attractive region with 28.8 percent of the migrants being attracted. These two migration streams are not differentiated solely in terms of geographic location within Sri Lanka. Colombo is the most urban district in Sri Lanka and this defines the nature of migrants to the Colombo District. Migrants to urban Colombo typify this stream rather than migrants to both rural and urban Colombo. In the case of the dry zone, the rural areas are the major destination.

The volume of migration to the dry zone districts of Sri Lanka during the last three or four decades was largely engineered by the government's land colonization program. As a result of growing unemployment, underemployment, and the necessity to produce an increasing quantity of food, the government proposed that the ideal situation would be to "hand over to the colonists a ready-made farm, complete with house" (Farmer, 1957:151). There were four categories of land allottees that benefited from the colonization program (Farmer, 1957). First, were those whose lands had to be acquired because they were needed for irrigation or related work within the program or to avoid the inclusion of small parcels of private land whose irrigation administration might cause difficulty. Although dispossessed landowners were paid monetary compensation, it was also their right to obtain land in the program. The second category of allottees was recruited from among the landless peasantry in the same Divisional Revenue Officer's Division in which the colony was situated. The third type of land allottee was the laborer who worked at least 500 days in the preparation of the program and was interested in obtaining land in the colony. This category was found more often in the large colonization programs. The last category was recruited from among the landless peasant applicants from other Divisions where there was recognizable overcrowding. They were least preferred because it had been "an established principle in the Ceylon colonies that an effort should be made to meet local needs before calling in outsiders." Considering this situation and also the volume of inter-district migration, the power of the stimulus to attract migrants was great. While no claim is made that each migrant bound for the dry zone was

112

TABLE 3.1

NUMBER AND PERCENT DISTRIBUTION OF MIGRANT
TYPES, SRI LANKA, 1971

Migrant Category		
Non-migrants	786,138	63.6
Total migrants	338,958	27.4
Missing Data	111,991	9.0
Total	1,237,087	100.0
Migrant Type (Total)	338,958	100.0
Primary	125,320	37.0
Within district	121,494	35.8
Repeat	13,382	3.9
Return	10,210	3.0
Uncertain	52,885	15.6
Foreign Born	15,667	4.6

Source: Census of Sri Lanka, 1971, 10 percent sample tape.

113

directly affected by the land development program of the government, it is maintained that government intervention was the major factor in precipitating migration to the dry zone hinterland.

Reflecting the widespread concern over rates of urban growth and the impact of migration on living and working conditions in urban places, research has disproportionately focused on rural-urban and urban-urban movements, while the study of the two streams destined for rural areas is conspicuous in its absence.

A review (Simmons et al., 1977) of research findings on internal migration makes the following observation on the nature of available literature pertaining to rural-rural migration in Asia:

> The bulk of the research has tended to be anthropological or semianthropological in scope with micro level observations often substituted for data. Others are policy oriented papers that set out to test whether or not a government's attempt to redirect migrants back to the countryside has been fruitful....There were few documented attempts to study patterns of migration other than rural-urban.

The situation is no better in Africa but perhaps slightly better in Latin America. However, even in Latin America, very few studies have been done on rural-rural movement. Martine (1975), for example, attempted to document the volume of migration to rural destinations in Colombia. He found a surprisingly high percent of all migrants in rural areas (35.9) as compared to 12.6 percent in Bogota and 51.5 percent in other urban places. Most studies concerned with migration to rural destinations have been in connection with colonization projects (e.g., Edelmann, 1967; Preston, 1969).

In the context of rural-rural migration, particularly considering the role of government policy on colonization, issues of land become central. We distinguish between two types of determinants of migration. One is the land utilization and land control pattern of villages; the other is the relationship of villagers to the means of production, which is basically land. Accordingly, it is possible to identify some of the more influential characteristics of villages and villagers which may precipitate out-migration.

In a relatively land scarce situation, it has been observed that an inverse relationship exists between land/man ratios and the propensity to migrate. Empirical results have been reported from Turkey (Turkey, Ministry of Village Affairs, 1965-68), Pakistan (Rochin, 1972), and New Zealand (Walsh and Trilin, 1973). However, this association does not apparently hold when land is generally found in abundance. Studies from Nigeria (Hill, 1972; Hunter, 1967) and Thailand (Fuhs and Vingerhoet, 1972) have revealed that an increase in population density does not lead to higher levels of out-migration. Apart from this conflicting evidence, Connell et al. (1976:8) suggest that land/man ratios are not the most potential predictors of migration. Many other mechanisms are brought to bear upon the village setting to alleviate the debilitating effects of acute fragmentation. A recent study of Sri Lanka (ESCAP, 1975: 103-104) briefly describes the operation of patron-client relationships which mitigate the effects of acute landlessness. The patrons who have more land than they can cultivate themselves are obliged to engage clients to cultivate their lands and share the fruits of land and labor in the interests of communal survival.

Connell et al. (1976:10-11) demonstrate from their analysis of 40 Indian villages that unequal distribution of land resources in a village tends to precipitate out-migration. Where private rather than communal ownership of land is established, unequal distribution of land among households (families) is an important predictor of out-migration from the village. Furthermore, village data show that households with lower caste status and/or with predominantly laborer statuses are more prone to migrate.

When one focuses on characteristics of individual villagers, it is tempting to assume that those with no land will show a higher propensity to migrate than those who own some land (Stiglitz, 1973). However, since migration requires some infrastructural support, it may not be the most deprived villager who has the opportunity to migrate but the person who has some 'maneuvering' space and is also relatively deprived. In a state-aided colonization program, however, the impact of the opportunity structure tends to be minimized for the colonists who are recruited by the government to receive land, since the government 'looks after' the allottee until he reaps his first harvest at destination. The voluntary migrants who encroach on government land are not in the same position as the migrant colonists, since they have to fend for themselves. It is thus possible that voluntary migrants are not selected from the most deprived stratum of villagers.

Social ties have been dealt with in both the sociologically and anthropologically oriented literature on migration. Emphasis has been placed on the link between the individual and the family (see, for example, Bieder, 1973; Choldin, 1973; Duncan and Reiss, 1956; Lansing and Mueller, 1967; Speare et al., 1976; Uhlenberg, 1973) and on the ways in which the links between the family and the community are related to the propensity to migrate (see Epstein, 1973; Solien De Gonzales, 1961; Singhe, 1958; Hilal, 1969).

Since the rural wet zone communities in Sri Lanka are relatively less differentiated societies, we focused on the link between the family and the community as the potential predictor of the propensity to migrate. Accordingly, patron-client relationships, the power structure of the community, the level of integration of families into communal activities, participation in voluntary communal services and in communal seeding and harvesting, utilization of communal credit facilities, and perception of close relatives and kin networks are pursued under social ties.

The sociological and anthropological orientations agree that there is a clear association between social ties and migration: the stronger the social ties, the less will be the propensity to migrate. We attempt to combine both the public policy considerations of the investment in peasant agriculture and the social ties orientation in guiding the analysis of the determinants of rural wet zone to rural dry zone migration in Sri Lanka.

Census data are seriously limited in providing the details on migration histories or on the social and economic correlates of migration. In order to analyze rural to rural migration in Sri Lanka, a series of sample surveys were undertaken in the dry zone and in the wet zone. Within the dry zone, the survey focused on five colonization schemes within three districts. A total of 1,439 male household heads were screened; 707 were selected for interview and 535 were interviewed. For comparisons, a sample of three villages within one district of the wet zone was selected. Of the 695 screened, 369 were selected for interviewing and 288 were successfully completed. A total of 823 interviews were collected to examine issues associated with rural to rural migration in Sri Lanka. The detailed procedures used and the limitations of the surveys are discussed in the Appendix of this chapter.

Determinants of Rural to Rural Migration

Why did the rural residents of the wet zone in Sri Lanka migrate to the rural dry zone? The determinants of rural to rural migration may be uncovered by examining the factors which differentiated the migrants from those who remained in the place of origin. The basic expectation is that migrants will disproportionately be selected from among the landless or the minimally landowning peasantry of the wet zone. Moreover, migrants are expected to be concentrated among those who were minimally integrated into communal activities at the place of origin.

The analysis of the determinants of migration focuses on the time around the movement. For migrants, there was no special technical problem in obtaining information about the situation at the time of the move, since it was a clear point of reference for them and a significant event. The comparable time reference for the socioeconomic situation of the natives of the wet zone was approximately 15 years before 1978, i.e., circa 1963. This was done since the largest volume of inter-district migration into the dry zone occurred during the 1953-63 intercensal period and 15 years was probably as far back as one could reliably probe details about social and economic conditions.

Four groups will be compared. Migrants were sub-divided into those who were resettled with government land and those who came to the dry zone on their own. The former will be referred to as *migrant colonists* and the latter as *voluntary migrants*. The wet zone natives have also been subdivided into natives who have never migrated out of their native village and those who have lived in two or more villages within the same district (i.e., within district migrants). The former will be referred to as *natives* and the latter as *mobile natives*.

Questions pertaining to the time of migration were asked of those migrants who were at least 18 years of age at the time of migration. While the same consideration applied to natives of the wet zone, it was decided to include the entire sample in obtaining the comparable measure, since they had not moved from their place of nativity and so memory lapses were hopefully less likely to occur. Only 6.6 percent of the sample of the wet zone natives were found to be less than 15 years of age during the time of the 'before' measure. Out of a total of 439 migrants found in the survey of the dry zone, 157 (i.e., 35.8 percent) were not asked the information pertaining to the time of migration since they were then under 18 years of age. Of these 157, 91 (57.9 percent) were among migrant colonists and 66 (42.0 percent) were voluntary migrants. Whenever the respondent's district of birth was not the same as the district of longest residence during his first 18 years, the latter was used as the district.

117

The analysis will be based on the responses of 538 ever married male heads of households; 282 were migrants in the dry zone and 256 were natives from the wet zone. Of the migrants, 179 were migrant colonists, while 103 were voluntary migrants. The majority (N=195) of the sample from the wet zone were natives who never resided outside their village of birth, while 61 were mobile migrants (i.e., those who resided in at least 2 villages within the Kegalle District).

In addition to testing the general hypothesis which pertained to the determinants of rural wet to dry zone migration, we shall examine the distribution of selected attributes of the four groups of migrants and natives at the 'time of migration' and assess the relative dissimilarity of distributions. Special emphasis will be given to the proportionate deviation from the marginals. We use a generalized index of dissimilarity (Sakoda, 1979). In addition to providing an index of dissimilarity for each of the four groups, an overall index of dissimilarity for the entire table is presented, based on the proportion of cases that can be reallocated maximally, and the proportionate deviation of each cell from the marginal. A single variable at a time will be pursued through the basic percentage table, the percentage deviation of each cell from its marginal will be presented, and the level of significance will be for each of the cell deviations.

Substantively, the analysis will be arranged under several themes and will refer to either the time just prior to migration (in the case of the migrants) or 15 years prior to the survey (in the case of the natives). These themes include: Age and educational selectivity; economic activity; ownership and control of land; housing conditions; non-farm and other sources of income; social ties; and contact with urban places.

Age and Educational Selectivity

There is a general consensus in the migration literature that young adults have a higher propensity to migrate (Thomas, 1938; Browning, 1971). However, the majority of migrant streams studied in the literature are voluntary. We included both a voluntary stream of migrants and a selected stream of migrants, screened through government eligibility criteria. A higher proportion of relatively older migrants are expected to be among the latter than among the voluntary migrants because the colonization program sought to select persons with families, possibly those with children who were old enough to contribute to farm labor.

118

The age distributions of migrants and natives are presented in Table 3.2. There are deficits in both migrant groups in the age groups below 15 (because of the elimination of those less than age 18 at the time of migration) and excesses among the natives. In the 15-19 age group, the migrant colonists show a slight deficit while the voluntary migrants show a statistically significant excess, which persists into the next two age groups and then turns into an equally significant deficit in the 30-34 age group and thereafter. The reverse characterizes the natives, where the deficit is very significant in the 15-29 age groups. In fact, these are the only age groups with a deficit among the natives (except for a very minute deficit in the oldest age group) and the proportion that has to be redistributed into these young adult age groups is 17.2 percent, the most dissimilar age distribution in comparison to the marginal distribution (I.D. = 27.5).

To ascertain whether young adults (age 18-29) were overrepresented among the two migrant groups, a one-tailed test of difference of proportions was carried out among three comparison groups. In each of the three comparisons--migrant colonists versus natives, voluntary migrants versus natives, and all migrants versus natives--the t-statistic was significant at the .01 level, reaffirming that migrants were over-selected among young adults.

The role of the selective process of government screening can be discerned by examining the 15-19 and 30-34 age groups; among the voluntary migrants the excess starts as early as ages 15-19, while among the colonists there is still a deficit. Conversely, the selectivity of voluntary migrants declines significantly in the 30-34 age group, while there is a slight excess among the migrant colonists. This is most likely because the government wanted married males with a family, rather than unmarried young adults, to colonize the dry zone.

There was approximately a gap of 5 years between the mean (or median) settlement periods of the migrant colonists and the voluntary migrants. Since the earliest migrant colonists were settled approximately 40 years before the date of the survey, which was the beginning of active colonization of the dry zone in the mid-1930s, it is very likely that the voluntary migrants did not make their move before 'testing' the performance of the migrant colonists. Almost half of the voluntary migrants (45.8 percent) migrated during the last 10 years compared to only 9 percent of the migrant colonists. Again, this reflects the earlier recruitment of colonists.

The basic expectation with respect to educational attainment

119

TABLE 3.2

PERCENTAGE DISTRIBUTION OF AGE AT THE TIME OF MIGRATION/15 YEARS
AGO, PROPORTIONATE DEVIATION FROM MARGINAL, MEDIAN AGE AMONG
MIGRANT TYPES, SRI LANKA, 1978

Age Group	Migrant colonist	Voluntary migrant	Native	Mobile native	Total
5-9	–	–	1.0	0.7	0.6
(% deviation)	(-0.6)	(-0.6)	(0.5)	(1.1)*	
10-14	–	–	6.7	3.3	2.8
	(-2.8)**	(-2.8)**	(3.9)**	(0.5)	
15-19	13.4	19.4	9.7	24.6	14.5
	(-1.1)	(4.9)**	(-4.8)**	(10.1)**	
20-24	25.1	29.1	12.3	16.4	20.3
	(4.9)**	(8.9)**	(-8.0)**	(16.3)	
25-29	16.2	17.5	7.7	4.9	12.1
	(4.1)**	(5.4)**	(-4.9)**	(-7.2)**	
30-34	14.0	7.8	15.4	13.1	13.2
	(0.8)	(-5.4)**	(2.2)	(-0.1)	
35-39	10.6	9.7	13.3	8.2	11.2
	(-0.5)	(-1.4)	(2.2)	(-3.0)	
40-44	8.4	9.7	13.3	13.1	11.0
	(-2.6)*	(-1.3)	(2.4)	(2.2)	
45-49	5.0	2.9	7.2	3.3	5.2
	(-0.2)	(-2.3)*	(2.0)*	(-1.9)	
50-54	3.4	2.9	6.2	4.9	4.5
	(-1.1)	(-1.6)	(1.7)*	(0.5)	
55-59	0.6	–	4.6	–	1.9
	(-1.3)**	(-1.9)**	(2.8)**	(-1.9)*	
60+	3.4	1.0	2.6	6.6	3.0
	(0.4)	(-2.0)*	(-0.4)	(3.6)**	
All ages	100.0	100.0	100.0	100.0	100.0
	(179)	(103)	(195)	(61)	(538)
Index of dissimilarity	15.2	23.7	27.5	20.1	21.8
Median age at migration	27.5	24.4	33.1	28.0	
Current median age	49.5	41.3	48.0	43.0	

* Significant at .05 level; ** significant at .01 level.

was that migrants to the dry zone would be selected from among those with lower levels of education. Since agricultural background rather than educational skills was a prerequisite for colonists, education would have discriminated between migrants and natives. The educational achievement of the four groups is presented in Table 3.3. In general, significant excess among the two lower educational categories (5 years or less) characterizes migrant colonists, while significant deficits are observed among voluntary migrants. Whereas migrant colonists have a consistent deficit among the better educated, the voluntary migrants reveal significant excesses in the 6-9 and 10+ years of education categories. Among the natives, there were significant excesses among those with 10 or more years of education, while the mobile natives reveal a significant excess in the 6-9 years of education category.

Thus, the best overall educational attainment characterizes the natives, followed by voluntary migrants, mobile natives, and lastly migrant colonists. The ratio of the number of persons with 9 years or less education to those with 10 years or more shows the low ratios among natives and voluntary migrants and the very high level (i.e., the low educational attainment) of migrant colonists.

However, it should be noted that free education came into operation in the mid-1940s, making the acquisition of educational skills easier with the passage of time. Thus the younger the average age of the group, the better the chance of receiving a higher level of education. The voluntary migrants were the youngest among the four groups; hence, some of the group differences reflect age compositional factors. We shall return to this in a subsequent section.

Economic Activity

Due to the operation of government selection criteria, we expect that the migrants were in large part of peasant background when compared with natives in the wet zone. None of the four groups reveal significant excesses or deficits among the employed; indeed, both groups of migrants have a slight excess of employed while both native groups show deficits (middle panel, Table 3.3).

It is difficult to classify occupations in rural areas of a developing country into a meaningful typology. As a first attempt, occupations were classified into eight categories: 1) white collar workers; 2) service personnel; 3) skilled craftsmen; 4) trade and retail related occupations; 5) blue collar workers; 6) skilled

121

TABLE 3.3

PERCENTAGE DISTRIBUTION OF EDUCATIONAL ATTAINMENT, PERCENT EMPLOYED,
AND INDUSTRY AT THE TIME OF MIGRATION/15 YEARS AGO AND PROPORTIONATE
DEVIATION FROM MARGINAL AMONG MIGRANT TYPES, SRI LANKA, 1978

Educational Attainment	Migrant colonist	Voluntary migrant	Native	Mobile native	Total
No schooling	16.4 (2.9)*	9.7 (-3.8)	13.0 (-0.6)	13.3 (-0.2)	13.5
1-5 years	55.4 (6.8)**	39.8 (-8.8)**	51.3 (2.7)	35.0 (-13.6)**	48.6
6-9 years	27.1 (-2.5)	38.8 (9.2)**	23.3 (-6.3)**	41.7 (12.0)**	29.6
10+ years	1.1 (-7.2)**	11.7 (3.4)*	12.4 (4.1)**	10.0 (1.7)	8.3
All levels	100.0 (177)	100.0 (103)	100.0 (193)	100.0 (60)	100.0 (533)
Index of dissimilarity	14.4	16.1	10.8	16.4	13.9
9 years or less/ 10+ years educated	87.5	7.6	7.0	9.0	11.0

Economic Activity

% employed	94.9 (6.2)	90.0 (1.3)	82.1 (-6.5)	86.3 (-2.4)	88.7

Industry

Agriculture	79.1 (16.5)**	55.1 (-7.6)	51.4 (-11.2)**	54.8 (-7.9)	62.7
Indeterminable	10.1 (-12.2)**	19.1 (-3.2)	33.8 (11.5)**	35.7 (13.4)**	22.3
Agric. & indet. primary sector	89.2 (4.3)	74.2 (-10.8)*	85.2 (0.3)	90.5 (5.6)	84.9
Secondary sector	3.8 (-3.9)**	10.1 (2.5)	10.6 (2.9)*	7.1 (-0.5)	7.7
Tertiary sector	7.0 (-0.5)	15.7 (8.3)**	4.2 (-3.2)**	2.4 (-5.0)*	7.4
Index of dissimilarity	16.2	40.2	12.0	20.8	20.2
All industries	100.0 (158)	100.0 (89)	100.0 (142)	100.0 (42)	100.0 (431)

* Significant at .05 level; ** significant at .01 level.

agricultural workers; 7) farmers; and 8) laborers.

Table 3.4 presents this classification of occupations among the four groups of migrant types. White and blue collar workers are perhaps the closest to the modern sector employment situation and account for only 11.2 percent of the entire sample, relative to the situation that prevailed 15 to 20 years before the survey. An excess (which is not significant) is found only among the natives. The proportionate prevalence of blue collar occupations points to small excesses among both migrant groups but deficits among the native groups. Trading and retail related occupations are the next closest to modern sector employment. Here, the voluntary migrants possess a very significant excess in this category while all other groups have deficits.

Skilled craftsmen are in excess among the migrant groups but in deficit among the native groups. Skilled craftsmanship has traditionally been highly associated with the caste system in Sri Lanka, with a few families in the village specializing in occupations such as laundry workers, barbers, potters, jewelers, blacksmiths, etc. These skilled craftsmen have invariably been in the minority caste situation and the general expectation is that migrants will be selected disproportionately from among the minority castes.

Farmers and laborers form more than three-quarters of the occupations in the rural wet zone villages. Although laborers need not necessarily be in agriculture, the majority are expected to be engaged in agricultural pursuits since this is dominant in the rural society. Only among the migrant colonists is there an excess in the farmer category, while both voluntary migrants and natives show significant deficits. At the same time, there is a very significant deficit among the migrant colonists and an equally significant excess among both native populations within the category of laborers. These data seem to contradict the expectation that migrants, especially the migrant colonists, would be disproportionately drawn from among the landless agricultural laborers and that the natives would represent predominantly the more economically viable peasant proprietor farmers and less of the landless laborers.

A predominance of farmers does not necessarily mean that they are economically viable farmers; they could be disproportionately representative of those who cultivate uneconomic land units, at marginally subsistence levels. They may be "farmers" who operate under unfavorable tenant conditions due to indebtedness or other socioeconomic obligations to the owner of the land. This too may result in semi-subsistence

TABLE 3.4

PERCENTAGE DISTRIBUTION OF OCCUPATIONAL STATUS AT THE TIME OF
MIGRATION/15 YEARS AGO AND PROPORTIONATE DEVIATION FROM
MARGINAL AMONG MIGRANT TYPES, SRI LANKA, 1978

Occupational Status	Migrant colonist	Voluntary migrant	Native	Mobile native	Total
Farmer	77.8	50.0	56.1	58.1	63.3
	(14.6)**	(-13.3)**	(-7.2)*	(-5.1)	
Laborer	3.0	16.3	23.0	27.9	14.5
	(-11.5)**	(1.8)	(8.5)**	(13.4)**	
Skilled worker in agriculture	–	2.2	3.6	2.3	1.8
	(-1.8)**	(0.4)	(1.8)**	(0.5)	
White collar worker	4.8	3.3	6.5	2.3	4.8
	(0.0)	(-1.5)	(1.7)	(-2.4)	
Blue collar worker	6.6	8.7	5.0	4.7	6.4
	(0.2)	(2.4)	(-1.3)	(-1.7)	
Trade and retail related	3.0	10.9	2.2	2.3	4.3
	(-1.3)	(6.6)**	(-2.2)*	(-2.0)	
Skilled craftsmen	4.8	6.5	3.6	2.3	4.5
	(0.3)	(2.0)	(-0.9)	(-2.2)	
Armed services	–	2.2	–	–	0.5
	(-0.5)	(1.7)**	(-0.5)	(-0.5)	
All occupations	100.0	100.0	100.0	100.0	100.0
	(167)	(92)	(139)	(43)	(441)
Index of dissimilarity	24.3	18.7	17.5	15.4	19.8

* significant at .05 level; ** significant at .01 level.

levels. Both these conditions would have satisfied the government's selective criteria of landlessness or marginal landownership and agricultural background for the receipt of dry zone land. Thus, the significant excess within the farmer occupation among the migrant colonists does not necessarily contradict the expected direction of the relationship.

What needs to be explained is how the predominance of laborers among the natives is reconcilable with non-migration. In rural Sri Lanka, peasant agriculture in general and paddy cultivation specifically is based on antecedent and continuing patron-client relationships. This system may be described as follows:

> Village resources are not shared equally; some have a larger share than others. It has been seen that, in land, there are mechanisms through which those who have less land can obtain an increase in income through working for those who have more land. To put this in the accepted phraseology, there is a "system of patrons and clients." In terms of the normal standards of behaviour, patrons do much more for clients than merely providing them with work. They are expected to help them at times of crisis and in many other ways. Similarly, the client has not merely to work for his patron but also be a follower in political and quasi-political contexts. In more recent times, patronage has been dispensed not only by land owners but also by those who have acquired other sources of income as well as by others who have some control over government funds flowing into the village.
>
> Parallel to this system of patronage is another of reciprocal services. Such a system ensures that village residents assist each other in agricultural work, in the construction of houses, and so forth. Together, the two systems may be regarded as something of an insurance. Where they function satisfactorily, the village is held together as a cohesive working entity. Land in such situations is not merely a resource but it is the "community" - the effective boundary of social relations. Village identity is clear, and there is little tendency towards disintegration (ESCAP, 1975:103-104).

Set within this social matrix, the laborers are the clients of patrons. In a land surplus situation, the clients have a greater bargaining position for self-improvement, since the patrons would be competing among themselves for the services of the limited supply of clients (Paige, 1975). In a labor surplus situation, the bargaining power of clients is drastically reduced, since the competition is among the potential clients for an economically and socially viable patron. Those who enter into mutually beneficial patron-client relationships in the village are an integral part of communal life. While their status is undoubtedly below that of the patrons, it is much more secure than the peasant proprietor cultivating his own piece of land when it is uneconomic to cultivate. Often, it would be beneficial for such a cultivator to sell or give up his land to the patron who has a large tract of land adjoining his and become his client. Thus, insofar as the laborers denote the essential complement of rural agricultural society, the excess of laborers among the natives need not necessarily be construed as an agricultural proletariat being expropriated by a fuedal landed gentry.

The fact that there were a mere 3 percent of laborers among the migrant colonists reveals that the attempt on the part of the government to reach out to clients who were boxed into an unfavorable patron-client relationship was not successful. This becomes more evident when it is observed that 16.3 percent of voluntary migrants were also laborers, who were in sufficiently marginal situations to precipitate migration to the dry zone.

Looked at within the power relations of the wet zone village, which were capable of manipulating the government screening process,[2] the minimization of the migration of one's clients into the dry zone was to the patron's advantage. Any loss of the labor surplus within the community would have amounted to a rise in paddy production costs. The nature of paddy production in the wet zone village requires large inputs of man-days during peak periods like seeding and harvesting. To that extent, the availability of large reserves of under and unemployed labor with varying degrees of linkage to the patron core maintained power

----

2
  All applications for land had to have the headman's report. A favorable report to the Land Kachcheri, where recruitment of colonists was decided upon, was a prerequisite to be a successful land alottee. The headman was invariably in a pivotal power position by virtue of his official status; being in a position of patrilineal inheritance also made him invariably a part of the power structure of the community.

relations and the status quo of the village.

The cardinal question then is how the power structure of the village turned this potential threat to their position into an advantage, while keeping the general spirit of the colonization policy intact. The obvious solution was the uneconomic landholding peasant proprietors, who could hardly make ends meet and were a source of irritation to the well-to-do patron. They often needed loans, were not available to work during the peak seasons since they were working their own plots of land, and were holding on to a small piece of land on the pretext that they would be doing irreparable wrong to their forefathers if they sold traditional family land.

Insofar as these marginal peasant farmers were under the influence of the patrons and the government was alienating land in the dry zone at no expense to the patron, the patron would facilitate peasant migration to the dry zone, perhaps by purchasing the peasant's small plot of land. From the perspective of the village, the net result may have been beneficial. Consolidation of land occurred on a minute scale. While it would have increased the gap in the ownership structure of village resouces, concentrated ownership per se does not exclude the use of land for the benefit of the community. Cultivation of land was essentially a communal activity. The intricate network of patron-client relationships saw to it that labor (at least the most important laborer clientele) was not exploited. As long as the patron's frame of reference was his native village and perhaps the adjacent ones, and once a stable economic foundation was created, the intentions of the patron were almost invariably concerned only with maintenance of his economic position.

The very traditional nature of the industrial classification of occupations in the rural wet zone of Sri Lanka is highlighted in the bottom panel of Table 3.3. More than three-quarters of the industrial distribution is concentrated within the 'agricultural' and the 'indeterminable.' The latter is primarily made up of the laborers, as there was no indication to which industry they belonged. The overwhelming majority of these would be engaged in agriculture as there was practically no other opportunity to be gainfully employed within the wet zone village.

Thus, when the population engaged in the 'indeterminate' industrial category was combined with the agricultural, a clearer picture of primary versus secondary and tertiary sectors comes into focus. The voluntary migrants are the only group to have a significant deficit within the combined agricultural category. While the migrant colonists and both groups of natives are a predominantly primary sector based industrial classification, the voluntary migrants are selected from among those with a significant deficit in agriculture-bound industry. Viewed in another way, voluntary migrants are more concentrated in the secondary and tertiary sectors, particularly in the latter. The natives are overrepresented within the secondary and underrepresented within the tertiary sector. The mobile natives are significantly underrepresented within the tertiary sector as well.

Two interesting observations may be made from this analysis of the four migrant types within the three sector industrial classification. First, the rank ordering of the four groups of migrant types within the secondary sector is similar to the ordering of educational level of the four groups. Pearson's r computed between the four groups in terms of educational attainment and the relative excess in the secondary sector yielded an extremely high positive coefficient of 0.89, signifying that educational attainment was a major determinant of secondary sector participation among migrant types.

The second observation relates to the high selectivity of voluntary migrants in tertiary sector employment compared to the significant negative selectivity of both groups of natives. This negative selectivity may be indicative of the low esteem for service oriented occupations (largely petty trading). It may also reflect the greater ties natives have to their place of origin and the higher propensities to move among those in the tertiary sector.

Ownership and Control of Land

The government's investment in peasant agriculture was explicitly geared to coping with the imbalance in the land/man situation at the national level by facilitating the combination of manpower resources with the availability of arable land and by the provision of effective irrigation. Set within this context, migration to the dry zone should be related to the ownership and control of land in the wet zone villages. The migrant colonists should have been selected disproportionaly from among the landless and/or the minimally landowning as well as from among those of predominantly agricultural background when compared to the natives as well as to the voluntary migrants. However, it may not be merely the landless and the minimally landowning that migrated but those who were both without viable units of land and also the least integrated into communal activity.

This section will examine the general issue of the nature of

128

landownership and control in the place of origin at the time of migration (15 years before the survey in the case of the natives). We include the following: 1) application for government land, 2) nature of possession of land, 3) succession to land, 4) location of land, 5) acreage cultivated, 6) crop cultivated, 7) nature of labor utilized for cultivation, 8) utilization of crop, and 9) relationship to the buyer of crop.

We begin the discussion on ownership and control of land with its relative demand, since that provides a basic indication of the prevalent landholding situation of the wet zone village. The assumption is that those who had land would not ask for it from the government because the government did not plan on alienating Crown land to landed proprietors and because those who were economically and socially viable in their native setting would not have considered migrating to the unknown of the dry zone.

Table 3.5 reveals, as expected, that migrant colonists are very significantly selected from among those who applied for land. The natives, on the other hand, are overrepresented among those who did not apply for land. Mobile natives are very similar to voluntary migrants. It is likely that they were less integrated into the community than the natives and, like most 'outsiders', had less ownership and control of village land. If in some cases the 'before' measure referred to the mobile natives' village of nativity rather than the current community of residence (i.e., the survey site), then they may have been in fairly deprived socioeconomic conditions vis-a-vis landownership. This may have been a major reason for their move within the district in search of a better economic situation.

Within the sample of applicants for Crown land, the relative success in obtaining it among the four migrant types shows that migrant colonists were the most successful while voluntary migrants were the least successful. However, the temporal and spatial referents between the voluntary migrants and the other three groups may not be identical. If the voluntary migrants received government land at the time of first migration (i.e., the temporal referent of the response), then, by definition, they could not be voluntary migrants but would be migrant colonists.

While the natives have a 19.7 percent deficit among those who applied and received land, the mobile natives, in fact, have a slight excess of 1.4 percent within the successful category. The lands which were received by almost three-fifths of the two groups of natives were small residential units of highland dispensed through the village expansion scheme rather than lands in the dry zone since the natives lived in the wet zone at the time of the

129

TABLE 3.5

PERCENT APPLIED FOR LAND, RECEIVED LAND, POSSESSED LAND AT THE TIME
OF MIGRATION/15 YEARS AGO AND PROPORTIONATE DEVIATION FROM MARGINAL
AMONG MIGRANT TYPES, SRI LANKA, 1978

	Migrant colonist	Voluntary migrant	Native	Mobile native	Total
% applied for land	91.1 (30.7)**	56.3 (-4.1)	34.4 (-26.1)**	60.7 (0.3)	60.4
Index of dissimilarity	68.0	7.5	60.5	0.4	42.8
% received land	88.3 (19.4)**	36.2 (-32.7)	49.3 (-19.7)**	70.3 (1.4)	68.9
Index of dissimilarity	45.3	76.4	45.9	3.1	46.2
Possession of land					
No land	18.0 (6.8)**	21.4 (10.2)**	1.7 (-9.5)**	3.4 (-7.8)**	11.2
Owned but uncultivated	9.3 (3.6)**	8.2 (2.5)*	2.2 (-3.5)**	1.7 (-4.0)**	5.7
Cultivated encroached land	4.1 (0.1)	2.0 (-1.9)	2.2 (-1.7)*	11.9 (7.9)**	3.9
Cultivated owned land	62.8 (-4.4)	60.2 (-7.0)	71.7 (4.5)	78.0 (10.8)*	67.2
Cultivated owned & unowned land	5.3 (-6.1)**	7.1 (-4.3)**	21.7 (10.3)**	5.1 (-6.3)**	11.4
Index of dissimilarity	16.0	16.3	22.8	21.2	19.0
Total	100.0 (172)	100.0 (98)	100.0 (180)	100.0 (59)	100.0 (509)

* Significant at .05 level; ** significant at .01 level.

survey.

Possession of land in rural Sri Lanka may be classified according to many criteria. One such schema ascends in rank ordering from the possession of no land to cultivating owned and unowned land (bottom panel Table 3.5). At the bottom of the hierarchy of landownership are those with no land, followed by those who own some land but did not cultivate it. In a land scarce agricultural economy, every bit of private land has to be cultivated. When there is land without cultivation, it generally signifies that the extent of the land is so meagre it is uneconomic to cultivate and serves more of a symbolic function of legitimizing one's membership in the community, or that the owner is unable to combine land, labor, and capital to yield an output from it.

Next in the ascending order of the hierarchy are the cultivators of encroached (mainly Crown) land, followed by those who only cultivate the land they own. A viable rural community in Sri Lanka should be recognized by the preponderance of its families within this last classification, which includes over two-thirds of the entire sample. The two top categories in the hierarchy are those who cultivate land they own and those who cultivate land owned by others. The latter are in a sufficiently powerful position to be able to persuade those in marginal landholding positions to either directly lease them the land or enter into patron-client relationships, augmenting the economic and socio-political base of the patron. Those persons with a combination of two or more landholding patterns entailed in the typology were classified with those who cultivate owned and unowned land.

The data show that within the two lowest categories of landownership, statistically significant excesses are found among both migrant groups, while both native groups reveal significant deficits in these two categories. Conversely, within the two highest landowning categories, excesses are found only among the natives. The mobile natives have a significant concentration in the two other ownership categories, i.e., those who cultivate their lands only and those cultivating encroached land. The voluntary migrants show a deficit in both these categories, while the migrant colonists show a very slight excess within the encroacher cultivator category but a deficit in the owner cultivator category.

Of those who possessed land, over three-fourths inherited the land. The natives are more concentrated among those who "inherited and bought" land. Again, this places the natives among those most socially and economically 'acceptable' within the rural community, followed by the mobile natives (some of whom seem to

131

have acquired land through marriage), and the two migrant groups.

The traditional village was mostly a self-contained unit and the elite of the community had the highest concentration of land within it. The further away the land was from the immediate vicinity of the village, the less its impact on the stratification and evaluation of the communal membership. The dominant mode of land location is within the territory of the village--fully 93 percent of the land owned was located in the village. Almost all the land owned by migrant colonists (98 pecent) before they moved was located in their village of origin. This further suggests that it was neither landownership or its location per se which precipitated their response to government policy. Both voluntary migrants and mobile natives had somewhat larger proportions owning land outside their village. This too reaffirms their "outside" status. The preponderance of voluntary migrants in trade activity may have provided them with resouces to acquire land outside the village perhaps from marginal proprietors in the vicinity. On the other hand, it may have moved them more easily into the provision of services needed for the maintenance of agricultural activity that was in short supply. It might be noted that "the real beneficiaries of dry zone investment were middlemen, who emerged as a new group of capitalists" (ESCAP, 1975: 111).

The necessary complement of the dimension of landownership and control is the extent of such ownership and control. This is obviously associated with the land colonization program of the government, which in turn was the major stimulus for migration.

In Table 3.6, the extent of land cultivated is arranged ordinally from those cultivating no land to those having five acres or more. Perusal of the two extreme categories alone suffices to reaffirm the expected association between acreage cultivated and the propensity to migrate. Each of the four groups shows statistically significant excesses or deficits; both migrant groups show an excess in the 'no land' category, the migrant colonists depicting a slightly greater excess (9.4 percent) than the voluntary migrants (7.5 percent). Both groups of natives, on the other hand, reveal deficits, greater among the mobile natives (11.4 percent) than among the natives (8.8 percent). At the upper extreme of the continuum, the only statistically significant excess is recorded among the natives. All other groups have deficits in this landholding category. Within the middle-range of the order of acreage cultivated, the best position as defined by the highest positive deviation from the marginal is found among the mobile

TABLE 3.6

PERCENTAGE DISTRIBUTION OF ACREAGE CULTIVATED AT THE TIME OF
MIGRATION/15 YEARS AGO AND PROPORTIONATE DEVIATION FROM
MARGINAL AMONG MIGRANT TYPES, SRI LANKA, 1978

Acreage Cultivated	Migrant colonist	Voluntary migrant	Native	Mobile native	Total
No land	29.0 (9.4)**	27.0 (7.5)**	10.8 (-8.8)**	8.2 (-11.4)**	19.6
Less than ¼ acre	4.6 (-0.2)	1.0 (-3.7)**	7.2 (2.5)**	3.3 (-1.4)	4.7
¼ - ½ acre	10.8 (-0.5)	12.0 (0.7)	10.8 (-0.5)	13.1 (1.8)	11.3
½ - 1 acre	11.9 (-2.4)	19.0 (4.7)**	12.3 (-2.0)	19.7 (5.4)*	14.3
1 - 2 acres	17.6 (-0.4)	20.0 (2.0)	16.4 (-1.6)	21.3 (3.3)	18.1
2 - 3 acres	13.6 (-0.5)	9.0 (-5.1)**	15.4 (1.3)	19.7 (5.6)*	14.1
3 - 4 acres	4.6 (-0.3)	2.0 (-2.9)**	7.2 (2.3)**	3.3 (-1.6)	4.9
4 - 5 acres	4.0 (0.2)	2.0 (-1.8)	3.1 (-0.7)	8.2 (4.4)**	3.8
5 or more acres	4.0 (-5.4)**	8.0 (-1.4)	16.9 (7.5)**	3.3 (-6.1)**	9.4
Total	100.0 (176)	100.0 (100)	100.0 (195)	100.0 (61)	100.0 (532)
Index of dissimilarity	14.4	18.3	21.4	23.2	18.8
Median acreage	0.74	0.76	1.27	1.13	1.01
Mean acreage	1.32	1.35	2.18	1.70	1.69
Mean acreage among lower 50%[1]	0.18	0.24	0.55	0.57	0.32
Mean acreage among upper 50%[2]	2.46	2.47	3.81	2.82	3.04
2 / 1	13.7	10.3	6.9	4.9	9.5

* Significant at .05 level; ** significant at .01 level.

133

natives (17.5 percent), followed by the natives (1.3 percent) with both migrant groups behind with net negative deviations of -4.0 percent (migrant colonists) and -6.1 percent (voluntary migrants).

In the bottom panel of Table 3.6, data are presented on the mean acreage cultivated by the bottom and upper half of each of the four migrant groups. The last row shows the number of units of land that the upper half cultivated per unit of land cultivated by the bottom half. This measure of disparity between an approximation of the 'haves' and the 'have-nots' reveals that the most equitable distribution of land cultivation was found among the mobile natives (4.9) followed by the natives (6.9). The largest disparities were found among the migrant colonists (13.7) and the voluntary migrants (10.3). The group with the most inequitable distribution of cultivatable land was the least able to survive in their community of nativity, while those with the lowest degree of disparity remained in the community. Since the migrants did not necessarily originate from the same three villages sampled in the wet zone, these patterns may be interpreted more broadly: Communities with a higher inequitable distribution of land were more likely to lose population to the dry zone. This conclusion is consistent with the more general argument based on migration data from rural areas of Third World nations that "intra-rural inequality is at once the main cause, and a serious consequence, of rural emigration" (Connell et al., 1976: 200).

The proportion cultivating more than 2 acres of land among the two migrant groups was substantial: 26.1 percent among the migrant colonists and 21.0 percent among the voluntary migrants. The important question is why they migrated at all to the dry zone. In this context, it needs to be recalled that the situation at the time of migration was in terms of the respondent's family's, and not in terms of the individual, situation. Thus, it is possible that those who had substantial land (i.e., more than two acres) moved because they were beginning to feel the pressure on land due to increased survivorship of siblings (Speare, 1974), since the tradition in Sri Lanka is to bequeath equally the immovable property (i.e., land) to sons and the movable property to daughters. An excessive number of male siblings within the family would have been detrimental to the generational maintenance of the same standard of living, while maintaining residency in the community of nativity.

An attempt was made to examine whether differential presence of male siblings was observable among the four migrant types. Within all acreage levels the natives show a noticeably lower mean in comparison to the other three groups. While a

134

more detailed statistical analysis did not show a stronger relationship among those with larger acres of land cultivated, the hypothesis is worthy of more systematic analysis.

Dependence on one crop cultivation is the least adaptive and flexible agricultural production situation. Mixed crop production is a more effective strategy of survival. In this context, it is significant that the natives and the mobile natives had a very positive net excess of mixed crop cultivation (83 percent were mixed crops). In contrast, both migrant groups had significant deficits in mixed crop cultivation and excesses in single crop cultivation (Table 3.7). Details not presented in tabular form show a heavy concentration of migrant groups in coconut cultivation, where the relative input of labor is minimal.

The organization of labor in the process of agricultural production in rural Sri Lanka has an important social as well as economic content, providing an additional dimension of the prestige hierarchy. The most popular form of labor utilized was that of family members. The family, while it need not be restricted to nuclear members, included at least three generations bonded together by filial lines and their immediate conjugal extensions. The preponderence of this type of cultivation (through family labor) indicates that the family and not the individual is the unit of production and this is the labor that is most easily mobilized and to which members have the least amount of obligation in terms of reciprocation since it is also the consumption unit. Most of the agricultural land possessed by the community was limited in size that it could viably be cultivated with the resources available within the family, except perhaps in the seeding and harvesting periods. This is amply reflected in the fact that at least three-quarters of the four migrant types utilize only the labor of their family members (Table 3.7, middle panel).

The natives are the only group to show an excess (4.2 percent) among those who use the kayya for cultivation. The kayya is a mutual-aid team of villagers who help in each other's fields throughout the cycle of cultivation. The mobile natives, on the other hand, show an equally significant deficit in the same category, perhaps indicating both smaller landownership as well as an inability to mobilize the community for purposes of cultivation. They are, however, found in significant excess (13.8 percent) among those who cultivate with family labor alone, signifying moderate farm size and/or larger families.

The crop that is cultivated can either be utilized solely for familial consumption or for both consumption and sale. The nature of the crop, however, has an impact on the possibility of

135

TABLE 3.7

PERCENT MIX CROP CULTIVATION, LABOR UTILIZED, CROP UTILIZATION,
AND RELATIONSHIP TO BUYER AT THE TIME OF MIGRATION/15 YEARS
AGO AND PROPORTIONATE DEVIATION FROM MARGINAL AMONG
MIGRANT TYPES, SRI LANKA, 1978

	Migrant colonist	Voluntary migrant	Natives	Mobile native	Total
Percent mixed crops	43.4	52.2	82.8	83.6	66.3
	(−22.8)**	(−14.1)**	(16.6)**	(17.4)**	
Index of dissimilarity	33.0	18.1	28.0	25.8	27.1
Labor Utilized					
Family members only	84.8	84.1	76.0	96.5	82.7
	(2.1)	(1.4)	(−6.7)	(13.8)*	
Family members and Kayya members	7.2	8.7	13.5	1.8	9.2
	(−2.0)	(−0.6)	(4.2)**	(−7.5)**	
Index of dissimilarity	4.3	3.8	11.5	15.9	8.6
Percent crops for consumption only	62.1	61.4	51.8	59.7	57.6
	(4.6)	(3.9)	(−5.8)*	(2.1)	
Index of dissimilarity	9.3	7.9	11.9	4.2	9.4
Percent buyer is in primary relationship	13.6	18.5	4.0	−	8.4
	(5.3)	(10.1)*	(−4.4)	(−8.4)	
Index of dissimilarity	31.9	54.1	35.6	42.9	39.4

* Significant at .05 level; ** significant at .01 level.

this dichotomous outcome. Within each migrant group, more than one-half of the respondents stated that the crop is only for consumption (Table 3.7, lower panel). This indicates the general pattern of agricultural production of the wet zone village, where increasing pressure on land would have forced more and more people to confine their produce for familial consumption.

The migrant colonists, voluntary migrants, and mobile natives consistently show small excesses within the 'consumption only' category. The proportionate deficit in the same category among the natives is statistically significant and is the only instance where a deficit is recorded.

Of those who said that their crops were sold as well as consumed, the relationship to the buyer of the crops was ascertained. When the responses are dichotomized into the 'predominantly primary' (relatives and family friends) and 'predominantly secondary' (non-relatives, co-operatives, mudalali or trader associations), both groups of migrants show that their dealings were within the 'primary' relationships, while both groups of natives disposed of their crops via secondary associations. The proportionate excesses are 5.3 percent and 10.1 percent among the migrant colonists and voluntary migrants, respectively. The deficits among the natives and mobile natives, on the other hand, are 4.4 percent and 8.4 percent, respectively. To the extent that disposal of one's surpluses through secondary associations is beneficial to the seller since he does not have to absorb losses on kinship grounds, both groups of natives appear to have been resorting to a more advantageous arrangement for the sale of their crops than either of the migrant groups.

Housing and Income

The general expectation was that since migrants were selected from the less well-off segments of the society, they would also be characterized by inferior housing conditions. Before analyzing the results of the survey, a more general description of rural housing in Sri Lanka is in order. Soysa (1979:170-172) provides a profile of rural housing in Sri Lanka and places it within the larger region of Southeast Asian housing situation.

Statistically, a typical rural house in Sri Lanka is a one- or two-room structure, 23 m in floor area, less than 30 years old. It is owned by one of the occupants who earns less than U.S. $30 per month. The house is a semi-permanent structure, with walls of wattle and daub, a roof thatched with cadjan, and a floor of dried mud. It has no toilet facilities. Lighting is from a lamp using kerosene oil. There are about five occupants, and they have access to drinking water from a well shared with others. For bathing, they make use of rivers and streams nearby.

This typical rural house looks attractive in that it appears clean and is located in a pleasant environment. However, a close view of the inside shows a shelter greatly in need of repair. In the dry season the house is cool, and, but for the smallest children, often empty during the day. In the rainy season, the floors and walls are constantly damp, and small children and domestic animals share living areas. Water has to be carried to the house and is stored in the backyard in open bins that are playgrounds for various insects and birds. Open cooking is done so close to the main living areas that the interior of the house is practically covered with soot. Outside, garbage is spread around to feed domestic animals, and the location of toilet facilities is a matter of daily decision.

Rural housing in Sri Lanka appears to be of better quality in both structural characteristics and amenities than that of countries like Indonesia, Philippines, and Thailand. However, even in Sri Lanka, which has invested heavily in welfare policies and has some key social indicators of a very developed country, the statistical profile of rural housing reflects the poor living conditions of the majority of its people.

Three questions pertaining to the structure of the respondent's house were posed, which related to the raw materials from which the roof, walls, and floor were constructed. The responses were then combined into an index on the basis of which the overall housing condition among the four migrant groups was assessed. Indicators such as availability of pipe-borne water, toilet facilities, and electricity were not pursued, since they do not effectively discriminate the rural Sri Lankan landscape.

The index was constructed as follows: Depending on their condition, the roof, walls, and floor were each assigned a score varying from one to three. The Cadjan/straw roof, mud walls, and mud floor were each allocated a score of one; tiled roofs, brick walls, and cement floors were given a score of three each. All other responses were given a score of two each. Scores ranged from a minimum of three to a maximum of nine on the overall housing index. This was further collapsed into four categories ranging from the worst housing (minimum score) to the best housing (maximum score) with two intermediate categories.

The rank ordering of the four migrant types in terms of overall housing conditions is presented in Table 3.8. The excesses among the groups are found in different housing conditions. The migrant colonists have their excesses in the worst housing, the natives are bimodal in the worst and the best, the mobile natives are in the intermediate categories of housing, and the voluntary migrants in categories three and four (the best).

When the housing categories are dichotomized and the net proportionate deviations from the row marginal are pursued in the combined categories of three and four (i.e., the best housing conditions), the voluntary migrants hold the best position with an excess of 7.7 percent, followed by the mobile natives with 3.8 percent, the natives with a deficit of -0.7 percent, and lastly the migrant colonists with a deficit of -5.4 percent. The overall housing index suggests that the general rank ordering observed on ownership and control of land with the natives followed by the mobile natives, migrant colonists, and the voluntary migrants is definitely not repeated in terms of rural housing conditions.

One possible explanation is that the ranking of migrant types in terms of housing conditions is brought about by the preponderance of skilled craftsmen and traders among the voluntary migrants and their relative absence among the natives. The presence of skilled craftsmen, mostly masons and carpenters, may facilitate the construction of better housing, since there is no need to spend money on these skills. The 'oversupply' of traders implies an above average usage of money among the voluntary migrants which in turn facilitates the acquisition of necessary raw materials like cement, tiles, limestone, and wood, which generally have to be purchased from outside the village. Being traders also may facilitate the acquisition of scarce construction materials within the village economy.

This speculation does not, however, explain why the mobile natives have better housing conditions than the natives, since both native groups have deficits of skilled craftsmen and traders within their ranks. Perhaps to improve their prestige positions, the mobile natives have to resort to a dimension other than land which could be as tangible and expressive. The mobile natives may invest their surpluses to a greater extent than the natives in improving their houses.

Although agriculture is by far the predominant livelihood of rural Sri Lanka, it is not the only source of sustenance. With declining land/man ratios and a stagnant agricultural base, the

TABLE 3.8

PERCENTAGE DISTRIBUTION OF OVERALL HOUSING CONDITIONS, INVOLVEMENT
IN NON-FARM ACTIVITY, AND ECONOMIC SITUATION AT TIME OF
MIGRATION/15 YEARS AGO AND PROPORTIONATE DEVIATION
FROM MARGINAL AMONG MIGRANT TYPES, SRI LANKA, 1978

	Migrant colonist	Voluntary migrant	Native	Mobile native	Total
Overall Housing Condition					
1 ('worst')	18.5 (1.8)	15.8 (-0.9)	18.9 (2.2)	6.8 (-10.0)**	16.7
2 ('bad')	50.0 (3.6)	39.6 (-6.8)**	45.0 (-1.4)	52.5 (6.1)	46.4
3 ('better')	24.1 (-4.6)*	31.7 (3.0)	27.8 (-0.9)	39.0 (10.3)**	28.7
4 ('best')	7.4 (-0.8)	12.9 (4.7)**	8.3 (0.2)	1.7 (-6.5)**	8.2
All conditions	100.0 (162)	100.0 (101)	100.0 (180)	100.0 (59)	100.0 (502)
Index of dissimilarity	7.9	9.6	3.6	18.6	8.5
Percent involved in non-farm activity	19.3 (6.7)**	15.4 (2.8)	7.9 (-4.7)*	6.8 (-5.8)	12.6
Index of dissimilarity	30.3	12.6	21.5	26.4	23.0
Economic Situation					
In debt	7.8 (-1.5)	4.3 (-5.1)**	14.8 (5.5)**	5.1 (-4.2)*	9.3
Just enough to live	84.4 (4.7)	85.1 (5.4)	70.5 (-9.3)**	96.4 (6.7)	79.7
Enough to live and save too	7.8 (-3.2)*	10.6 (-0.3)	14.8 (3.8)**	8.5 (-2.5)	11.0
Total	100.0 (154)	100.0 (94)	100.0 (176)	100.0 (59)	100.0 (483)
Index of dissimlarity	14.3	13.9	30.2	15.9	19.6

* Significant at .05 level; ** significant at .01 level.

140

inhabitants of the wet zone had to seek and secure extra-agricultural employment. ESCAP (1975:109) presents the major mechanisms through which the bulk of the wet zone resisted the attraction of the dry zone as well as that of urban Colombo.

If forms of intensive agriculture had been devised and popularized at this stage (i.e., circa late 1930s and early 1940s), agriculture might have been an effective income alternative to extra-village employment. As it was, the relative position of agriculture only continued to worsen. The wet zone recognized, particularly those parts of the wet zone which had urban contact, that significant upward mobility could not be obtained through agriculture alone. The concomitant of this was that agricultural labor as the sole source of income was looked down upon and education with its potential for extra-village employment was elevated. At the level of aspirations, education and extra-village employment came to be looked upon as the polar opposite of agricultural work. This continued to be so even after education ceased to be an automatic guarantee of employment, for, even by then, agriculture had not taken a significant upturn.

The middle panel of Table 3.8 reveals the wet zone village situation approximately two decades prior to the survey with respect to the prevalence of non-farm activity. Only 12.6 percent engaged in any non-farm activity. However, even with this imbalanced distribution of non-farm activity, the four migrant types are characterized by different patterns. While both migrant groups reveal an excess of those with non-farm activity, both native groups show very significant deficits.

This is, perhaps, an indication of the complementary adjustment to the landownership pattern in the village which favored the native groups and showed that the migrant groups possessed minimal land. With less land from which to derive a sustenance, they resorted to non-farm activity. More than one-half of all those engaged in any non-farm activity were occupied in trade.

Similarly, the proportion who had family members receiving income from any other source varied by migration status. There are excesses among the two migrant groups, while both native groups show deficits in the proportion receiving any other source of income.

The survey asked if the respondent (his family) was in debt, had just enough income to live, or had enough to live and save at the time of migration (15 years before the inquiry in the case of the natives). The results in the lower panel of Table 3.8 show that natives are clearly distinctive relative to the other groups. The migrant colonists, voluntary migrants, and mobile natives are less likely to be in debt than natives but are more likely to have just enough to live. In contrast, the natives are more likely to be in debt and also more likely to have enough to live on and save as well. The excesses in the two polar categories of income among the natives suggest the existence of a small core of patrons who were capable of gainfully employing the less well-off sections of the native membership of the community. The proportionate deviation from the row marginals among the other three groups reveals that the mobile natives were the most viable in terms of the income situation (excess of 8.5 percent), followed by the voluntary migrants (5.4 percent), and the migrant colonists (2.8 percent).

Social Ties

Agriculture being the dominant way of life requires the combination of all resources of the community for its perpetuation. In the rural hinterland, social relationships and kin ties are the means as well as the goal of existence. Unlike the more urban environment where differentiation has taken place and division of labor is conspicuously visible by the levels of specialization achieved, separation of occupation from social relationships is almost impossible to achieve in rural areas.

Social ties have been among the most emphasized in social and economic anthropological literature covering traditional societies. Social ties are the essence of traditional peasant societies like that of the contemporary rural wet zone Sri Lanka. We define them in the broad sense, not limited to ties within the nuclear or extended family but more to relationships of familial integration into communal activity. This is most important in the Sri Lankan context because it is not the mere fact of landlessness that stimulates 'push' propensities but the combined impact of marginal landownership and minimal integration into communal activity. The latter, if present, will provide the social security for survival within the community through the elasticities of patron-client relationships, in spite of 'push' pressures. Thus, the basic hypothesis that guided the analysis in this section is that, the higher the level of integration into the community, the lower the propensities to migrate.

Two questions on communal participation were included: 1) participation of the respondent's family in voluntary social services, and 2) participation in communal cultivation on other's land. Voluntary social services were defined in the questionnaire as "mediating in disputes of others, offering advice and guidance in conflicting situations, and taking an active role in matters pertaining to the village school, temple, or other voluntary society in the community on a regular basis."

While both groups of natives show excesses among those reporting participation in voluntary services, the two migrant groups reveal significant deficits in the same category (Table 3.9). In terms of proportionate deviations, the natives show 11.8 percent of the cases needing to be reallocated, followed by voluntary migrants (9.7 percent), migrant colonists (8.1 percent), and lastly by mobile natives (4.9 percent). Thus, those who did not take part in communal voluntary social services, that is, those who were marginally integrated into the community, were disproportionately selected for migration, both voluntarily and through government sponsorship.

The second dimension of communal participation, that is, taking part in the seeding or harvesting of other people's lands, is a more specific question attempting to capture the crucial juncture between economic activity and social ties in rural Sri Lankan life. The seeding and harvesting times are the peak periods of labor utilization and require the full mobilization of all available manpower. It is in the community's general interest to do the seeding of tracts of paddy lands within the shortest possible span because it facilitates the coordination of irrigation activities which have to be effected communally. Harvesting also has to be accomplished within a short period because, once the crop is ready for harvesting, a thunderstorm could destroy the crop and endanger the viability of the community. Thus, there is a compelling necessity to engage in communal seeding and harvesting. Communal coordination optimally serves individual and familial interests, except for those who are completely independent of land and its cultivable potential, which is rare in rural Sri Lanka.

While both groups of migrants show significant deficits among those participating in communal cultivation activities, both groups of natives show highly significant excesses. The proportionate deviations are larger among the voluntary migrants (20.1 percent), followed by natives (18.9 percent), mobile natives (12.6 percent), and migrant colonists (12.0 percent). Thus, migrants are clearly different from natives along these dimensions

143

TABLE 3.9

PERCENT PARTICIPATING IN VOLUNTARY COMMUNITY SERVICES,
PARTICIPATING IN SEEDING AND/OR HARVESTING WITH OTHERS,
BORROWING MONEY FOR CEREMONY, PRESENCE OF POTENTIAL
LENDER, RELATIONSHIP TO POTENTIAL LENDER AT TIME OF
MIGRATION/15 YEARS AGO AND PROPORTIONATE DEVIATION
FROM MARGINAL AMONG MIGRANT TYPES, SRI LANKA, 1978

	Migrant colonist	Voluntary Migrants	Native	Mobile native	Total
% participating in voluntary commu- nity services	75.1 (-8.1)*	73.5 (-9.7)*	95.0 (11.8)**	88.1 (4.9)	83.2
Index of dissimilarity	28.9	34.6	42.2	17.6	33.3
% participating in seeding and/or harvesting on others' land	63.6 (-12.0)**	55.5 (20.1)**	94.4 (18.9)**	88.1 (12.6)**	75.6
Index of dissimilarity	32.4	54.6	51.1	34.0	43.3
% borrowing money for ceremony	12.1 (-1.8)	9.8 (-4.0)	18.0 (4.1)*	13.5 (-0.4)	13.8
Index of dissimilarity	7.4	16.9	17.4	1.6	12.2
Presence of potential lender	74.7 (-8.2)**	81.1 (-1.8)	88.0 (5.2)*	97.7 (14.9)**	82.9
Index of dissimilarity	26.0	2.7	30.1	86.7	22.9
Primary rela- tionship to potential lender	70.1 (-11.2)**	73.3 (-8.0)*	93.8 (12.4)**	87.8 (6.5)	81.3
Index of dissimilarity	26.6	11.5	66.5	34.7	33.8

* Significant at .05 level; ** significant at .01 level.

144

of communal participation, suggesting that migration is selective of those with lesser integration into village life.

Credit in rural Sri Lanka is as much a way of life as it is in the urban metropolises of the developed world. The basic difference lies in the amount of credit that is given or taken. Credit has an ambiguous status in the lives of the rural people. On the one hand, norms of self-sufficiency, self-reliance, and frugality indicate that one should live within one's means. This reinforces a negative value on those who borrow. However, rural inhabitants are part of a gamut of social obligations which propel them towards borrowing in order to fulfill these obligations. Puberty, matrimony, and death are the most common occasions when the peasant is driven to 'over-perform', which in turn compells him to secure consumption oriented credit.

The responses to the general question of whether or not the interviewee's family borrowed any money in connection with a ceremony are presented in the middle panel of Table 3.9. A casual perusal of the marginal reveals that this dimension does not discriminate the sample to a large degree. Only 13.8 percent admit to borrowing money for a ceremony, and only the natives depict an excess among those who have borrowed money.

The ambivalent moral connotations associated with the admission of obtaining credit may have motivated respondents to deny the fact of borrowing money. While the moral connotations of borrowing are derogatory, the fact of borrowing symbolizes the possibility of a higher level of integration into the community. It signifies that there is a person (or group) to whom one can go and get some money; since money or any other goods and services is not dispensed without the expectation of reciprocation, the act of borrowing symbolizes the continuity of social obligations. In that sense, the natives appear to be the most integrated in the community, followed by the mobile natives.

A hypothetical situation was created and respondents who did not admit to borrowing money were asked: 'In case you (your family) needed some money for unforeseen reasons, does your family have a source to borrow from?' The responses disclose that more than four-fifths of the sample admit to having a potential lender. However, the excesses are among the two native groups (significant among the mobile natives), while there are deficits among both migrant groups (significant among the migrant colonists) within the affirmative category (Table 3.9, lower panel).

We separated the potential lender into two broad categories: the 'predominantly primary' and 'predominantly secondary' associations with the potential lender. Consistent with previous findings, the data show that both native groups depict a consistent excess among the primary associations, while both migrant groups depict a deficit.

The major limiting factor in being able to obtain personalized credit is tied to the level of integration into communal life. Marginal integration means that one would have had to resort to impersonal credit. Thus, the overrepresentation of both groups of migrants who potentially were able to solicit the services of the money lender could be taken as an indicator of minimal integration into communal life. The complementary observation reinforcing this same pattern is found in the underrepresentation of credit relations with close relatives among the migrant groups.

Some have argued that the migration stream to the rural dry zone in part contained those who "were attempting to improve an adverse caste situation" (ESCAP, 1975: 110). If that were the case, we would expect that those belonging to a minority caste, would have a higher propensity to migrate. The results of our analysis do not confirm this hypothesis.

Two questions on the caste situation at the place of origin were posed: one attempted to elicit the percentage of families that belonged to the respondent's caste, and the other inquired whether or not the majority of families belonged to the respondent's caste or to another caste. Both queries reveal the same pattern (Table 3.10, top panels). The two native groups show a deficit of cases among those stating the majority of community households belonged to their own caste (proportionate deficits of 3.5 percent among natives and 16.2 percent among mobile natives) or that more than 50 percent of the households belonged to their caste (7.9 percent deficit among natives and 19.7 percent among mobile natives).

The strength of the results is not derived from the observations on the native groups. The latter were drawn from three locations and had at least two survey sites with multi-caste situations. The migrants, on the other hand, were drawn from a more representative spectrum of rural wet zone villages. Over 60 percent of both migrant groups came from places of origin where they belonged to a caste which contained 75 to 100 percent of the community. The relative excesses of 7.2 percent and 12.4 percent among the migrant colonists and the voluntary migrants, respectively, are highly significant statistically.

Kinship ties are generally known to be highly elastic (Leach, 1960, 1961; Thambiah, 1958). The imposition of a definition of 'close relative' was not attempted in this study because it may have been meaningless to a majority of respondents. While

TABLE 3.10

PERCENT IN CASTE AND LOCATION OF CLOSE RELATIVES
AT THE TIME OF MIGRATION/15 YEARS AGO AND PROPORTIONATE
DEVIATION FROM MARGINAL AMONG MIGRANT TYPES,
SRI LANKA, 1978

	Migrant colonist	Voluntary migrant	Native	Mobile native	Total
Most families were in R's caste	75.6 (3.5)	80.9 (8.7)**	68.7 (-3.5)	56.0 (-16.2)**	72.2
Index of dissimilarity	8.6	21.6	8.7	10.6	14.5
More than 50% were in R's caste	77.9 (8.2)**	83.7 (14.0)**	61.8 (-7.9)**	50.0 (-19.7)**	69.7
Index of dissimilarity	26.9	46.3	16.7	28.3	24.9
% close relatives in village	56.4 (-21.5)**	64.0 (-13.9)**	98.9 (21.0)**	98.3 (20.4)**	77.9
Index of dissimilarity	62.5	40.3	35.9	59.1	57.1
% close relatives outside village	36.8 (-28.9)**	38.8 (-26.8)**	96.1 (30.5)**	98.3 (32.7)**	65.6
Index of dissimilarity	63.9	59.5	67.6	72.5	65.4

* significant at .05 level; ** significant at .01 level.

147

kinship may be defined, 'closeness' is highly susceptible to underlying variability in terms of mutual utility, social status, volume of interaction, residential proximity, and many other such dimensions. Leach (1961), for instance, differentiates between the 'family' and the 'effective family', the latter being the inner core where important problems are discussed and decisions made. Kinship is the legitimate vehicle through which membership in a rural community is galvanized into economic, social, and political action.

The presence of 'close relatives' is regarded as an important proxy for the prevalence of social ties, which, in turn, represents integration into the community. The presence of 'close relatives' is contingent upon the perception of a part or the whole of one's kin group as 'close'. The absence of this perception is regarded as the relative scarcity of social ties and minimal communal integration.

The data relate to the presence of close relatives in and outside of the village of origin. They show (Table 3.10, lower panel) that migrant groups are more likely not to have close relatives either in or outside the village of origin. In sharp contrast, almost all of the native groups have close relatives in and outside the village. Thus, migrants in general were drawn disproportionately from among those who did not think they had close relatives in or outside their village of nativity. If having close relatives is a proxy indicative of a higher level of integration into the community, then the lack of integration into one's social environment appears to facilitate further estrangement consequent of undertaking physical dissociation through migration.

Multi-variate Analysis

A large number of variables have been introduced to investigate the determinants of rural migration to rural areas. We now focus on the broader picture, in particular on how much of the propensity to move can be accounted for and which variables or sets of variables are relatively more important.

Fourteen independent variables were selected on the basis of theoretical considerations and from the insights gained from the empirical analysis. These variables were selected to represent four dimensions which were expected to discriminate between migrants and natives: 1) a land dimension; 2) a non-land-based economic dimension; 3) a socioeconomic status dimension consisting of housing conditions, education, and self-evaluation; and 4) social ties. Each of these variables is at best at an ordinal

148

level, although each was implicitly assumed to have interval level properties when entered into the regression equation.

The land dimension consisted of four variables. Nature of possession of land (POSESLIND) was scored from one through five, in ascending order from no land, owned land but did not cultivate, cultivated encroached land, cultivated owned land, and cultivated owned and unowned land. The acreage cultivated (ACRECULT) was the second land-based variable and was scored from zero to eight ascending from no land to those cultivating more than 5 acres. Location of land (LOCLAND) was scored from one to three; in ascending order, they were those having land only inside the village, those with land outside the village, and those with land both in and outside the village. Succession to land was the last variable (SUCCLAND) and was also scored one through three; in ascending order, they were those who had acquired land by purchase, and those who had obtained land through both inheritance and purchase. The basic expectation was that each of the land related variables would display an inverse relationship with propensity to migrate.

The economic dimension had three variables. Whether or not one sold one's crop was the first variable (CROPSALE), which was dichotomous. Qualitative evaluation of one's income situation (INCMSITU) was the second and was scored from one through three; in ascending order, they were being in debt, having just enough to live, and having enough to live as well as save. The last variable was involvement in non-farm activity (NONFARM), which was also dichotomous. In actuality it was a negative land variable since its effect on migration was expected to be positive, the rationale being that a preponderance in non-farm activity would signify minimal landownership. The other two variables were expected to have an inverse relationship with migration.

The socioeconomic status dimension had three variables. Overall housing conditions (HOUSE) was scored one through four as noted above. The achievement related SES variable was education (EDUCATN), which was scored zero through 16. The subjective indicator of SES was that of self-evaluation of social status (SELFEVAL) scored from low to high in four categories. Each of these was expected to vary inversely with migration.

The dimension of social ties had four variables. Whether or not one participated in the seeding or harvesting on land owned by others (HARVEST) was the first. The second was whether or not one participated in communal voluntary service (VOLUNSER). The third determined if one belonged to a minority caste in the community of nativity (LESSCAST). The last was an additive index created by the answers to two questions on close relatives; i.e., whether or not one had close relatives in the community of nativity as well as outside the community of nativity (CLOSEREL). The dichotomized responses to each question were added together after coding the affirmative answer one and the negative answer zero. Each respondent could have a score of zero through two. All four variables were expected to have an inverse relationship with migration, although there were some doubts about LESSCAST since it revealed a positive association when examined in the bi-variate situation.

The same sets of regression models were run on three samples. The first one contrasted the migrant colonists with the combination of the native groups; the second, the voluntary migrants against the combined natives; and the third combined both migrant groups against both native groups. Within each comparison, a list-wise deletion procedure as well as a pair-wise deletion procedure were adopted. The difference in the multiple R in the two runs within the same sample differed by no more than three percentage points. Therefore, the results of the pair-wise deletion procedure are presented in Table 3.11 as the latter included a much larger proportion of the sample.[3]

All variables pertaining to each of the four dimensions were entered step-wise into the regression equation in the same order as appearing in the table. For each of the four models, the simple r and the beta coefficient when all variables in each dimension were entered are presented, as well as the multiple R contribution of each variable and the number of cases in each of the three comparisons.

The most striking observation consistently found in all three comparisons is the power of the social ties dimension (especially that of CLOSEREL and HARVEST) and the relative weakness of the other three dimensions in explaining the variance in propensity to migrate. Social ties and the land dimensions are the only variable sets which have significant predictive potential in each of the three comparisons. The economic dimension is not significant for the voluntary migrant-native comparison, while the

----

[3] The list-wise deletion procedure included between 57 to 67 percent of the eligible respondents in each comparison; the pair-wise deletion procedure included an average of approximately 90 percent of the cases.

TABLE 3.11

PREDICTABILITY OF PROPENSITY TO MIGRATE BY SELECTED SOCIOECONOMIC VARIABLES
WITHIN THREE COMPARISON GROUPS IN SRI LANKA, 1978

VARIABLE	MIGRANT COLONISTS AND NATIVES				VOLUNTARY MIGRANTS AND NATIVES				ALL MIGRANTS + NATIVES			
	r	beta	R^2	# of cases	r	beta	R^2	# of cases	r	beta	R^2	# of cases
POSESLND	-.04	.06	.002	435	-.10	-.01	.010	359	-.07	.04	.004	538
ACRECULT	-.23	-.23**	.054	432	-.19	-.18**	.027	356	-.22	-.23**	.048	532
LOCLAND	-.07	-.03	.001	365	-.08	.10	.010	309	-.01	.03	.001	445
SUCCLAND	-.12	-.06	.004	343	.07	-.06	.001	292	-.12	-.08	.004	413
(LAND)			.061**				.048**				.057**	
CROPSALE	-.07	-.09	.001	359	-.03	-.04	.001	297	-.06	-.07	.004	429
INCMSITU	-.01	-.01	.000	398	.05	.04	.003	333	.01	.01	.000	494
NONFARM	.17	.18**	.033	377	.15	.15**	.022	328	.16	.16**	.027	468
(ECONOMIC)			.034**				.026				.031**	
HOUSE	-.05	-.05	.002	401	.07	.09	.001	340	.00	.01	.000	502
EDUCATN	-.16	-.18**	.023	430	.08	.11	.000	356	-.07	-.08	.005	533
SELFEVAL	.03	.10	.008	416	-.04	-.12	.010	340	.00	.02	.001	518
(S.E.S.)			.033*				.011				.006	
HARVEST	-.36	-.14**	.133	415	-.44	-.24**	.196	340	-.37	-.17**	.014	516
VOLUNSER	-.26	-.06	.011	416	-.28	-.03	.010	341	-.26	-.06	.007	518
LESSCAST	.16	.07	.012	361	.22	.07	.017	311	.20	.10*	.018	448
CLOSEREL	-.71	-.65**	.382	398	-.68	-.59**	.314	337	-.66	-.59**	.321	496
(SOCIAL TIES)			.538**				.528**				.586**	

* Significant at .05 level; ** significant at .01 level.

151

SES dimension is significant only for the migrant colonist-native comparison. Only four variables have significant betas in all three comparisons. They are ACRECULT, NONFARM, HARVEST, and CLOSEREL, all of which are either land- or social ties-based.

The summary results of a slight variation in the same regression model are presented in Table 3.12. All four dimensions are entered into the equation in a step-wise manner in the same order they appear in the table. However, all variables associated with each dimension are entered into the equation at the same time. All R^2s for each of these comparisons are significant at the .01 level. The total variance explained ranges between 52.8 percent and 60.3 percent; the social ties dimension dominates the other three dimensions in its predictive potential of migration behavior. The other three dimensions which were entered into the equation before social ties jointly explained between 10.1 percent to 14.5 percent of the variance in the propensity to move.

The most unexpected result that emerges from these regression analyses is the unimpressive predictive power of the land dimension. Within a socioeconomic context where land is scarce in the community of origin and available in the place of destination, it is reasonable to expect the land-based variables to explain more of the variance in the propensity to migrate. However, while the scarcity of land is the fundamental situation at the time of migration, the level of integration into communal life is of overwhelming importance in determining migration. The level of integration of the respondent and his family is related to patron-client relationships which provide the substantive base for stable and continuing social ties and link the family units of a village into a communal network. None of the land-based variables managed to identify the relative presence of these all-important patron-client relationships. The most pertinent in this context would be the HARVEST variable which explained 13.3 percent to 19.6 percent of the variance in migration. This variable, as was mentioned earlier, captured the crucial juncture in rural social life where infra-structural necessity is translated into a social tie which, in turn, reflects the integration of families into communal life.

The other variable that proxied for the level of integration as well as explained over 30 percent of the variance was the perception of close relatives. In traditional society, the kin group provides the social security for individual survival. The 'we' feeling within the kin group brings fellow kinsmen into the mainstream of communal activity by providing them with a livelihood, the mechanisms of which have come to be recognized as

TABLE 3.12

PREDICTABILITY OF PROPENSITY TO MIGRATE BY FOUR SELECTED
SOCIOECONOMIC DIMENSIONS WITHIN THREE COMPARISON GROUPS,
SRI LANKA, 1978

	Comparison Groups					
	Migrant Colonists + Natives		Voluntary Migrants + Natives		All Migrants + Natives	
Socioeconomic Dimension	R	R^2	R	R^2	R	R^2
Land	.245	.060**	.217	.047*	.240	.057**
Land + Economic	.326	.106**	.288	.083**	.307	.095**
Land + Economic + S.E.S	.380	.145**	.317	.101**	.324	.105**
Land + Economic + S.E.S + Social Ties	.776	.603**	.749	.560**	.727	.528**

* Significant at .05 level; ** significant at .01 level.

153

'involution' (Geertz, 1963).

The basic point which emerges from the foregoing analysis is that the scarcity of land was a fundamental fact of life in the rural area but it did not effectively discriminate between those who migrated to the dry zone and those who remained in the wet zone. If marginal landownership or landlessness was the major criterion for selection (as was partly the case in terms of the government policy), then there was a potential oversupply of migrants at the origin. There was also a concomitant undersupply of land in the dry zone as well as some availability of residential plots of land within the wet zone village itself. The more important infrastructural necessity of the wet zone village was the retention of a surplus of labor in the community in the interest of communal survival. The power structure of the village saw to it that government policy was not allowed to undermine the integrity of the village. The joint effects of these cross pressures likely coincided in differently selecting the least integrated families of the community for migration to the dry zone. Non-control of a viable unit of land thus became a 'push' factor precipitating migration only if the respondent and his family were less integrated into communal activities and lacked supportive social ties.

In attempting to identify the determinants of rural dry zone-ward migration in Sri Lanka, we have compared the characteristics at the time of migration of migrants and natives on a host of variables which have not been regularly included in previous research on internal migration. The more orthodox indicators like socioeconomic status were found to be quite unimportant in explaining the propensity to migrate. Instead, landownership and control, patron-client relationships, level of integration into communal life, and manipulations of the local power structure were of key significance.

Social ties have been a fairly commonly pursued theme in migration literature. As observed by Ritchey (1976:389-390), the literature could be broadly organized under three interrelated hypotheses: 1) the 'affinity hypothesis' states that the more kinship ties, the less is the propensity to migrate; 2) the 'information hypothesis' proposes that the location of relatives in distant places increases the awareness of the opportunity structure of unknown places and so stimulates migration; and 3) the 'facilitating hypothesis' expects the destination of migration will be most selective of places where one's relatives are in residence since they would facilitate the adaptation of the new migrant.

The vast literature which inquires into the general

154

association between social ties and migration (see, for example, Bieder, 1973; Choldin, 1973; Duncan and Reiss, 1956; Lansing and Mueller, 1967; Speare et al., 1976; Uhlenberg, 1973) primarily focuses on the link between the individual and the family. These studies have investigated primarily urbanward migration processes, where the inhabitants concerned are at least a part of a semi-urban complex. The present study differs in that the migration process under scrutiny is directed towards the rural hinterland and originates in comparatively undifferentiated communities (Smelser, 1968). Goldscheider (1971:93-94) provides an outline of such communities which closely parallels the rural wet zone village of two decades ago and still is intact to some extent.

To illustrate these major processes we may note the dominance of kinship groupings in premodern societies. Prior to modernization, economic production, exchange, and consumption occur largely within family and kinship groupings and are located typically in local community settings. Subsistence farming and supplementary small scale industry are attached to local villages and are controlled by extended family units. Economic activities are, therefore, relatively undifferentiated from kinship groupings. Furthermore, occupational position is established by extended kin, perhaps caste, as is status and rank. Ascription, inherited privilege, political, and religious positions are intertwined with kinship position and confined spatially to the local village or community. Moreover, the educational-socialization function takes place under the aegis of the kinship group either directly through the family or indirectly through kinship-dominated religious institutions. The dominance and multifunctionality of kinship units result in the expression of loyalty and identification through kin and the investment of political and social control within the localized kin group, clan, or tribe. In short, rewards and sanctions, survival and growth, social structure and process are dependent on, controlled by, and located in local kinship groups.

In his study on cost benefits of migration in Taiwan, Speare (1971:130) observed:

A great many of the non-migrants we interviewed

155

appeared to have never given any serious consideration to the thought of moving anywhere. If this is true, then a model based on the decision-making process cannot be applied to all people. This suggests that the next step in trying to build a comprehensive understanding of the process of individual migration may be to investigate factors which may influence whether or not a person considers moving.

It is, however, not the 'model based on the decision-making process' that has to be abandoned because most voluntarily made changes are arrived at through a decision-making process. What needs to be modified are the basic propositions that are considered vital by the researchers in recapitulating decision-making processes. The decision to migrate is arrived at (including the initial consideration of migration itself) through the interaction of three levels of the social order, i.e., the community, the family, and the individual. It is not necessarily explained satisfactorily by the last two alone where the bulk of research has focused.

The relative weight on the outcome of the interaction of these three levels may change with the level of differentiation of the community of origin. The lower the level of differentiation of the community, the greater will be the influence of the family-community interaction, with the individual's power minimal. In this context, the higher the level of integration of the family into communal life, the less will be the propensity for migration of the family or its individual members. As differentiation takes root, the community no longer depends for its survival upon the joint and coordinated contributions of familial units. It increasingly requires specific and specialized services to be performed; as long as they are fulfilled, its continuity is not threatened. The basic necessities of communities are fulfilled by the variety of skills internalized by individuals. At this level of differentiation, each community can be considered a microcosm of the society at large, demanding specific services which are performed by individuals mostly for monetary remuneration and with minimal social obligations of a lasting kind. The attraction or repulsion of individuals from a particular community thus becomes mostly dependent upon supply and demand for necessary services. Then, the social ties between family and individual become critical for migration. That is the situation where the underlying dynamics of the three hypotheses outlined by Ritchey (i.e., 'affinity', 'information', and 'facilitating') come into operation. Individual preferences to be with the family or to be away from it are given

156

greater weight in the decision-making processes. With further advances in differentiation, and changes in the centrality of the family as in many more developed societies (Ross and Sawhill, 1975; Weir and Wilson, 1973), the interaction along the social ties dimension will increasingly be reduced to the linkage between the community and the individual: the impersonal community demanding specialized services and the individuals who have the speciality stepping in to fulfill them.

In the rural communities where differentiation is at a minimum, the functional equivalent of 'unemployment' in more differentiated societies becomes the lack of integration into communal life. This absence of integration undermines the very source of livelihood since at the subsistence level, all members of the community need to cooperate for joint survival.

The unifying theme emerging from the analysis is that the less differentiated the society, the more will be the weight of family-community linkage in individual life changes (migration is a particular example); a 'medium' level of differentiation will shift the more determinant effect on life changes into the realm of family-individual linkage; while in the very differentiated society, life changes will be determined more by individual preference in interaction with the supply and demand structures of communities for essential services. The rural wet zone village in Sri Lanka is closest to the lower end of the continuum where minimal differentiation is the hallmark. Hence, the analyses have emphasized the family-community linkage. The general conclusion supported by the bi-variate and multivariate analyses is that the lower the level of integration into communal activity, the higher the propensity to migrate.

Consequences of Rural to Rural Migration

The analysis of the consequences of migration to the rural dry zone focuses on one major question: what socioeconomic and demographic changes occurred among those who migrated to the dry zone? To assess these changes, we compare migrant colonists and voluntary migrants with natives in the place of destination, i.e., the dry zone. To take into account changes in the place of origin, we also include the natives of the wet zone for comparisons. The analysis focuses on the current characteristics of five groups: in the dry zone--migrant colonists, voluntary migrants, and natives; in the wet zone--natives and mobile natives. We compare current with past characteristics at the aggregate and individual levels. Many of the variables used in the analysis of the determinants of out-migration are included here. We shall refer to previous tabular materials for aggregate comparisons of the current situation relative to the time of migration.

Our first set of questions revolve around the educational and occupational changes brought about by migration to the rural dry zone. Before examining these issues at the aggregate and individual levels, we look at age compositional variation among the migrant groups.

Age, Education, and Occupation

We have shown earlier that migration to the dry zone was selective of those in the younger ages. An examination of the current age of the five groups in the wet and dry zones reveals that the migrant colonists are underrepresented among the young: fully 74 percent of those 20 years of age and older were over age 45. In contrast, 61 percent of the voluntary migrants were age 20-44 (Table 3.13). This reflects the abating of the government colonization program in the survey sites and the continued voluntary movement of familied males to the dry zone. For the voluntary migrants to the dry zone, the pull of non-farm based employment opportunities plus push factors in the wet zone operate.

Another observation relates to the preponderance of young male heads of households in the dry zone compared to both groups of natives in the wet zone. Dry zone natives are concentrated in the 20-29 age group, while the wet zone natives and mobile natives reveal moderate deficits in the same age categories. This suggests that young males in the dry zone are getting married at an early age and that they have the resources to be heads of households. They have a higher probability of achieving economic viability at an earlier age, and they are more likely to break away from their parental families and establish a neo-local residence. Economic viability in the dry zone is primarily reducible to the availability of land, which, unlike in the wet zone, is relatively available. With the concentration of government investment in peasant agriculture, the productive potential of land appreciated due to increased irrigation. Furthermore, the policy of the government to fill its quota of land allottees from within the local area over those in the wet zone favors the young male native of the dry zone who has an agricultural background.

Another factor favoring dry zone natives over those in the wet zone relates to the generally lower educational levels of dry zone natives. Educational attainment of the population of Sri

TABLE 3.13
PERCENTAGE DISTRIBUTION OF CURRENT AGE AND PROPORTIONATE
DEVIATION FROM MARGINAL AMONG MIGRANT TYPES, SRI LANKA, 1978

Age Group	Migrant colonist	Voluntary migrant	Wet Zone native	Mobile native	Dry Zone native	Total
20-24	–	4.0	1.0	1.6	4.3	1.8
	(-1.8)*	(2.2)	(-0.7)	(-0.1)	(2.5)*	
25-29	3.5	9.0	6.7	3.2	20.2	7.9
	(-4.4)*	(1.1)	(-1.2)	(-4.6)	(12.4)**	
30-34	5.2	11.0	9.7	24.6	17.0	11.2
	(-6.0)**	(-0.2)	(-1.5)	(13.4)**	(5.8)	
35-39	4.6	16.0	12.3	16.4	12.8	11.2
	(-6.6)**	(4.8)	(1.1)	(5.2)	(1.5)	
40-44	12.7	21.0	7.7	4.9	6.4	10.8
	(2.0)	(10.3)**	(-3.1)	(-5.8)	(-4.4)	
45-49	21.4	15.0	15.4	13.1	5.3	15.3
	(6.1)**	(-0.3)	(0.1)	(-2.1)	(-9.9)**	
50-54	20.2	5.0	13.3	8.2	10.6	13.0
	(7.2)**	(-8.0)**	(0.3)	(-4.8)	(-2.4)	
55-59	11.0	6.0	13.3	13.1	3.2	10.0
	(1.0)	(-4.0)	(3.4)	(3.2)	(-6.8)*	
60-64	7.5	6.0	7.2	3.3	5.3	6.4
	(1.1)	(-0.4)	(0.8)	(-3.1)	(-1.1)	
65-69	3.5	4.0	6.2	4.9	9.6	5.5
	(-2.0)	(-1.5)	(0.7)	(-0.5)	(4.1)	
70+	10.4	3.0	7.2	6.6	5.3	7.1
	(3.3)*	(-4.1)	(0.1)	(-0.5)	(-1.7)	
Total	100.0	100.0	100.0	100.0	100.0	100.0
	(173)	(100)	(195)	(61)	(94)	(623)
Index of dissimilarity	28.8	21.9	9.5	24.0	30.9	22.0
Mean Age	51.1	43.4	48.4	44.4	42.7	47.2

* significant at .05 level; ** significant at .01 level.

159

Lanka has been one characteristic that has changed greatly over the past three decades, reflecting largely the advent of free education in the mid-1940s. We dichotomized the sample at age 40 to capture these changes (Table 3.14).

Older males are consistently less educated than their younger counterparts. This is shown in the ratios computed which show the number of persons with nine years or less of schooling in relation to persons with 10 years or more. The wet zone natives are the best educated and the dry zone natives the least educated. The better educational achievement of wet zone natives is not due to an overrepresentation of younger cohorts. In fact, the youngest persons are found mostly among the dry zone natives, who have the lowest level of education. Moreover, the higher indices of dissimilarities among the young suggest that disparities in educational attainment among migrant types have widened over time, especially after the advent of free education. While only 10.9 percent of the older males have to be reallocated, 16.0 percent of the younger males have to be redistributed to achieve comparability across migrant types. To further address the question of growing educational divergences, the groups were subdivided into three age categories. Average educational levels differentiated among the groups of the youngest ages (below age 30) and showed the strongest association (eta = .29). However, for those of the two oldest age categories (ages 30-44 and 45+), no significant educational differences emerged among the five migrant groups.

Comparisons of the distributions of the current occupational status of the four groups (migrant colonists, voluntary migrants, wet zone natives, and mobile natives) with that at the time of migration (or 15 years ago) presented in Tables 3.15 and 3.4 suggest that few changes have taken place. This was not surprising since the major attraction of the dry zone was land availability and more than three-fourths of the occupations are in farming. Indeed, fully 95 percent of the dry zone natives are engaged in agriculture.

It appears, however, that the largest decrement in the aggregate land-bound population occurred among migrant colonists: at the time of migration, 77.8 percent were farmers which dropped to 62.3 percent by 1978. The decline in the farmer population is found among the other three migrant groups as well. Among the two migrant groups, the exodus from farmer occupations appears to be in the direction of blue collar jobs. The increase in the latter is 8.3 and 7.8 percentage points among the migrant colonists and voluntary migrants, respectively. Other

160

TABLE 3.14

PERCENTAGE DISTRIBUTION OF EDUCATIONAL ATTAINMENT OF RESPONDENT
AND PROPORTIONATE DEVIATION FROM MARGINAL AMONG
MIGRANT TYPES, SRI LANKA, 1978

Educational Attainment	Migrant colonist	Voluntary migrant	Wet Zone native	Mobile native	Dry Zone native	Total
YOUNG (BELOW AGE 40)						
No schooling	– (-1.1)	– (-1.1)	3.6 (2.5)*	– (-1.1)	– (-1.1)	1.1
1-5 years	43.5 (2.7)	26.3 (-14.4)**	44.6 (3.9)	37.0 (-3.7)	48.9 (8.2)	40.7
6-9 years	39.1 (1.6)	55.3 (17.7)*	21.4 (-16.1)**	40.7 (3.2)	40.0 (2.4)	37.6
10+ years	17.5 (-3.1)	18.4 (-2.2)	30.4 (9.8)*	22.2 (1.6)	11.1 (-9.5)	20.6
Total	100.0 (23)	100.0 (38)	100.0 (56)	100.0 (27)	100.0 (45)	100.0 (189)
9 yrs or less/10+ yrs education	4.8	4.4	2.3	3.5	8.0	3.8
Index of dissimilarity	4.9	22.2	23.7	7.4	13.9	16.0
OLD (AGE 40 AND OVER)						
No schooling	– (-1.9)	1.8 (-0.1)	3.2 (1.3)	6.9 (5.0)*	– (-1.9)	1.9
1-5 years	69.5 (9.5)**	50.0 (-10.0)	55.9 (-4.0)	48.3 (-11.7)	64.7 (4.8)	60.0
6-9 years	29.0 (-4.7)	41.1 (7.4)	33.1 (-0.6)	41.4 (7.7)	35.3 (1.6)	33.7
10+ years	1.5 (-3.0)	7.1 (2.6)	7.9 (3.4)	3.5 (-1.0)	0.0 (-4.5)	4.5
Total	100.0 (131)	100.0 (56)	100.0 (127)	100.0 (29)	100.0 (34)	100.0 (377)
9 yrs or less/10+ yrs education	64.5	13.0	11.7	28.0	–	21.2
Index of dissimilarity	14.6	12.1	7.0	13.8	7.0	10.9

* Significant at .05 level; ** significant at .01 level.

161

TABLE 3.15

PERCENTAGE DISTRIBUTION OF CURRENT OCCUPATIONAL STATUS OF
RESPONDENT AND INDIVIDUAL CHANGES BETWEEN FARMER/LABORER
AND NON-FARMER/NON-LABORER OCCUPATIONS AND PROPORTIONATE
DEVIATION FROM MARGINAL AMONG MIGRANT TYPES, SRI LANKA, 1978

Occupational Status	Migrant colonist	Voluntary migrant	Wet Zone native	Mobile native	Dry Zone native	Total
Farmer	62.3	49.5	50.8	47.5	95.2	59.6
	(2.7)	(-10.0)*	(-8.8)**	(-12.0)*	(35.7)**	
Laborer	3.4	8.7	21.0	29.5	–	12.0
	(-8.6)**	(-3.2)	(9.1)**	(17.5)**	(-12.0)**	
Skilled worker in agriculture	1.1	1.0	6.7	3.3	–	2.9
	(1.8)	(-1.9)	(3.8)**	(0.4)	(-2.9)	
Blue collar worker	14.9	15.5	4.6	8.2	2.4	9.4
	(5.5)**	(6.2)*	(-4.8)**	(-1.2)	(-7.0)*	
Trade and retail related	6.3	12.6	5.1	3.3	1.2	6.0
	(0.3)	(6.6)**	(-0.9)	(-2.7)	(-4.8)*	
Skilled craftsman	6.9	5.8	4.6	1.6	–	4.5
	(2.3)	(1.3)	(0.1)	(-2.9)	(-4.5)*	
White collar worker	4.0	4.9	7.2	6.6	1.2	5.0
	(-1.0)	(-0.2)	(2.2)	(1.5)	(-3.8)	
Armed services	1.1	1.9	–	–	–	0.7
	(0.5)	(1.3)	(-0.7)	(-0.7)	(-0.7)	
All occupations	100.0	100.0	100.0	100.0	100.0	100.0
	(175)	(103)	(195)	(61)	(84)	(618)
Index of dissimilarity	15.8	18.4	22.0	21.6	41.3	22.6
FROM FARMER/LABORER TO NON-FARMER/NON-LABORER						
Changed	20.5	16.4	7.3	8.1	0.0	12.3
	(8.2)**	(4.1)	(-5.0)	(-4.2)	(-12.3)**	
N	127	61	110	37	47	382
Index of dissimilarity	33.1	6.3	40.9	34.1	100.0	31.2
FROM NON-FARMER/NON-LABORER TO FARMER/LABORER						
Changed	10.5	9.7	13.3	–	–	13.0
	(-2.5)	(-3.3)	(0.3)	(-)	(-)	
N	38	31	30	6	3	108
Index of dissimilarity	18.8	25.3	1.1	–	–	16.0

* Significant at .05 level; ** significant at .01 level.

162

occupational shifts occurred as well. There was a relative increase in white collar occupations among wet zone natives and mobile natives, while voluntary migrants increased their proportions in occupations associated with trade. The relative distribution of the dry zone natives' current occupation is unique in that they have an excess in only one occupational category, viz., farmers.

The foregoing changes have been observed at the aggregate level. Two basic individual level changes are important: 1) the relative change from farm and/or laborer occupations to any other and 2) the change from non-farm and/or non-laborer occupations to either farm and/or laborer statuses. In the lower panel of Table 3.15, only the two migrant groups have an excess among those who changed from farmer to non-farmer jobs. The three groups of natives have a deficit among those who changed away from farming. The excess among the migrant colonists and the deficit among the dry zone natives are significant statistically. Consistent with these data are the very small shifts in the other direction, from non-farmer/laborer occupations to farmer/laborer occupations. A greater influx into farm occupations characterized only the native groups. Insofar as changes away from farming occupations constitute 'upward' social mobility and changes toward farming occupations constitute 'downward' social mobility, both groups of migrants emerge as having achieved 'upward' mobility and resisted 'downward' mobility. Nevertheless, the dominant characteristic of all five groups is stability over time in farm occupations.

Any change in residential location is likely to generate some change in occupational status in comparison with spatial stability. Therefore, it was expected that greater changes in occupational status would characterize migrants. The more interesting observation is that despite the attraction of acquiring land in the dry zone, there has been a relative decline in the agricultural occupations among migrants there. Moreover, there has been hardly any movement from non-agricultural to agricultural occupations since migration.

An analysis of the changing industrial classification of migrant groups adds depth to this conclusion. When the industrial classification is collapsed into three sectors (primary, secondary, and tertiary), the general direction of aggregate change over time is different for migrants and natives. While both groups of wet zone natives have gained in the primary sector, the migrant groups have moved away from that sector. The data in Table 3.16 reveal that the significant excesses and deficits are found among the voluntary migrants, the wet zone natives, and the dry

TABLE 3.16

PERCENTAGE DISTRIBUTION OF CURRENT INDUSTRY (BY SECTOR) AND
INTER-SECTOR MOBILITY AND PROPORTIONATE DEVIATION FROM MARGINAL
AMONG MIGRANT TYPES, SRI LANKA, 1978

	Migrant colonist	Voluntary migrant	Wet Zone native	Mobile native	Dry Zone native	Total
Primary sector	84.1 (-2.7)	70.9 (-15.9)**	90.8 (4.0)*	93.4 (6.7)	97.6 (10.9)**	86.8
Secondary sector	3.4 (0.7)	4.9 (2.1)	2.6 (-0.2)	1.6 (-1.1)	– (-2.8)	2.8
Tertiary sector	12.5 (2.0)	24.3 (13.8)**	6.7 (-3.8)*	4.9 (-5.6)	2.4 (-8.1)**	10.5
Total	100.0 (176)	100.0 (103)	100.0 (195)	100.0 (61)	100.0 (84)	100.0 (619)
Index of dissimilarity	8.0	23.9	30.3	50.5	82.0	28.9
			INTER-SECTOR MOBILITY			
Remain in primary	91.4 (-2.1)	86.4 (-7.1)*	96.7 (3.3)	94.7 (1.3)	100.0 (6.6)	93.4
From primary to secondary sector	– (-1.0)	3.0 (2.1)	0.8 (-0.2)	2.6 (1.7)	– (-1.0)	1.0
From primary to tertiary sector	8.6 (3.0)	10.6 (5.0)	2.5 (-3.1)	2.6 (-3.0)	– (-5.6)	5.6
Total	100.0 (139)	100.0 (66)	100.0 (121)	100.0 (38)	100.0 (46)	100.0 (410)
Index of dissimilarity	24.4	20.5	49.8	27.4	100.0	33.4

* Significant at .05 level; ** significant at .01 level.

164

zone natives. While the two native groups show excesses in the primary and deficits in the tertiary, the voluntary migrants have a deficit in the primary and an excess in the tertiary. Within the secondary sector, all three groups of natives have deficits, while the two migrant groups show an excess.

Thus, it appears that migrants have, at the aggregate level, managed to change away from the primary sector more than the natives at either location. Among both the migrant colonists and voluntary migrants, the pattern of inter-sectoral distribution was similar. When contrasted with the entire sample, both migrant groups were less concentrated within the primary sector and more in the tertiary sector. The pattern is stronger among voluntary migrants who continue to move into petty trade and service jobs.

The sectoral changes that took place at the individual level are presented in the lower panel of Table 3.16. The aggregate pattern is repeated at the individual level. While migrants are less likely to have remained in the primary sector over time, the three groups of natives have an excess in this category. The deficit among the voluntary migrants is the only deviation from the row marginal that is significant. Migrant colonists who moved out of the primary sector have been concentrated in the tertiary, while voluntary migrants have moved into both the secondary and the tertiary sectors.

Data not presented in tabular form show that very few moved from the secondary and tertiary sectors into primary sector employment. Migrants (colonists and voluntary) are significantly underrepresented among the small proportion moving to the primary sector.

Land Changes

Land was a critical factor which precipitated out-migration from the wet zone as well as attracted migrants to the dry zone. Although we argued that selection for migration to the dry zone was primarily on the basis of integration in the community of origin rather than on ownership and control of land, from the perspective of government policy, land still assumes a central position. Here we raise the question of whether or not migration to the dry zone resulted in greater benefits to those who migrated and the impact of limited out-migration on landownership and control in the wet zone village.

A comparison of the current possession of land with the pre-migration pattern reveals that far-reaching changes have taken place over time (Tables 3.17 and 3.5). The most outstanding

TABLE 3.17

PERCENTAGE DISTRIBUTION BY CURRENT POSSESSION OF LAND AND CHANGES
IN LAND POSSESSION, PROPORTIONATE DEVIATION FROM MARGINAL AMONG
MIGRANT TYPES, SRI LANKA, 1978

Possession of land	Migrant colonist	Voluntary migrant	Wet Zone native	Mobile native	Dry Zone native	Total
No land	1.1 (-0.5)	2.9 (1.3)	1.6 (-0.0)	3.4 (1.8)	– (-1.6)	1.6
Owned but uncultivated	– (-0.6)	– (-0.6)	1.0 (0.4)	– (-0.6)	2.1 (1.5)*	0.6
Cultivating encroached land	3.4 (-14.74)**	63.1 (45.0)**	6.7 (-11.4)**	5.1 (-13.0)**	28.4 (10.3)**	18.1
Cultivating owned land	93.9 (19.6)**	30.1 (-44.2)**	80.9 (6.6)*	83.1 (8.8)	66.3 (-8.0)	74.3
Cultivating owned and unowned land	0.6 (-2.6)*	1.9 (-1.2)	6.7 (3.5)**	5.1 (1.9)	1.1 (-2.1)	3.2
"Other" arrangements	1.1 (-1.1)	1.9 (-0.3)	3.1 (0.9)	3.4 (1.2)	2.1 (-0.1)	2.2
Total	100.0 (179)	100.0 (103)	100.0 (194)	100.0 (59)	100.0 (95)	100.0 (630)
Index of dissimilarity	27.3	55.4	16.5	15.1	13.9	25.7

CHANGES IN LAND POSSESSION

Deteriorated	7.1 (-12.7)**	46.3 (26.5)	17.4 (-2.4)	9.1 (-10.7)*	27.6 (7.8)	19.8
Stable	60.7 (1.0)	22.1 (-37.6)**	72.7 (13.0)**	74.6 (14.8)*	64.5 (4.8)	59.7
Improved	32.1 (11.7)**	31.6 (11.1)**	9.9 (-10.6)**	16.4 (-4.1)	7.9 (-12.6)**	20.5
Total	100.0 (168)	100.0 (95)	100.0 (172)	100.0 (55)	100.0 (76)	100.0 (566)
Index of dissimilarity	23.3	34.3	32.2	36.8	17.9	30.5

*Significant at .05 level; ** significant at .01 level.

changes are the marked decline among the landless from 11.2 percent to 1.6 percent, and the large increase in the proportions holding encroached land from 3.9 percent to 18.1 percent. Those who had land which was not cultivated declined from 5.7 percent to 0.6 percent, indicating that there is currently greater utilization of privately owned land. The marginal plots of land which were not being cultivated before migration have now been brought under the plough; this indicates a functional realization of land consolidation (ESCAP, 1975:87). The proportion that own and cultivate their own land has increased from 67.2 percent to 74.3 percent, while there has been a decline among those who cultivated both owned and unowned land from 7.5 percent to 3.2 percent.

Comparison of the patterns of land possession among the five migrant types reveals important differences. Fully 94 percent of the migrant colonists cultivate owned land, while 63 percent of the voluntary migrants cultivate encroached land. Dry zone natives and voluntary migrants are significantly underrepresented among cultivators of owned land, while the wet zone natives, continue to be overrepresented among those who cultivate owned and unowned land.

The changes that have occurred at the aggregate level are quite marked. The proportions landless among the two groups of migrants have declined from 18.0 percent and 21.4 percent to 1.1 percent and 2.9 percent among the migrant colonists and voluntary migrants, respectively; among the two wet zone natives it has remained almost the same. Very few own but do not cultivate the land they own. The proportion cultivating encroached land among the migrant colonists and mobile natives has declined, quite substantially among the latter. This probably reflects the general improvement in the landownership position among them with increasing duration of residence. The increase among the voluntary migrants from 2.0 percent to 63.1 percent follows from the observation that they migrated without the promise of land from the government. The substantial increase in the cultivators of encroached land among the wet zone natives from 2.2 percent to 6.7 percent signifies the growing population pressure on land in the wet zone village and also the reluctance of many villagers to leave their place of nativity if there is any land available in the vicinity.

Apart from the voluntary migrants, whose position deteriorated from 60.2 percent to 30.1 percent among those who cultivated the land they owned, the other three migrant types (except the dry zone natives) improved their position over time.

While the improvement among the two native groups of the wet zone was moderate (since they already possessed a higher proportion in this category), the improvement of the migrant colonists was extremely high, from 62.8 to 93.8 percent. The government land they received is considered their own, since, apart from the restrictions on outright sale and protected tenureship, the land is functionally the property of the peasant who receives the grant. All other groups, except the mobile natives, have declined among those who cultivated both owned and unowned land; the mobile natives have managed to remain unchanged over time. The decline of the wet zone natives from 21.7 percent to 9.8 percent (among the combined categories of those who cultivated owned and unowned land and those who combined two or more arrangements) reflects the general depreciation of the patron core in the wet zone village. If any land consolidation took place, it was barely sufficient to offset the devastating joint impact of multi-geniture inheritance and growing population pressure. The surplus land once bequeathed to the male issue would have left the long-standing patron-client relationships in disarray. The former patrons would have most likely swelled the ranks of those who cultivated their own land, while those who were displaced from being a client would have invariably encroached on available Crown land, or migrated out of the village (the latter, of course, would not be included in the sample).

While these changes occurred at the aggregate level, what of the changes that took place at the individual level? Land possession categories were ordered hierarchically into those whose position improved, remained unchanged, or deteriorated. The row marginals reveal that the majority of the sample maintained their positions in terms of land possession (59.7 percent), while the remainder almost split equally into relative improvement and deterioration (Table 3.17, lower panel).

The natives of both the wet and dry zones are the most stable over time; voluntary migrants are the least stable. Both voluntary migrants and migrant colonists were more likely to have improved their situation regarding land possession than any of the native groups. Thus, at the individual level, the migrant colonists are an unconditional success story, when the span of time is restricted to the first generation of migrants. The voluntary migrants have also improved themselves substantially. The three native groups have not performed as well as either of the migrant groups in terms of landownership. Most have managed to conserve their positions; the wet and dry zone natives deteriorated

168

more than improved.

Two dominant patterns of succession to land emerge from the results presented in Table 3.18 and they are distinctly location-bound. The two wet zone native groups are concentrated in the traditional methods of succession, viz., either through inheritance, purchase, or a combination of both. Residents of the dry zone have primarily come to control the land either through government alienation (i.e., legal and peaceful disbursement) or by encroachment (acquisition by force).

Given the diversity of the dominant modes of succession, the only legitimate comparison to be made is with respect to the change in the aggregate level of succession to land among the two groups of wet zone natives. The wet zone natives have generally managed to restrict almost 90 percent of their land acquisitions to the two traditional forms at both points in time. Although there is a reduction in the proportion inheriting land from 74.1 percent to 62.7 percent, there is a rise among those who acquired land through joint inheritance and purchase from 11.5 percent to 20.0 percent. Among the mobile natives, inheritance has dwindled markedly from 66.1 percent to 47.4 percent. The gain is concentrated mainly among those who received government land, an increase from 17.9 percent to 33.3 percent.

The relatively large proportion of voluntary migrants (41.0 percent) found in the government land recipient category relative to those in the encroacher category (18.1 percent) is perhaps due to the regularization of encroachments by the Land Commissioner. A very similar proportionate distribution exists within these two categories of land acquisition among the natives of the dry zone. The presence of a positive deviation in land acquisitions made through purchase among voluntary migrants denotes that they had financial resources available to them.

A casual glance at acreage cultivated presented in Table 3.19 reveals that the migrant colonists and the dry zone natives have the largest acreage under cultivation, while the voluntary migrants, wet zone natives, and the mobile natives have comparatively less land. Although the relative ranking has changed somewhat and the migrant colonists rank highest rather than the wet zone natives, as was the case at the time of the 'before' measure, each of the four groups (except the dry zone natives) has improved its mean acreage cultivated over time. While the increase of the two migrant groups is high (from an average of 1.3 to 4.9 acres among the migrant colonists and 1.4 to 2.7 acres among voluntary migrants), gains of the two groups of natives from the wet zone have been very moderate (from 2.2 to

TABLE 3.18

PERCENTAGE DISTRIBUTION BY METHOD OF SUCCESSION TO LAND AND
PROPORTIONATE DEVIATION FROM MARGINAL AMONG MIGRANT TYPES,
SRI LANKA, 1978

Method of succession to land	Migrant colonist	Voluntary migrant	Wet Zone native	Mobile native	Dry Zone native	Total
Inherited	2.3	3.6	62.7	47.4	16.3	28.1
	(−25.8)**	(−24.5)**	(34.6)**	(19.3)**	(−11.8)**	
Bought	1.2	7.2	4.9	8.8	4.7	4.5
	(−3.3)*	(2.8)	(0.4)	(4.3)	(0.2)	
Inherited and bought	−	−	20.0	3.5	2.3	7.0
	(−7.0)**	(−7.0)**	(13.0)**	(−3.5)	(−4.7)	
Encroached	14.4	18.1	1.1	1.8	20.9	10.5
	(4.0)*	(7.6)*	(−9.4)**	(−8.7)*	(10.5)**	
Alienated by government	78.6	41.0	7.6	33.3	40.7	40.8
	(37.9)**	(0.2)	(−33.2)**	(−7.4)	(−0.1)	
"Other"	3.5	30.1	3.8	5.3	15.1	9.3
	(−5.8)**	(20.9)**	(−5.5)**	(−4.0)	(5.9)*	
Total	100.0	100.0	100.0	100.0	100.0	100.0
	(173)	(83)	(185)	(57)	(86)	(584)
Index of dissimilarity	59.5	36.7	70.3	26.2	19.4	48.4

* Significant at .05 level; ** significant at .01 level.

TABLE 3.19

PERCENTAGE CURRENT ACREAGE CULTIVATED AND PROPORTIONATE
DEVIATION FROM MARGINAL AMONG MIGRANT TYPES, SRI LANKA, 1978

Acreage cultivated	Migrant colonist	Voluntary migrant	Wet Zone native	Mobile native	Dry Zone native	Total
No land	1.7 (-1.8)	5.8 (2.3)	4.1 (0.6)	4.9 (1.4)	2.1 (-1.4)	3.5
5 or more acres	38.4 (14.8)**	11.7 (-11.9)**	16.9 (-6.7)**	8.2 (-15.4)**	32.3 (8.7)*	23.6
Number	177	103	195	61	96	632
Index of dissimilarity	42.7	27.8	29.6	31.1	28.2	32.7
Median acreage cultivated	3.9	2.3	1.8	1.2	3.4	2.7
Median acreage cultivated	4.9	2.7	2.8	2.0	4.5	3.6
Mean acreage among lower 50%[1]	2.8	1.3	0.7	0.5	2.0	1.3
Mean acreage among upper 50%[2]	5.6	3.9	4.1	3.1	5.4	4.7
2 / 1	2.0	3.0	5.9	6.2	2.7	3.6
Age Group	MEAN ACREAGE CULTIVATED					
Less than 30 years ** Eta = .32	3.5	1.9	1.9	1.6	3.1	2.5
30 - 44 years ** Eta = .47	5.5	2.9	2.3	2.0	4.0	3.5
45 years or more ** Eta = .22	3.5	3.6	3.9	1.8	2.2	3.4
All ages ** Eta = .36	4.9	2.7	2.8	2.0	4.5	3.6

* Significant at .05 level; ** significant at .01 level.

171

2.8 acres among the wet zone natives and from 1.7 to 2.0 acres among the mobile natives). It becomes evident that through the joint incidence of land alienation under Village Expansion Schemes and the consolidation of land due to out-migration of marginal landowning peasants, the wet zone too had increased in terms of acreage cultivated. While the mobile natives may have benefited more from the Village Expansion Scheme (33.3 percent received government land), it is likely that the wet zone natives benefited from both land consolidation and the Scheme.

Comparing the mean acreage cultivated by the lower 50 percent and top 50 percent of the migrant groups shows that the most equitable distribution of land is found among the migrant colonists (1:2.0), followed closely by the dry zone natives (1:2.7), and the voluntary migrants (1:3.0). Over time the amount of land that was alienated per colonist deteriorated drastically and this, in all probability, should lower the 'true' level of equity that was generated within the program. Farmer (1957) pointed out that the earliest colonists in the mid-1940s had as much as 10 acres, while toward the late 1960s they had as low as 3 acres (Administrative Report of the Land Commissioner, 1975). Thus, if this decline did not take place, the disparity between the top and bottom halves of the distribution would have been nearer parity. From the situation that prevailed at the time of migration (13.7 and 10.3 per unit of land cultivated by the top half among migrant colonists and voluntary migrants, respectively), the current level of distribution is a vast improvement among the two migrant types in addition to the elevation of the mean unit of acreage cultivated.

The equity performance in terms of the acreage cultivated among the two wet zone native groups is not consistent. While the distribution improved (i.e., greater equity) among the wet zone natives, it deteriorated among the mobile natives. The improvement among the former is primarily through Village Expansion Schemes and a moderate improvement in the top half through land consolidation. The relative impact of the same two mechanisms has reversed in the case of the mobile natives. Perhaps the power structure of the community constituted predominantly by the wet zone natives managed to favor their own clients to be differentially recipients of the land alienated through the Village Expansion Scheme. They may have indirectly benefited from the bounty of Crown land, since the added land accruing to the clients may have enhanced their surpluses; in turn, this would have reduced the obligations on the part of the patrons to their clients.

172

Do these patterns of acreage cultivated apply to all age groups? To examine this, we subdivided the sample into the young (less than 30 years old), the middle aged (30-44 years old), and the old (45 years or more). The data in Table 3.19 show that the mean acreage cultivated for each of the three age groups as well as among the entire sample are significantly different among groups at the .01 level. The mean acreage cultivated by the migrant colonists within the three age groups reveals a partial failure of the colonization program. The program at its inception alienated more land per allottee than in its subsequent phases. Assuming that the age of recruitment within the program remained relatively stable over time, there should be a monotonic decline in the acreage cultivated associated with the declining age of the colonist. The pattern that emerges, however, is that of an inverted U-shaped distribution. The highest mean acreage is concentrated among the middle aged (5.5 acres), while both the young and the old cultivate 3.5 acres. In all probability, the older colonists received more than six acres on the average,[4] but since they are old enough to have married children, they have managed to undermine the protected tenure regulation of land alienation by transferring the use of part of their property to their children. The middle-aged colonists, yet to face the realities of fragmentation, have managed to keep the land they received intact. The mean acreage cultivated by the young reflects the general decline in the unit of land that is alienated per colonist. The dry zone natives closely parallel the situation of the migrant colonists since they, too, benefited from the same colonization program.

The voluntary migrants and the two groups of wet zone natives show a different pattern. The wet zone natives have managed to withstand the rigors of fragmentation, since the mean acreage cultivated declines monotonically with age. This reflects a strategy of securing extra-agricultural opportunities by young adults, which probably results in a relatively higher incidence of out-migration from the community of nativity. This is correlated

----

[4] The oldest colony in the sample is Katiyawa, established in 1944. The extent of land alienated per colonist there was 5 acres of lowland and 3 acres of highland. Farmer (1957:264) shows that among the colonies established by 1951, 6 acres per colonist was the minimum.

with educational attainment and supremacy in landownership, which are higher among the wet zone natives when compared to the mobile natives or the two migrant groups. The relatively lower level of education and land-based affluence may have detracted the mobile natives from following the same pattern that characterized the wet zone natives.

The relative changes over time in the extent of acreage cultivated at the individual level are presented in Table 3.20 for the five migrant types. Migrant colonists have improved the most, followed by the voluntary migrants with just under two-thirds upwardly mobile. All three groups of natives are clustered together with the dry zone natives, followed by the wet zone natives and mobile natives; among all three groups, well below half experienced upward mobility.

If the voluntary migrants were likely to be downwardly mobile had they stayed at their place of nativity, then the fact that 62.0 percent of them improved their positions and an additional 17.0 percent maintained their positions while being outside the official colonization program implies the powerful impact of migration. Perhaps it should be considered more remarkable than the improvement of the migrant colonists who were aided by the government program. The fact that the improvement of the dry zone natives has not been as spectacular as those of the two migrant groups suggests that it took more than proximity of residence to achieve what was accomplished by the migrants, especially the voluntary migrants. They, nevertheless, have benefited from the program since they have the second highest average acreage cultivated.

The comparatively moderate improvement among the two native groups of the wet zone indicates how difficult it is to increase acreage cultivated in a land-scarce situation. This becomes more evident when the proportionate deviation from the row marginals is examined within the five categories of cultivation. The mobile natives have deficits in the three upwardly mobile categories (so do the dry zone natives), while the wet zone natives reveal an excess in the least upwardly mobile category and the other two 'hyper' mobile categories show deficits. In contrast, the voluntary migrants have significant excesses among those who moved up by 3-4 categories. The migrant colonists have consistent excesses in all three upwardly mobile categories.

These data indicate that the government policy provided the marginally landowning with adequate land, rather than enhancing the land owned by the "haves". The fact that more than half the

174

TABLE 3.20

PERCENTAGE DISTRIBUTION OF INDIVIDUAL LEVEL CHANGE IN ACREAGE
CULTIVATED AND PROPORTIONATE DEVIATION FROM MARGINAL AMONG
MIGRANT TYPES, SRI LANKA, 1978

Nature of change	Migrant colonist	Voluntary migrant	Wet Zone native	Mobile native	Dry Zone native	Total
Downward	7.5 (-11.7)**	21.0 (1.8)	22.6 (3.4)	31.2 (12.0)*	24.0 (4.8)	19.2
Stable	5.2 (-19.1)**	17.0 (-7.3)	38.0 (13.7)**	34.4 (10.2)	32.3 (8.0)*	24.3
Upward 1-2	22.4 (0.1)	18.0 (-4.4)	27.7 (5.3)*	21.3 (-1.1)	16.7 (-5.7)	22.4
Upward 3-4	24.1 (7.4)**	28.0 (11.2)**	9.7 (-7.0)**	9.8 (-6.9)	10.4 (-6.4)	16.8
Upward 5 or more	40.8 (23.4)**	16.0 (-1.4)	2.1 (-15.4)**	3.3 (-14.1)**	16.7 (-0.8)	17.4
Total	100.0 (174)	100.0 (100)	100.0 (195)	100.0 (61)	100.0 (96)	100.0 (626)
Index of dissimilarity	42.7	15.5	32.5	24.5	15.1	28.3
Percent upwardly mobile	87.3	62.0	39.5	33.4	43.8	56.6

*significant at .05 level; ** significant at .01 level.

175

dry zone natives did not increase their acreage cultivated denotes that merely living in the dry zone did not favor them to possess disproportionate amounts of land under the aegis of the colonization program. The main beneficiaries were the migrant colonists and voluntary migrants. Both had marginal amounts of land before migrating to the dry zone.

The Organization of Agriculture

Has the organization of rural agriculture changed over time? Data in Table 3.21 address this issue with various indicators. Both migrant groups have experienced sharp declines in the proportions utilizing only family labor for cultivation: the migrant colonists from 84.8 percent to 48.9 percent and the voluntary migrants from 84.1 percent to 67.0 percent. This signifies in part changes in the organization of agicultural production due to increases in acreage cultivated. While the wet zone natives have slightly increased their proportion using family labor only (reflecting the effects of incipient fragmentation), the mobile natives reveal a slight decline (indicating the effects of consolidation of land through purchase). This latter trend is further substantiated among the mobile natives by the small increases in the proportion utilizing both family members and kayya members (from 1.8 percent to 3.5 percent) as well as in those using both family members and laborers (from none to 5.2 percent). Thus, while the mobile natives may have acquired more land over time, they still have not mobilized the community for labor on a non-monetary level. The wet zone natives, on the other hand, have declined in the proportion utilizing family members and laborers for cultivation from 4.7 percent to 2.7 percent, another indication of declining acreage cultivated.

The migrant colonists reveal a marked increase in the family and kayya member utilization category from 7.2 percent to 18.5 percent, while the voluntary migrants have declined from 8.7 percent to 6.2 percent. Both migrant groups show increases in utilizing laborers only.

The basic divergence in the organization of production becomes more apparent when the current situation is compared across migrant types. While over four-fifths of the wet zone are dependent upon family labor for cultivation, only one-half of the dry zone utilize family labor exclusively. The next most utilized combination of manpower is family members and laborers among the dry zone residents, particularly among the dry zone natives and the migrant colonists. Combining family members and kayya

176

TABLE 3.21

PERCENTAGE DISTRIBUTION OF CURRENT LABOR UTILIZATION,
OWNERSHIP OF AGRICULTURAL IMPLEMENTS, AND CROP
UTILIZATION AND PROPORTIONATE DEVIATION FROM
MARGINAL AMONG MIGRANT TYPES, SRI LANKA, 1978

Nature of labor used	Migrant colonist	Voluntary migrant	Wet Zone native	Mobile native	Dry Zone native	Total
Family members only	48.9 (-14.0)**	67.0 (4.1)	79.8 (16.9)**	91.4 (28.5)**	35.4 (-27.5)**	62.9
Family members & Kayya members	18.5 (6.0)**	6.2 (-6.4)*	14.2 (1.6)	3.5 (-9.1)*	10.4 (-2.2)	12.6
Family members & laborers	25.8 (6.7)**	19.6 (0.5)	2.7 (-16.4)**	5.2 (-13.9)**	45.8 (26.7)**	19.1
Index of dissimilarity	20.1	8.6	26.8	31.5	35.2	23.8
Ownership of Agricultural Implements						
Own all	8.0 (-17.4)**	15.5 (-9.9)*	48.2 (22.9)**	51.1 (25.8)**	22.2 (-3.1)	25.3
Own some & rent some	56.3 (22.1)**	25.8 (-8.4)	20.9 (-13.3)**	9.3 (-24.8)**	32.2 (-1.9)	34.1
Rent all	31.8 (-4.7)	49.5 (13.0)**	29.5 (-7.0)*	39.5 (3.0)	41.1 (4.6)	36.5
Index of dissimilarity	33.6	25.7	30.8	32.7	7.0	28.2
Current crop utilization for consumption only	22.9 (-12.9)**	44.8 (9.7)*	49.2 (14.1)*	45.6 (10.5)	14.7 (-20.4)**	35.1
Index of dissimilarity	36.8	15.0	21.8	16.2	58.0	30.1
Individual change from consumption to sale	48.5 (20.9)**	33.3 (5.8)	13.8 (-13.8)	25.9 (-1.6)	18.2 (-9.4)*	27.5
Index of dissimilarity	28.9	9.6	19.2	11.8	31.8	23.7

*Significant at .05 level; ** significant at .01 level.

members is found to be in excess among the migrant colonists. Thus, even among migrants, the kayya participation has been transplanted.

The foregoing has established that more dynamic changes characterized the dry zone and greater improvement in socioeconomic conditions occurred in the dry zone than in the wet zone. One set of factors facilitating these changes is technology. We look at the possession of agricultural implements and the use of mechanical sources of energy. Almost three-quarters of the sample rent at least some of their implements. However, the proportionate distribution within the migrant types varies to a great degree as is evidenced by the high indicies of dissimilarity. While both native groups in the wet zone show very significant excesses among those owning all agricultural implements, the dry zone residents depict deficits, particularly among migrants. The type of implements referred to range from mammoties and axes to ploughs, cattle, and tractors.

However, the relative advantage of the wet zone natives reflects the agricultural technology utilized. Not a single member of either group of wet zone natives uses any mechanical sources of energy for cultivation, while 55 to 75 percent of the dry zone residents do. Mechanical sources of energy, in this instance, translate more specifically into the use of either the hand (two-wheeled) tractor or the four-wheeled tractor. A hand tractor is 20-30 times as costly as a pair of bullocks (cattle), the latter being the most expensive agricultural 'implement' used in the wet zone. This is the main reason for the apparent advantageous position of wet zone natives in terms of ownership of agricultural implements.

It appears that migrant status per se has not helped to improve the relationship to the moveable means of production. Among the residents of the dry zone, the natives have the highest proportion of overall ownership of the moveable implements of production, while at the same time the highest proportion of tractor utilization. The migrant colonists occupy the next best situation, with the voluntary migrants holding the last position.

With the secular increase in the mean acreage cultivated across all migrant types and the increasing dominance of the market economy, the expectation is for an increase in the proportion of the rural agricultural households engaged in production for sale. There has indeed been an increase from 42.4 percent to 64.9 percent (cf. Tables 3.21 and 3.7). However, there is marked variation among migrant types. While gains have been recorded among all migrant types (except the dry zone natives), only very moderate increases characterize the natives of the wet zone, while there are marked increases among the migrants.

The current situation in terms of utilization of crops for consumption only reveals that only the migrant colonists and the dry zone natives have deficits while the other three groups, including the voluntary migrants, have excesses. Although consolidation of land has taken place in the wet zone village, it has not been of sufficient proportion to convert into market oriented production. The increasing population pressure has absorbed any increase in absolute output or improvements in productivity. The voluntary migrants, too, were in the possession of land units that were better than those enjoyed by both groups of wet zone natives. Not being directly aided by the irrigation sources and probably cultivating sub-fertile land in comparison to those that were cultivated either by the migrant colonists or the dry zone natives, the voluntary migrants were also capable of producing mostly for consumption. Farming may have been more auxiliary to the voluntary migrants, in light of their non-agricultural occupation concentration in trading and blue collar work.

Changes in the utilization of crops at the individual level (Table 3.21, bottom half) show that out of the entire sample, over one-quarter (27.5 percent) have changed from consumption to production for sale. Only the two migrant groups have an excess in this category and the excess among the migrant colonists is significant statistically. Natives of the wet and dry zone have deficits. However, the deficit of dry zone natives is mainly due to the fact that 70 percent were producing for sale at the time of the 'before' measure, while 63.6 percent are still producing for sale.

The surplus crop is disposed of mainly through secondary sources. The secondary sources constitute the non-relative villagers, the cooperative, and the Mudalali (traders). However, the distribution within these three secondary sources has changed markedly over time. The non-relative villager has dropped from 22.2 percent to 5.9 percent and the Mudalali from 47.9 percent to 34.3 percent. The cooperative has become a main outlet for surplus produce, increasing from 18.6 percent to 52.5 percent.

The cooperative is basically a characteristic of the dry zone, and the dominant position held by the Mudalali as the main purchaser of surplus crop is maintained in the wet zone. The government-backed cooperative was the instrument through which the state actively executed the Guaranteed Price Scheme which bought the surplus paddy of the peasant at approximately 50 percent above the prevalent world market prices and thus forced middle-men to raise their purchasing price of peasant produce. In the wet zone this did not have that much of an impact mainly

179

because there was not enough land to cultivate for sale of produce. The few well-to-do patrons who produced for sale apparently did not wish to change their channels of distribution even though the prices paid by the trader would have undoubtedly increased because of the Guaranteed Price Scheme. The cooperative thus became the crucial juncture where the peasant farmer was drawn into the market system of the world outside his immediate community.

In sum, migrant colonists have gained the most in terms of possession and acreage cultivated. The dry zone natives have benefited from the colonization program as well. Voluntary migrants are a somewhat distant third in sharing the bounty of the government investment; however, in comparison to the situation they faced in their place of nativity, the improvements have been substantial. The native residents of the wet zone, on the other hand, though benefiting to a moderate extent by both land consolidation and annexation of residential plots (and marginal tea. and/or rubber plantation acquired by the government) through Village Expansion Schemes have remained comparatively static.

The increase in the acreage cultivated has facilitated the emergence of surplus production for sale in the dry zone but not in the wet zone. Market oriented production has reorganized the nature of labor utilized for cultivation in the dry zone which appears to favor the recruitment of wage labor over communal self-help teams which continues to be the case in the wet zone. Tractors are being utilized in the cultivation of crops which in turn has encouraged differentiation and division of labor. The surplus produce is increasingly being disposed of through secondary channels and the government sponsored cooperative has become the pivotal institution for monetizing the rural dry zone economy. Within this scale of operation, the attempt to establish stable communities based on the traditional principles of communal self-help has not been too successful. Since the incentive of the dry zone has been the potential for surplus food production and its ready conversion into money, structural and functional differentiation and intermediate mechanization appear to be the bases upon which a relatively stable future of the dry zone's communal organization lies.

Changing Housing Conditions and Income

What have been the changes in the housing conditions of migrants and non-migrants over time? Before the move, 36.9

percent had either 'better' or 'best' housing conditions; at the time of the survey, 49.0 percent were in the same two categories (Tables 3.22 and 3.8). Of the four migrant types (except the dry zone natives), only the voluntary migrants who displayed the 'best' housing conditions at the time of migration have deteriorated from 44.6 percent to 22.3 percent. The migrant colonists have improved from 31.5 percent to 48.3 percent, the wet zone natives from 36.1 percent to 55.4 percent, and the mobile natives from 40.7 percent to 64.4 percent at the aggregate level. The inter-migrant type comparison at the time of the survey reveals that voluntary migrants have the 'worst' housing conditions, with significant excesses in the two lower categories and deficits in the two better categories. The two wet zone native groups show the 'best' housing conditions, with the dry zone natives closely following them.

To facilitate individual level comparisons, the four category hierarchical ordering of overall housing conditions was classified into five categories of relative change. Those whose housing conditions 1) deteriorated by two or more categories, 2) deteriorated by one category, 3) remained unchanged, 4) improved by one category, and 5) improved by two or more categories. These individual level changes in housing conditions for the entire sample are presented in the lower panel of Table 3.22. The migrant colonists are the most susceptible to major improvement (27 percent improved the most). None of the four other migrant types have more than 15 percent in these categories. The deterioration of housing conditions among the voluntary migrants is significant at the individual level with excesses only in the two deteriorated categories. The highest level of stability characterizes the wet zone natives who have a proportionate excess of 13.5 percent in the stable category. The mobile natives have either improved moderately or deteriorated. The dry zone natives have either remained stable, moderately improved, or deteriorated in housing.

As might be expected, a change of locality results in the most drastic change in housing conditions. While the state-aided migrant colonists improved vastly and some moderate improvement among the dry zone natives who participated in the program also took place, the housing of the voluntary migrants, who were left to their own resources, deteriorated markedly. The change among the latter was greatly accentuated because they possessed the best housing conditions prior to migration. Although there is general improvement in the realm of landownership and control among the voluntary migrants, this improvement has not

181

TABLE 3.22

PERCENTAGE DISTRIBUTION OF CURRENT OVERALL HOUSING CONDITIONS,
INDIVIDUAL LEVEL CHANGE AND PROPORTIONATE DEVIATION FROM
MARGINAL AMONG MIGRANT TYPES, SRI LANKA, 1978

Current housing conditions	ALL AGES					
	Migrant colonist	Voluntary migrant	Wet Zone native	Mobile native	Dry Zone native	Total
1 ('Worst')	8.4 (-6.3)**	28.2 (13.4)**	16.9 (2.2)	8.5 (-6.3)	11.5 (-3.3)	14.7
2 ('bad')	43.3 (7.0)*	49.5 (13.2)**	27.7 (-8.6)**	27.1 (-9.2)	32.2 (-4.0)	36.3
3 ('better')	19.1 (-5.6)*	16.5 (-8.2)*	28.7 (4.0)	40.7 (16.0)**	26.0 (1.3)	24.7
4 ('best')	29.2 (5.0)	5.8 (-18.4)**	26.7 (2.4)	23.7 (-0.5)	30.2 (6.0)	24.3
Total	100.0 (178)	100.0 (103)	100.0 (195)	100.0 (59)	100.0 (96)	100.0 (631)
Index of dissimilarity	14.5	28.3	9.6	21.2	7.2	17.9

Individual Level Change						
Deteriorated by 2 or more	6.2 (1.9)	11.9 (7.6)**	1.7 (-2.7)*	– (-4.3)	– (-4.3)*	4.3
Deteriorated by 1	11.2 (-3.4)	35.6 (21.1)**	4.4 (-10.1)**	17.5 (3.0)	15.2 (0.7)	14.5
Stable	32.3 (-9.7)**	38.6 (-3.4)	55.6 (13.5)**	29.8 (-12.2)*	44.3 (2.3)	42.0
Improved by 1	23.0 (-0.7)	9.9 (-13.8)**	23.9 (0.2)	42.1 (18.4)**	29.1 (5.4)	23.7
Improved by 2 or more	27.3 (11.9)**	4.0 (-11.4)**	14.4 (-1.0)	10.5 (-4.9)	11.4 (-4.0)	15.4
Total	100.0 (161)	100.0 (101)	100.0 (180)	100.0 (57)	100.0 (79)	100.0 (578)
Index of dissimilarity	19.2	34.7	19.9	23.8	9.6	21.4

* Significant at .05 level; ** significant at .01 level.

been translated into better quality housing. The fact that their dwelling units are built mostly on encroached government land and most of them do not have legitimate titles to land may inhibit the improvement of housing conditions. The threat of eviction may act as a deterrent to building houses with more permanent structures.

It is expected that with the increase in landholdings and land units cultivated especially among the residents of the dry zone, there would be a concomitant decline in the involvement in non-farm activity as well as in the dependence on other sources of income. Data not presented in tabular form show that non-farm activity is engaged in by only one-tenth of the sample, having declined somewhat from 12.6 percent. At the aggregate level, the largest drop in non-farm activity is found among the migrant colonists followed by voluntary migrants; the receipt of land is a major factor. Among both groups of wet zone natives, however, there is a small but perceptible rise among those engaged in non-farm activity. The wet zone natives have increased from 7.9 percent to 11.3 percent and the mobile natives have grown from 6.8 percent to 8.3 percent. This possibly reflects changing socioeconomic behavior in the face of harsh economic realities. While the pressure on land is sufficient to 'push' marginal proportions of people into non-farm activity concentrated mainly in the service sector, the absence of a ready demand for such employment is an inhibiting factor substantially curbing its growth in the wet zone village.

At the individual level, the voluntary migrants and the dry zone natives gained in non-farm activity. About 15 percent of the dry zone natives and 10 percent of the voluntary migrants gained, higher than the other groups. In contrast, a larger proportion of migrant colonists than other groups lost non-farm activity, followed by voluntary migrants. Similarly, data not shown in tabular form show that the overwhelming majority of the five groups do not have other sources of income apart from land and non-farm activity. Over time, there has been but a small decline.

A final indicator of the current economic situation of the migrant groups relates to the assessment of indebtedness. The data in Table 3.23 show that the proportions in debt have increased from 9.3 percent to 20.3 percent (see Table 3.8). The proportions who had just enough income declined by 13.8 percentage points, while those having enough income to live and save as well increased very moderately from 11.0 percent to 12.9 percent.

Among the migrant types, two patterns of aggregate change

183

TABLE 3.23

PERCENTAGE DISTRIBUTION OF CURRENT ECONOMIC SITUATION AND
PROPORTIONATE DEVIATION FROM MARGINAL AMONG MIGRANT
TYPES, SRI LANKA, 1978

Economic Situation	Migrant colonist	Voluntary migrant	Wet Zone native	Mobile native	Dry Zone native	Total
In debt	29.2 (9.0)**	21.8 (1.5)	13.4 (-6.9)**	11.7 (-8.6)	22.1 (1.8)	20.3
Just enough to live	56.1 (-9.7)**	65.4 (-0.5)	73.2 (7.3)**	81.6 (15.8)**	59.0 (-6.9)	65.9
Enough to live and save too	14.6 (1.7)	9.9 (-3.0)	12.9 (0.0)	6.7 (-6.2)	16.8 (4.0)	12.9
'Other'	— (-1.0)	3.0 (2.0)*	0.5 (-0.5)	— (-1.0)	2.1 (1.1)	1.0
Total	100.0 (171)	100.0 (101)	100.0 (194)	100.0 (60)	100.0 (95)	100.0 (621)
Index of dissimilarity	13.9	4.3	17.5	46.3	6.2	16.5

* Significant at .05 level; ** significant at .01 level.

184

seem to have occurred over time. The two migrant groups have lower proportions in the ranks of those who had enough income to get by and they have swelled the proportions in debt. The native groups of the wet zone have managed to conserve their high proportion in the middle economic category, although there is some loss among the mobile natives who have joined the ranks of the indebted.

The current economic situation also tends to differentiate the two locales. The dry zone residents have one-half to two-thirds in the middle income category and one-fifth to just over one-quarter in debt. The wet zone residents have more than three-quarters in the middle income category and about one-eighth among those in debt. Accordingly, while the wet zone residents have an excess among those having a sufficient income to live, the dry zone residents have a deficit. The pattern is reversed in the case of those who are in debt.

In the wet zone where there was extremely limited room for economic advancement via land, the residents managed to conserve their economic situation; at the time of the survey, more than three-quarters of the natives were capable of living without being in debt. The dry zone, on the other hand, which held out the potential for economic improvement (via land), has over one-half in the economically viable state while over one-quarter are in debt. Being in debt in the dry zone need not necessarily denote indebtedness associated classically with peasant livelihood and unequivocal poverty. Production loans raised from rural banks would also designate those obtaining them as debtors. The fact that even the dry zone natives, with the highest income range, also have 22.1 percent of their group in debt reveals that being in debt is becoming an acceptable way of economic life in the dry zone. However, it is possible that there are two strata of dry zone residents. One has not moved into the realm of commercial crop production but still conforms to the basic lifestyle of the subsistence farmer, the norm of whose life is being in debt associated with poverty. The other stratum has transcended the traditional peasant lifestyle and encompasses those who have become small-time entreprenuer farmers.

Social Ties

One goal of the colonization program was to replicate wet zone type communities which had high levels of interdependence and integration in the colonies of the dry zone. A more equitable distribution of land meant that the chance for the emergence of a patron core as found in the wet zone was minimized and a more atomized cultivation pattern would likely prevail. Surplus production for profit was undermining the communal mobilization potential, while encouraging the growth of wage labor. Therefore, we expected that among the residents of the dry zone, there would be a decline in communal participation and an underutilization of credit facilities within the scope of primary relations in comparison to the natives of the wet zone. Due to indiscriminant selection and relocation, communal caste composition in the dry zone was also expected to be more heterogeneous.

As seen in the top half of Table 3.24, almost nine of every ten in the sample participate in communal voluntary services. When compared to the 'before' situation (compare Table 3.9), there is a slight increment among those who participate from 83.2 percent to 86.6 percent. Among the migrant types, this is true among all except the voluntary migrants who declined from 73.5 percent to 62.1 percent. Their deficit of 24.4 percent with respect to the current situation and the excess of 11.4 percent among the wet zone natives are statistically significant. Because they do not own large areas of land, the small farms can be cultivated by family labor and they do not need the labor of others to farm their lands. Furthermore, since more than 40 percent of their members were engaged in non-agricultural occupations, self-reliance rather than communal reliance among the voluntary migrants is more likely.

In comparison to the situation that prevailed at the time of the 'before' measure, there has been practically no change in participation in seeding and harvesting on land owned by others within the entire sample. However, there have been perceptible changes in the proportions involved in this activity among the two migrant groups; while the migrant colonists have increased participation since migration into the dry zone from 63.6 percent to 70.2 percent, the voluntary migrants have reduced participation from 55.5 percent to 46.1 percent.

In comparing the current situation across migrant types, it can be observed that the dry zone still lacks the same degree of communal activity which characterizes the wet zone. However, the difference between the natives of both locations is not large. Despite the fact that tractors are used in paddy cultivation, only the ploughing is done this way, even in the dry zone; all other activities like ridging, seeding, transplanting, and harvesting are still done with manpower and with little or no use of non-biological energy. To that extent, communal activity is still very much in 'demand' and the ability to mobilize it is a distinct advantage in

TABLE 3.24

PERCENT DISTRIBUTION OF CURRENT COMMUNAL PARTICIPATION,
MONETARY BORROWING STATUS, PRESENCE OF POTENTIAL
LENDER, AND RELATIONSHIP TO POTENTIAL LENDER AND
PROPORTIONATE DEVIATION FROM MARGINAL AMONG
MIGRANT TYPES, SRI LANKA, 1978

	Migrant colonist	Voluntary migrant	Wet Zone native	Mobile native	Dry Zone native	Total
% participating in voluntary cummunal service	83.2 (−3.3)	62.1 (−24.4)**	98.0 (11.4)**	91.7 (5.1)	92.7 (6.1)	86.6
Index of dissimilarity	9.8	35.4	84.7	37.9	45.7	42.3
% participating in seeding and/or harvesting on others' and	70.2 (−5.4)*	46.1 (−29.5)**	91.8 (16.2)**	88.3 (12.7)*	76.0 (0.5)	75.6
Index of dissimilarity	8.6	39.0	66.4	52.2	1.8	34.1
% borrowing money for ceremony	17.4 (−0.1)	14.6 (−2.9)	22.3 (4.8)*	16.7 (−0.8)	11.2 (−6.3)	17.5
Index of dissimilarity	0.5	16.8	12.3	4.7	35.8	10.3
% presence of potential lender	79.8 (−3.9)	73.0 (−10.8)**	88.3 (4.6)	95.7 (12.0)*	86.7 (3.0)	83.7
Index of dissimilarity	10.2	13.7	28.3	73.9	18.1	22.1
% primary relationship to potential lender	44.7 (−25.7)**	34.2 (−36.3)**	91.2 (20.7)**	88.6 (18.2)**	87.0 (16.5)**	70.5
Index of dissimilarity	36.5	51.5	70.2	61.5	55.8	55.6

* Significant at .05 level; ** significant at .01 level.

187

the augmentation of production.

Viewed from another angle, the dry zone's mode of production is much more differentiated than the wet zone's production processes. With increasing differentiation, the ties between the family and the community become less pervasive and the individual has greater freedom of choice with respect to vocation. Both the scale of production and increasing differentiation change communal participation in the dry zone. Indeed, the scale of production is such as to question the validity of continued usage of 'peasant production' to describe the economy of the dry zone. The peasant mode of organization of production remains largely land and labor; the emergence of capital in any pervasive form is still in its incipient stages.

Borrowing money for social occasions appears to have increased only slightly as can be seen from a comparison of the middle panels of Tables 3.24 and 3.9. Among each of the four migrant types, a consistent increase is observable. As was the case with the 'before' situation, the wet zone natives are the only group to show an excess among those who borrowed money.

Being 'in debt' and borrowing for ceremonial occasions are not coincidental and depict different dimensions. While the two groups of wet zone natives have a lower proportion 'in debt' than admit to borrowing in connection with ceremonies (13.4 percent and 11.7 percent versus 22.3 percent and 16.7 percent among migrant colonists and voluntary migrants, respectively), the three groups of residents of the dry zone have the reverse pattern. It is possible that the excess of 'indebted' over those borrowing for ceremonies among the latter consists mainly of production loans obtained from state credit agencies. Among the wet zone native groups, it is likely that those in debt are the ones whose economic condition is associated with poverty. The proportionate excess found among those borrowing for ceremonies may not be considered by them a 'debt' in the sense of being associated with poverty, but may possibly be subsumed under the general rubric of rights and obligations entailed in patron-client relationships.

The same hypothetical question with respect to the presence of a potential lender was inquired of all respondents. The results indicate that there has been hardly any change in the proportions having a potential lender. The migrant colonists have gained from 74.7 percent to 79.8 percent and the voluntary migrants have declined from 81.1 percent to 73.0 percent (Table 3.24, lower panel). The current situation differentiates between the natives and the migrants; while all three groups of natives have an excess of potential lenders, migrants have a deficit. Migrant status, thus,

188

appears to be somewhat of a hinderance in the quest to establish 'social security' within the community of residence.

The relationship to the potential lender shows a sharp increase in 'secondary' sources from 18.7 percent to 29.5 percent. However, variations are more discriminating by migration status. While the migrants experienced drastic reductions in the proportion soliciting (potential) credit from primary sources, the two native groups of the wet zone remained relatively stable. The migrant colonists have declined from 70.1 percent to 44.7 percent and the voluntary migrants have declined even more from 73.3 percent to 34.2 percent. In other words, more than half the sample of migrants cited secondary sources as their potential lender, while approximately one-eighth of the natives of both the wet and dry zones mentioned them. As might be expected, all deviations from the row marginals at the time of the post-migration measure exhibit significant deficits among the migrants and significant excesses among the three native groups with respect to primary relationships.

Another indicator of the changed social ties brought about by migration relates to changes in caste composition. In comparison with the situation before migration, the post-migration situation resulted in more multi-caste localities (Table 3.25). While there were 27.8 percent who lived in communities whose dominant caste was other than their own at the time of the 'before' measure, after migration 35.5 percent are in the same situation and another 13.2 percent say that they are unsure of the caste situation. The latter category suggests that the communities consist predominantly of other castes than that of the respondent. If this is so, the current caste composition in the sample has dramatically changed from one in which three-fourths of the respondents were in majority caste situations to one in which only one-half were in such situations.

While the caste situation within the three wet zone communities surveyed remained stable, the changes were significant in the dry zone communities where the influx of migrants from different communities with different castes has made them multi-caste communities. Migrant colonists who before migration had 75.6 percent of their membership from dominant caste communities have now dwindled to 34.8 percent, and the voluntary migrants have declined from 80.9 percent to 44.9 percent. Since the voluntary migrants had more choice of destination than the migrant colonists, it is possible that they searched for communities which had a larger number of their own caste before migration.

TABLE 3.25

PROPORTIONATE DISTRIBUTION BY CURRENT CASTE COMPOSITION, NUMBER
OF CONSUMER DURABLES, AND SATISFACTION WITH LIFE AMONG MIGRANT
TYPES, SRI LANKA, 1978

	Migrant colonist	Voluntary migrant	Wet Zone native	Mobile native	Dry Zone native	Total
Most families were in R's caste	34.8 (−16.5)**	44.9 (−6.3)	70.0 (18.7)**	59.3 (8.1)	42.2 (−9.1)	51.3
Index of dissimilarity	21.8	12.8	38.4	20.9	14.0	25.5
More than 50% were in R's caste	30.7 (−14.6)**	34.6 (−10.7)*	59.7 (14.4)**	40.3 (−5.0)	41.6 (−3.7)	45.3
Index of dissimilarity	28.5	22.3	36.4	16.5	26.8	28.1
No. of consumer items possessed						
None	22.9 (−12.4)**	38.8 (3.5)	44.6 (9.3)**	59.0 (23.7)**	20.8 (−14.5)**	35.3
One	22.9 (−2.2)	27.2 (2.1)	26.2 (1.1)	21.3 (−3.8)	27.1 (2.0)	25.1
Two	32.4 (11.0)**	12.6 (−8.8)*	15.4 (−6.1)*	13.1 (−8.3)	28.1 (6.7)	21.5
Three	13.4 (3.0)	10.7 (0.3)	8.7 (−1.7)	3.3 (−7.1)	12.5 (2.1)	10.4
Four	6.2 (1.3)	4.9 (−0.0)	4.1 (−0.8)	1.6 (−3.3)	6.3 (1.4)	4.9
Five	2.2 (−0.6)	5.8 (3.0)*	1.0 (−1.8)	1.6 (−1.2)	5.2 (2.4)	2.8
Total	100.0 (179)	100.0 (103)	100.0 (195)	100.0 (61)	100.0 (96)	100.0 (634)
Index of dissimilarity	21.2	10.6	15.0	26.2	17.1	17.5
Proportion satisfied or very satisfied with life	74.6 (−1.0)	53.4 (−22.2)**	83.6 (8.0)*	71.6 (−3.9)	87.5 (11.9)**	75.6
Index of dissimilarity	2.0	27.7	13.9	5.4	14.0	12.3

* Significant at .05 level; ** significant at .01 level.

190

Moreover, while 77.9 percent of the migrant colonists came from communities where their own caste had at least 50 percent or more families, the current situation in the colonization schemes reveals that the proportion has declined to 30.7 percent. Similarly, the voluntary migrants have declined from 83.7 to 34.4 percent.

Caste in traditional and current Sri Lanka remains an active force in the ordering of social relations in the country, whether it be in the rural hinterland or in the cities. Nevertheless, there have been changes toward greater caste heterogeneity in rural areas brought about in part by rural-rural migration.

Consumerism and Quality of Life

Indicators of personal characteristics, changing land relationships, housing, and income as well as changing social ties portray the broad transformations associated with rural-rural migration. In general, the evidence points to the improved standard of living of migrants and their families. Combined with the changing monetization of rural areas, we would expect changes in the possession of consumer durables.

The possession of consumer durables has been studied mainly in the urbanward migration literature and has been used to assess the acculturation of migrants to the city (Green, 1977; McCutcheon, 1977; Tirasawat, 1977). As such, the possession of consumer durables has come to symbolize city values and indicates relative modernity. Since our focus is on ruralward migration, the possession of consumer durables will be viewed as a proxy for relative affluence and as an indicator of incipient penetration of 'modern' values.

Ten consumer durables were identified in the questionnaire and the respondent answered whether he (or his family) possessed any of the items listed. In ascending order of value attached, they were: 1) radio, 2) wall clock, 3) bullock cart, 4) sewing machine, 5) bicycle, 6) kerosene oil cooker, 7) motor cycle, 8) hand tractor, 9) four-wheeled tractor, and 10) automobile. The number of objects that were possessed by the respondents is presented without regard to the value of each item.

When the distribution is dichotomized by collapsing the first three categories and the last three categories, the residents of the dry zone reveal a net excess and the wet zone residents display a net deficit among those owning three or more objects (Table 3.25). The dry zone natives possess the largest number of items with a

191

net excess of 5.8 percent, followed by the migrant colonists (3.7 percent) and the voluntary migrants (3.3 percent). The mobile natives possess the least with a deficit of 11.6 percent and the wet zone natives depict a deficit of 4.3 percent.

If the possession of consumer durables is an indication of modernity, then the residents of the dry zone appear to be more modern than the residents of the wet zone who live in the more developed parts of the country. However, other characteristics, e.g., educational attainment, suggest that the residents of the dry zone are less modern than their wet zone comrades. A partial reconciliation of this inconsistncy is found in the contrasting dynamism of the two economies. The dry zone, though less developed than the wet zone, has in the last two decades generated more productive output than the wet zone and consequently it has attracted an unprecedented amount of money into the hands of its residents, especially those involved with land-bound economic activity. The possession of many consumer durables can be seen as the result of money becoming a relatively available commodity in the dry zone. The dynamism of the dry zone economy has helped its residents to acquire symbols of modernity before they have begun to internalize and manifest norms and behavior patterns of modernity.

A subjective assessment of quality of life at the current residence was solicited of all respondents. Nine dimensions were scored on a five-point Guttman Scale varying from 'very satisfactory' to 'very unsatisfactory'. The nine dimensions that were obtained included: 1) physical environment, 2) housing conditions, 3) job, 4) cost of living, 5) income, 6) children's education, 7) relationship with relatives, 8) relationships with friends, and 9) relationship with neighbors.

The response on each dimension was scored from one through five, 'very unsatisfactory' being scored one and 'very satisfactory' being scored five, summed, and averaged. Only one percent of the sample stated that they were either dissatisfied or very dissatisfied with these aspects of life, while just under one-quarter (23.5 percent) were 'indifferent' to their current situation. The overwhelming majority were either satisfied or very satisfied with their quality of life. Most of the migrant types closely paralleled the marginal distribution, which is reflected in the relatively low magnitude of the indicies of dissimilarity (Table 3.25, lower panel).

The dry zone natives were the most satisfied (with an excess of 11.9 percent), followed by the wet zone natives (8.0 percent). The other three groups had deficits, least among the migrant colonists (1.0 percent), followed by mobile natives (3.9 percent), and by voluntary migrants (22.2 percent).

It appears that the dry zone natives were the most capable of exploiting the improvement in the dry zone. The fact that they (or their kinship network) may have already held other private land, which had appreciated in value (mainly because of irrigation), may have provided them with the additional edge over the migrant colonists who were restricted to an allocation of land. The voluntary migrants, on the other hand, had a frame of reference setting their aspirations higher than those of either the dry zone natives or the migrant colonists. They were better educated, had much better housing conditions, and in all probability better living conditions in general at their place of origin. Left to their own resources, they were unable to surpass either the achievements of the dry zone natives or the migrant colonists; neither did they achieve quite the same standards which they enjoyed at their place of origin.

Concluding Observations

Many of the broad objectives that guided the colonization program have been achieved. A fairly equitable distribution of land has been maintained in the program nearly four decades after its inception. Increased food production has resulted in progressively reducing the burden on the budget allocations for food importation (Samarasinghe, 1977) and the money has been redistributed among the peasant farmers (Yost, 1978). The technological base of agricultural production has been altered somewhat by the usage of intermediate technology on a limited scale and the norm of surplus production for the market has become the motivating force for cultivation of the dry zone. Consequently, the peasant economy has become increasingly monetized and differentiated.

Some degree of failure of the program is also conspicuous. Its basic shortcoming lies in not being able to provide the children and the grandchildren of the migrants with a livelihood. The Land Development Ordinance of 1935 incorporated protected tenureship to most Crown land grants. As a result, one male heir was provided for but the other children of the colonist technically had not much to look forward to. It was seen that protected tenure was ineffective in maintaining the land units intact since the older migrants had allowed the use of their land to their children. If only some children were to remain on the land, there were no other formal arrangements made for the alternative absorption of the others within the rest of the national economy. In the meantime, welfare measures on food, education, and medical care were transforming the population but without the infrastructural base for ushering in modernization at the material level.

The future success of the colonization program lies in the ability of the government to generate productive employment opportunities for the unemployed youth of the country, the majority of whom are also educated. Several Youth Settlement Schemes in agriculture have already been initiated (Land Commissioner's Department, 1972; Department of Agriculture, n.d.; Ellman and Ratnaaweera, 1974). Attempts were also being made to create a viable industrial base with the collaboration of foreign investment. The absorption capacity of both the agricultural and industrial investment will be crucial for Sri Lanka in the decade of the 1980s in its effort to grapple with problems of development, population, and social change.

Appendix

Study Design of the Rural Samples in Sri Lanka

The absence of adequate statistical information on the large number of rural villages in Sri Lanka resulted in the decision to restrict the survey sites to major colonization schemes only. There were several stages to select eligible respondents for interviewing.

Stage 1

The first question to be resolved was which major colonization schemes were to be selected. The Administrative Report of the Land Commissioner for the financial year of 1968-69 (the last one before the field work began), listed 98 major colonization schemes throughout the whole Island. Of them, 60 schemes were in the dry zone districts and the rest were either in the intermediate or the wet zones. The 60 colonies were scattered among all the districts of the dry zone, viz., Anuradhapura, Trincomalee, Polonnaruwa, Amparai, Hambantota, Batticaloa, Mannar, Vavuniya, and Jaffna.

Of these districts, the last three had a predominantly Tamil population and were situated in the northern part of the country. Batticaloa had a mixed population of both Ceylon Tamils and Ceylon Moors and the language of communication was, for the major part, Tamil. The principal reseacher and his staff of interviewers were Sinhalese and therefore were unable to communicate in Tamil; this was a biasing factor that militated against including colonization schemes from these four districts. The advantages of having a native researcher conversant with the indigenous population conducting research would have been lost had any colony from these districts been included in the sample. Furthermore, the communal violence which had erupted between the Sinhalese and the Tamil communities as recently as late 1977 was still fresh in the minds of the people and the wounds were yet to heal to warrent undertaking any form of research.

This left five predominantly Sinhalese districts from which colonies were to be selected. Amparai had one vast colonization scheme within its boundaries, viz., the Gal Oya Left Bank, holding over 7,000 land allottees and making it an atypical scheme in terms of its vastness. Once Amparai District was eliminated, the question was whether at least one colonization scheme from the four remaining districts should be included in the study. At least three reasons prevailed in arriving at the decision to drop Hambantota from the sample. (1) Though possessing 3 colonies within its boundaries, the intercensal net migration rates reveal that between 1946 and 1971, Hambantota consistently lost population (ESCAP, 1976:45-57). This indicated that Hambantota was not a good location for studying migration and the input of the government's investment on lifestyles in the dry zone. (2) Hambantota District is generally not considered an area which has felt the full impact of the government's investment in agriculture. (3) The inclusion of Hambantota would have meant increasing travel time and costs since it was in the deep south of the country.

By a process of elimination, therefore, it was decided to select colonization schemes only from within the districts of Anuradhapura, Polonnaruwa, and Trincomalee.

Stage 2

Before the six colonization schemes could be identified, there was a need for more information on the characteristics of the colonies and colonists. The information sought included: (1) how many inhabitants (households) resided within the boundary of the colony; (2) what was the proportion of legitimate land allottees to that of encroachers; (3) when was the recruitment of colonists started, has it ended, and if so, when did it end; (4) from what districts were the colonists recruited; and (5) have there been pre-existing old villages that were absorbed into the colonization scheme? This was considered valuable input information in the selection of the survey sites since we wanted to include both legitimate land recipients and encroachers, as well as non-migrants and migrants. Most of the information was neither available in the scanty literature nor in the Administrative Reports of the Land Commissioner and had to be solicited through personal interviews with the field staff of the Land Commissioner.

Contact was first established with the three Senior District Land Officers in each of the three districts. They too were unable to provide all the information sought in the selection of the colonies. It was discovered that this information, if at all, was available with the individual Colonization Officers in charge of the colonization schemes. The C.O.s are the last rung of a chain administrative command, who are resident in situ. Consequently, a decision was made to mail a brief outline of the research to be undertaken along with a two page questionnaire to 27 C.O.s within the three districts. These did not constitute the entire universe of C.O.s in the 3 districts; elimination of some colonization schemes had already ensued during the course of discussion with the D.L.O.s.

Twenty-four completed questionnaires were received from among the 27 mailed and one was returned because the addressee could not be located. Based on the responses obtained, 8 C.O.s were chosen to be visited. The major limiting criterion in selecting these 8 locations was the existence of old villages either absorbed into the scheme or lying on the fringe of it, facilitating some element of integration between the two. Common to the 8 locations was the presence of people originating from the same district as well as from other districts, and the presence of legitimate allottees and encroachers in sufficient numbers. There was, however, variation across the schemes with respect to land area held by each colonist as well as to the period of establishment and the last date of recruitment of colonists.

After visiting these 8 C.O.s, it was decided to select Galmetiyawa Colonization Scheme from Trincomalee District, Pimburathewa and Thopawewa Schemes from Polonnaruwa District, and Katiyawa, Rajangana Left Bank, and Mahawilachiya Schemes from Anuradhapura District as the survey sites.

Stage 3

Since these schemes in their entirety would have run from several hundred up to several thousand households scattered through a large land area, the screening sites had to be demarcated. During the discussions with the C.O.s, the 'best' contiguous areas were identified by their boundaries so as to optimize the location of migrants, non-migrants, land allottees, and encroachers. As a general rule, the area marked out to be screened contained between 200 and 350 households.

Before the interviewers (male undergraduates majoring in Sociology) began screening and while the householders' lists were being copied in each of the selected survey sites, it was discovered that Thopawewa Scheme had more than 60 percent of its inhabitants residing in an urban area as defined by the Department of Census and Statistics. Since we focused the study on rural wet zone to rural dry zone migrants, we excluded Thopawewa from the study.

The colonization schemes selected as survey sites were similar in some respects and varied in others. Each had an allocation of lowland and highland per colonist; they all had some man-made irrigation component which fed the lowlands they cultivated, and were all located in the dry zone; the main crop cultivated was rice and the colonists depended upon it as their main source of income; each survey site contained both legitimate government colonists as well as encroachers; recruitment of colonists was done by the same government agencies using practically the same criteria.

There was also variability in several respects. The unit of land alienated to each colonist within each colonization scheme, though consistent, varied across the schemes. Katiyawa Scheme had the highest land unit alienated (8 acres), while Pimburathewa and Galmetiyawa had the lowest (3-4 acres). There was variation in the degree of irrigatability of land. Rajangana, being one of the country's largest schemes, was better irrigated than either Mahawilachchiya or Galmetiyawa. The date of establishment of colonies spanned from the mid-1940s to the late 1950s, and as a result, the duration of residence of the migrants varied. While these differences raise questions about combining respondents from these five survey sites into one sample, it was expected that taken together, they would very roughly replicate the spectrum of colonization projects undertaken by the government during the last 3 to 4 decades.

Stage 4

The interviewers resided in or in the vicinity of each of the identified survey sites for approximately 3-1/2 weeks. During this time they were instructed to visit all households in the area; householder lists from either the C.O. or the GRAMA SEWAKA (headman) were obtained and the services of at least one local informant were secured in facilitating the location of all households.

The screening interview was designed to ascertain the characteristics of the household and eligible respondent. All ever-married male heads of households were stratified according to five criteria: (1) non-migrants, those who had lived in the same community they were born in all their lives; (2) non-migrants, those who had lived in their district of birth all their lives, though not in their village of birth; (3) primary migrants, those who had moved once from their district of birth into a different district where they were presently living; (4) repeat migrants, those who had moved at least twice across district boundaries since birth; and (5) return migrants, those who had come back to reside in their district of birth after moving out of it at least once across district lines.

Once the screening operation was completed, a sample of respondents was selected. In all five locations of the dry zone, the guiding principle was to include between 100 and 120 respondents from each site so that each migrant type would have at least 20 cases. To ensure this, it was soon discovered that some migrant types would have to be oversampled. All return migrants and all repeat migrants who were screened were included in the sample. Even with this extreme measure, only 7 return migrants were found. Such a situation was anticipated before the field work began when cross tabulation of the 1971 sample census tapes revealed a small number of return migrants in the country.

The sample to be intensively interviewed was selected by using a random numbers table according to the varying sampling factors appearing on Row 3 in each panel of Table A.1. In Rows 4 and 5, the numbers and proportions actually interviewed from each site are given. The discrepancy between the two marks the failure to secure an interview with the male head of the household after three attempts. In all, there were 535 completed interviews obtained from the 5 dry zone colonization schemes.

A similar selection procedure was adopted in choosing 3 villages from the wet zone. The objective was to ensure a comparison group that could be contrasted with the dry zone sample. The literature on rural-urban migration is abundant with critiques directed at studies which concentrated only on the place of destination and did not include the place of origin of the migrants (Macisco & Myers, 1975; Martine, 1975; Zarate & Zarate, 1975).

The village typology was once again developed from the literature review (ESCAP, 1975). The utility of this typology was also contingent upon the availability of information pertaining to land alienation records. However, it was discovered that there were no recorded lists of villages from which colonists were recruited to settle in the dry zone. Thus, it was decided that in selecting the wet zone villages, expert opinions were to provide the basis for ensuring that each village selected had experienced some degree of out-migration.

Selection of districts had to be done before the identification of the villages. Of the seven districts situated entirely within the wet zone, Colombo, Kalutara, Galle, and Matara were on the coast and Kandy, Nuwara Eliya, and Kegalle were in the mountainous interior of the country. Consideration was also given to the districts of Matale, Kurunegala, Ratnapura, Puttalam, and

199

SELECTION OF SAMPLES IN DRY ZONE AND WET ZONE

| Category | MIGRANTS | | | NON-MIGRANTS | | |
	Primary	Repeat	Return	One Village	Several Villages	Total
TOTAL DRY ZONE						
Number screened	1,034	105	8	116	176	1,439
Selected for interview	465	105	8	45	84	707
% Selected for interview	45.0	100.0	100.0	38.8	47.7	49.1
Number interviewed	360	72	7	28	68	535
% Interviewed	34.8	68.6	87.5	24.1	38.6	37.2
% Non-response	22.6	31.4	12.5	37.8	19.0	24.3
TOTAL WET ZONE						
Number screened	32	6	14	524	119	695
Selected for interview	32	6	14	240	77	369
% Selected for interview	100.0	100.0	100.0	45.8	64.7	53.1
Number interviewed	19	5	8	194	62	288
% Interviewed	59.4	83.3	57.1	37.0	52.1	41.4
% Non-response	40.6	16.7	42.9	19.2	19.5	22.0

Badulla which were situated in both the wet and dry zones. Lifetime net out-migration as of 1971 was recorded in Matara, Galle, Kandy, Kegalle, Nuwara Eliya, Badulla, and Kalutara (ESCAP, 1976:57). Matara, Galle, and Kalutara were eliminated from consideration because of their geographic, socio-historical, and urban configuration. These districts, along with Colombo, were the most urban areas, predominantly inhabited by the Sinhalese and therefore hardly qualified as a group likely to go into the dry zone as peasant farmers en masse. They were more likely to have migrated as petty traders or as those engaged in other tertiary sector services.

Kandy District, with a net out-migration rate of 10 per 1,000, was the next to be considered but was passed on in favor of Kegalle because the former contained the second city of the country (also called Kandy) and was therefore too urban. Although Kegalle and Nuwara Eliya had an identical net migration rate of -7.26, the former was preferred since the latter's out-migration would have incorporated the South Indian plantation laborer population, fairly large numbers of whom were being repatriated to South India under the provisions of the Sirima-Shastri Pact of 1964.

It was decided to concentrate on locating the three villages within the same district rather than spread the resources too thinly with no commensurate gain from the endeavor. The expert opinions solicited consisted of the three District Land Officers attached to the Government Agent's Office at Kegalle. Five villages scattered within Kegalle District were identified for on-the-spot evaluation and, subsequent to the visits to these locations and discussions with the Grama Sewakas of the area, three villages were selected as survey sites. Rangalla was a village that had tea land alienated to the village resulting in expansion of the same; Arama had a limited amount of land alienated explicitly for homesteads rather than for any form of viable cultivation and these constituted no more than one-quarter acre per allottee; Dunukewela had not benefited at all from the government's Village Expansion Program.

As in the dry zone, two interviewers were resident in each village for approximately 3-1/2 weeks. Screening of all households in the village was carried out first and then stratified according to the same criteria as in the dry zone. Sampling factors differed once again from site to site and between migrant types. However, this time it was the non-migrants who were found in abundance (as was expected) and very few migrants were in the sample. All types of migrants who were screened were to be included in

201

intensive interviewing, while it was only possible to select a simple random sample from among the non-migrants. The bottom panel of Table A.1 shows the very meagre supply of return and repeat migrants found in the villages. In all, there were 288 completed interviews obtained from the three wet zone villages.

There is a gap between the number identified for intensive interviewing after screening and the number of actually completed interviews. The interviewers were instructed to locate each of the identified households and secure an interview with the male head of household which lasted approximately 75 minutes. At least 3 attempts were to be made to locate each eligible respondent. However, in anticipation of problems associated with locating the respondent, the number selected for interviewing was consciously overdrawn with the intention of eventually securing approximately 100 to 120 completed questionnaires from each site. By nature the Sinhalese peasant family is fairly easygoing and hospitable. But they are not over-eager to answer scores of questions pertaining to their lifestyle, especially when the questions are asked by young university students who are strangers in the community.

Considering the limited resources and objectives of this study, no claims regarding the representativeness of the sample are made. It would be technically correct to say the results of this study are not generalizable beyond the boundaries of the communities that were studied. At best, they may reflect the colonization scheme or village in which the study was done (as in most survey sites only part of a scheme or village was screened). Under no circumstance should the results be generalized to the whole stream of migrants from the rural wet zone to the rural dry zone.

The rates of non-response from each survey site are provided in Table A.1. The overall non-response rate for each of the 8 survey sites ranges markedly from 12.3 to 34.0 percent. All respondents who were ear-marked for selection after screening were to be interviewed intensively. However, the number identified to be interviewed exceeded the expected number of completed interviews at the end of the field work. This was done after the pre-test revealed there would be problems locating and securing an interview from respondents.

References

Administration Report of the Land Commissioner for 1968-69. 1975. Part I - Civil (G). Colombo.

Bieder, R.E. 1973. "Kinship as a Factor in Migration." *Journal of Mariage and the Family* 35: 429-439.

Browning, Harley L. 1971. "Migrant Selectivity and Growth of Large Cities in Developing Societies." In *Rapid Population Growth*. Ed. Roger Revelle et al. Baltimore: Johns Hopkins University Press, pp. 273-314.

Choldin, H.M. 1973. "Kinship Network in the Migration Process." *International Migration Review* 7: 163-175.

Connell, John, Biplab Dasgupta, Roy Laishley, and Michael Lippton. 1976. *Migration from Rural Areas*. Institute of Development Studies, Village Studies Programme. Delhi: Oxford University Press.

Department of Agriculture. n.d. *Economic Evalution of Youth Settlement Schemes at Muttu-Iyan-Kaddu Special Project*. Peradeniya.

Department of Town and Country Planning. n.d. *Urbanization*. Colombo. (mimeo).

Duncan, Otis D. and A.J. Reiss, Jr. 1956. *Social Characteristics of Urban and Rural Communities*. New York: John Wiley and Sons.

Edelmann, A.T. 1967. "Colonization in Bolivia: Progress and Prospects." *Interamerican Economic Affairs* 20(4) (Spring): 39-54.

Ellman, A.O. and D. de S. Ratnaaweera. 1974. "New Settlement Schemes in Sri Lanka: A Study of Twenty Selected Youth Schemes, Co-operative Farms, DDC Agricultural Projects and Land Reform Settlements." Colombo: Agrarian Training and Research Institute.

Epstein, T.S. 1973. *South India: Yesterday, Today, and Tomorrow*. London: Macmillan.

E.S.C.A.P. 1975. *Comparative Study of Population Growth and Agricultural Change: Case Study of Sri Lanka.* Asian Population Studies Series, No. 23:D E/CN.11/1224. New York: United Nations.

_____. 1976. *Population of Sri Lanka: ESCAP Country Monograph Series No. 4.* New York: United Nations.

Farmer, B.H. 1957. *Pioneer Peasant Colonization in Ceylon: A Study in Asian Agrarian Problems.* London: Oxford University Press.

Fuchs, F.W. and Vingerhoet. J. 1972. "Rural Manpower, Rural Institutions and Rural Employment in Thailand." Bangkok: Manpower Planning Division, National Economic Development, pp. 96-103.

Geertz, Cliford. 1963. *Agricultural Involution: The Process of Ecological Change in Indonesia.* Berkeley: Published for the Association of Asian Studies by University of California Press.

Goldscheider, Calvin. 1971. *Population, Modernization and Social Structure.* Boston: Little Brown and Company.

Green, Sarah Clark. 1977. "Dimensions of Migrant Adjustment in Seoul, Korea." Unpublished Ph.D. Dissertation. Providence, Rhode Island, Brown University.

Hilal, J.M. 1969. "Family, Marriage and Social Change in Some Libyan Villages." Unpublished Manuscript. Litt. Thesis. University of Durham.

Hill, P. 1972. *Rural Hausa, a Village and a Setting.* Cambridge: Cambridge University Press.

Hunter, J.K. 1967. "Population Pressure in Part of West African Savanna." *Annals of the Association of American Geographers,* pp. 110-114.

Lansing, John B. and Eva Mueller. 1967. *The Geographical Mobility of Labor.* Ann Arbor: Survey Reseach Center,

204

University of Michigan.

Leach, E.R. 1961. *Pul Eliya, A Village in Ceylon: A Study of Land Tenure and Kinship.* Cambridge: Cambridge University Press.

_____. 1960. *Aspects of Caste in South India, Ceylon and North West Pakistan.* Cambridge: Cambridge University Press.

Macisco, John J. Jr. and George C. Myers. 1975. "Introduction." *International Migration Review* 9(2): 11-114.

Martine, George. 1975. "Volume, Characteristics and Consequences of Internal Migration in Colombia." *Demography* 12(2): 193-208.

McCutcheon, Laurie. 1977. "Migrant Adjustment in Surabaya, Indonesia." Unpublished Ph.D. Dissertation. Providence, Rhode Island, Brown University.

Paige, Jeffery M. 1975. *Agrarian Revolution: Social Movements and Export Agriculture in the Underdeveloped World.* New York: Free Press.

Preston, D.A. 1969. "Rural Emigration in Andean America." *Human Organization* 28(4) (Winter): 279-286.

Ritchey, P. Neil. 1976. "Explanations of Migration." In *Annual Review of Sociology.* Eds. Alex Inkeles, James Coleman, and Neil Smelser. Vol. 2. California: Annual Reviews Inc. pp. 363-404.

Rochin, R.I. 1972. "Inter-relations between Farm Environment, Off-farm Migration and Rates of Adoption: Dwarf Wheats on Irrigated Small-Holdings in Pakistan." Workshop on Empirical Studies of Small Farm Agriculture in Developing Nations. Indiana, Purdue University, November.

Ross, Heather L. and Isabel V. Sawhill. 1975. *The Time of Transition: The Growth of Families Headed by Women.* Washington, D.C.: The Urban Institute.

Sakoda, James M. 1979. "Generalized Index of Dissimilarity:

205

Computer Program 'DISSIM'." Unpublished paper. Providence, Rhode Island, Brown University.

Samarasinghe, S.W.R. de S. 1977. "Introduction." In *Agriculture in the Peasant Sector of Sri Lanka.* Ed. S.W.R. de S. Samarasinghe. Peradeniya: Ceylon Stuies Seminary, pp. ix-xiv.

Simmons, Alan, Sergio Diaz-Briquets, and Aprodicio A. Laquian. 1977. *Social Change and Internal Migration: A Review of Research Findins from Africa, Asia and Latin America.* International Development Research Centre. IDRC-Ts6e.

Singhe, B. 1958. *Next Step in Village India.* Department of Economics, University of Lucknow.

Smelser, Neil J. 1968. *Essays in Sociological Explanation.* New Jersey: Prentice-Hall.

Solien de Gonzales, N.L. 1961. "Family Organization in Five Types of Migratory Wage Labor." *American Anthropologist* 63: 1264-1281.

Speare, Alden Jr. 1971. "A Cost-Benefit Model of Rural to Urban Migration in Taiwan." *Population Studies* 25: 117-130.

_____. 1974. "Migration and Family Change in Central Taiwan." In *The Chinese City Between Two Worlds.* Eds. Mark Elvin and William G. Skinner. California: Stanford University Press.

Speare, Alden Jr., Sidney Goldstein, and William H. Frey. 1976. *Residential Mobility, Migration, and Metropolitan Change.* Cambridge, Mass: Ballinger Publishing Company.

Stiglitz, J.E. 1973. "Alternative Theories of Wage Determination and Unemployment in LDCs." IDS. Nairobi. Discussion Paper 125.

Thambiah, S.J. 1958. "The Structure of Kinship in Pata Dumbara, Central Ceylon." *Jounal of the Royal Anthropological Institute* 88: 21-44.

206

Thomas, Dorothy, S. 1938. *Research Memorandum on Migration Differentials. Bulletin No. 43. New York: Social* Science Research Council.

Tirasawat, Penporn. 1977. "Urbanization and Migrant Adjustment in Thailand." Unpublished Ph.D. Dissertation. Providence, Rhode Island, Brown University.

Turkey, Ministry of Village Affairs. 1965-1968. *Koy Evanter Etudierine Gore.* 1-26 Ankara. (quoted in Connell et al., 1976).

Uhlenberg, P. 1973. "Noneconomic Determinants of Nonmigration: Sociological Considerations for Migration Theory." *Rural Sociology* 38: 296-311.

Walsh, A.C. and A.D. Trilin. 1973. "Niuean Migration: Niue Socio-Economic Background, Characteristics of Migrants and Settlement in Auckland." *Journal of Polynesian Society* 82(1): 47-85.

Wier, Angela and Elisabeth Wilson. 1973. "Women's Labor and Women's Discontent." *Radical America* 7 (July): 80-95.

Yost, Charles. 1978. "Showcase for Foreign Aid Results." *Providence Journal Bulletin,* February 22.

Zarate, Alvan O. and Alicia Unger de Zarate. 1975. "On the Reconciliation of Research Findings of Migrant-Nonmigrant Fertility Differentials in Urban Areas." *International Migration Review* 9(2): 115-156.

4
Rural Out-Migration
and Labor Allocation in Mali

Robert E. Mazur

Introduction

Increasing attention is being paid by governments, policy makers, and scholars to patterns and rates of population redistribution in developing countries. The governments of almost all developing countries find the spatial distribution of their populations undesirable, with the vast majority favoring substantial or radical intervention to slow or reverse current rates of rural to urban migration (U.N., 1978:27-28; U.N., 1979:72-73). In West Africa, the proportion perceiving radical intervention as appropriate to further socioeconomic development is particularly high.

One reason for interest in migration from rural areas is the continued rapid growth of cities in recent decades and the consequences of urban growth. In a fundamental way, however, the marked attention given to the "urban" aspects of migration has perpetuated the neglect of the "rural" context of migration. The changes associated with moving out of rural areas can only be understood through reference to the social, economic, and demographic characteristics of the households, villages, and regions from which migrants come.

----

*Support from the National Institute of Health, Purdue University and its A.I.D. grants AF-1257 and AF-1258, and The University of Montana is gratefully acknowledged. I owe a special debt of gratitude to Stan Cohen, Allen Fleming, and Tom Whitney.

209

A substantial amount of evidence indicates that economic considerations underlie most migration. In various circumstances, labor migration contributes to the material welfare of individuals, households, and villages. Demographic, social, and political factors are important as well and may at times be the major causes of migration. Migration studies focusing on the economic dimension have tended to be of two general types. The first places primary emphasis on individualistic, "rational" behavior without specifying the social, economic, and demographic context at the household, village, or regional level. The second type describes what should occur at a societal level under the assumptions of the classical economic equilibrium model, without providing an understanding of the macro context as an historical confluence of social, economic, political, and demographic factors. In both views, migration is treated relatively abstractly as a logical, rather than a social, process. Neither approach relates specifically to the broadly-defined environment within which migration occurs.

The identification of characteristics of migrants is useful but relatively trivial compared to the need for explaining the role of migration in the transformation of the socioeconomic structure of society, in general, or of the processes of production and distribution, in particular. While it is often assumed that rural areas have substantial labor surpluses, there is growing evidence that rural to urban migration may take place despite labor shortages in rural areas and may result in reductions in agricultural production. Underlying economic policies may determine the existence of a local labor surplus or shortage by affecting the viability of local economic activities and the income which can be derived from them. Indeed, out-migration of labor from agriculture has been one factor leading to national food deficits and rising food prices in many African countries (Byerlee, 1974). An approach to the study of migration which incorporates individual and structural considerations, with attention to the historical context of the society and its transformation, is essential to understanding migration patterns in the transformation of developing societies.

This research focuses on the development of an integrated approach to the empirical study of rural out-migration in sub-Saharan Africa. A comprehensive theoretical framework is formulated to analyze survey data on population movements which are part of the broader, structural transformation of societies as a whole (Goldstein, 1976: 427-428; Gerald-Scheepers and Van Binsbergen, 1978: 30; Van Binsbergen and Meilink,

1978: 11; Wood, 1980: 1-2). In this way it may be possible to specify the primary, or underlying, causes of migration (Shaw, 1975: 100), and permit a more systematic interpretation of contemporary patterns and differentials in migration. The objectives of the present research are to understand the immediate and broader causes of labor out-migration in rural Mali, a country in Sahelian West Africa.

Several levels of analysis are incorporated in this research. The first consists of analysis within an historical-structural perspective to examine the origins and present structure of the distribution of productive assets among households and differences in the level of development of productive forces in areas from which migrants come. More specifically, this includes policies of labor recruitment and remuneration, colonial and neo-colonial patterns of investment and "development assistance", and the institutions governing access to land, labor, and capital. The second involves analysis of contemporary structural conditions within which decisions regarding labor allocation and migration occur. Imbalances or inequalities in access to productive resources among regions, villages, and households are at the core of understanding rural out-migration (Connell et al., 1976). Finally, there is a need to examine and explain the strategies of labor allocation and migration adopted by households, in different villages and regions, by reference to the opportunities and constraints they face.

The central hypothesis guiding our research is that both the socioeconomic circumstances (social class position) of a household and its socio-demographic structure significantly affect its pattern of labor allocation and migration. In addition, inequalities among villages and regions are expected to further define the range of opportunities and constraints and, therefore, patterns of labor allocation and migration. A major goal of the data analysis is to assess the independent and joint effects of these factors.

The Demographic and Economic Context of Mali

The Republic of Mali is one of the least developed countries in the world, with a long history of labor migration out of the country. On the surface, Mali appears rather unlike most other developing countries today. However, the characteristics and processes found in contemporary Mali, and their historical origins, exist in numerous countries throughout Africa and indeed throughout the developing world. The mix of commercial and subsistence agricultural production, agro-ecological conditions,

211

types of colonial labor recruitment policies, the nature of its development policies, and the types of labor migration found in Mali as part of the West African region are similar to those which exist in varying combinations throughout the developing world.

Throughout the history of what is known today as Mali, migration has assumed a variety of forms corresponding to different contexts. Long-distance migration coincided with the flourishing trans-Saharan trade from 800 to 1600; wealth and slave labor circulated under the protection of various great empires at that time (Jones, 1976:13,16). The bases of these systems were undercut by the impact of Europeans. Beginning with Portuguese commercial contact in the 15th century, followed by Atlantic slave trade, this region was most profoundly changed by the French military, political, economic, and social conquest from 1878 onward (Crowder, 1968; Hopkins, 1973). Despite efforts to establish railways and improve roads, the French were unable to realize a significant profitable surplus for export to Europe from Mali (Jones, 1976:22-26). Exportation of peanuts, and particularly cotton, failed to materialize; only cattle production eventually became a profitable export commodity. Instead, the French undermined local craft production with cheap imported goods and imposed head taxes to mobilize the Malians (as well as those from Niger and Upper Volta) as laborers who met their cash needs by migrating to work on peanut farms in Senegal, on cocoa plantations in Ghana and the Ivory Coast, and in the French army (Jones, 1976:24-25). During this phase of the colonial period, the seasonal movement from the interior regions to the farms and plantations of the coastal regions of West Africa amounted to perhaps 400,000-500,000 adult males (Adepoju, 1977:209; Amin, 1974:71,74; Hance, 1970:33,146; Hopkins, 1973:224; Hoyt; 1962:21; Mabogunje, 1975:157).

This massive migration was exacerbated by the French strategy of "contrived stagnation" and unbalanced investment in the interior regions of West Africa (Amin, 1972:520; Gregory and Piche, 1979:42-43; Standing, 1979). Vastly disproportionate investment occurred throughout this period, particularly between 1945-60, in the coastal areas (Jones, 1976:28). Investments in Mali modified the structure of the economy somewhat by expanding transport firms, trucks, and improved roads for a growing trade with the Ivory Coast and Ghana, notably in fish and cattle exports. These investments, however, failed to affect more than a small portion of Mali's population.

Most people in Mali continued to rely on self-sufficiency in farming. Increasing reliance on producing peanuts for sale was met during World War II by a collapsed market as terms of trade deteriorated dramatically. Most of the economic surplus accruing to the colonial administrators in Mali resulted from head taxes, obtained through labor migration, rather than from productive activities in Mali.

The structure of a comparatively large, dependent bureaucracy without an industrial base to support it was passed from the French to an independent Mali in 1960 (Meillassoux, 1970a:97; Diop, 1977a:406; 1977b:263). Offering a socialist political and economic ideology as a guise for state capitalism, the Malian government nationalized the transportation, commercial, and banking sectors and implemented a program to collectivize agriculture (DuBois, 1975:8; Diop, 1977b:263). Besides the subsequent lack of capital investment in the economy, disruption of transportation networks, and declining agricultural production, an even larger government bureaucracy emerged. New "taxes" were levied on the agricultural sector, both by directly taxing each farming household (and livestock) and by enforcing sales of agricultural produce to the state at unrealistically low prices.

Declining output from commercial agriculture, stemming from peasant discontent, undermined the government's capacity to pay its bills, obtain imports, and feed cheaply the urban population. Forced to reaccept French control of its monetary and fiscal policies in March 1968, the Keita government was overthrown in November 1968 (Jones, 1972:44). As a result, subsidies to cooperatives ended, peasant membership in co-ops was no longer compulsory, rural prices were raised, and price controls were no longer enforced. However, the class of politicians and bureaucrats maintained their position and standard of living (Wolpin, 1975:612).

In Mali, as in West Africa generally, there is no intense pressure on the land. There is a widespread feeling of disadvantage among the rural population and high levels of motivation to find a job that pays a regular wage.

> The migration experience and transition to urban life can be successful in both social and economic senses. However, for the majority such a movement is an invidious last resort; many have chosen not to participate, or have and then rejected it. There is also evidence that given viable economic alternatives at home, there is a strong tendency for migration not to occur (Riddell, 1978:243).

The inability, or unwillingness, of successive Malian governments

213

to reform their policies has produced conditions which continue to be generally unfavorable for commercial agricultural production and favorable for rural out-migration.

After the severe drought of 1973-74, government programs were strengthened to improve cultivation techniques, chemical fertilizers, better seed varieties, subsidies, credit, and marketing facilities. However, most of these programs were designed to increase the cultivated area and productivity of export crops. The result has been an increasing gap between the few growing export crops and the masses producing staple food crops. Gains in accumulating foreign exchange through crop exporting are likely to be eroded by Mali's increasing food imports (Berg, 1975).

The tendency of economic assistance to contemporary African states has been toward infrastructural investments that facilitate exploitation and exportation of natural resources and cash crops and that reinforce centralization of public infrastructure. These "policies" have reinforced social, political, cultural, and ideological conditions which in themselves have encouraged an exodus from rural areas (Adepoju, 1977:208; Gerald-Scheepers and Van Binsbergen, 1978:30; Lipton, 1977; Riddell, 1978:248).

The French colonial policies in Mali, and in West Africa as a whole, produced a semi-proletarian class; that is, a significant portion of the population was involved both as a migrant labor proletariat while remaining essentially a peasantry. Non-capitalist modes of production, based on the subsistence economy, continued to reproduce the cheap migrant labor force for coastal agricultural and industrial development, despite observable surpluses of labor in areas of commercial development (Cliffe, 1976:115; Foster-Carter, 1978:50; Meillassoux, 1970b:102-103; 1975) and labor shortages in areas of emigration (Gregory and Piche, 1978:45; Van de Walle, 1975:142; Gerald-Scheepers and Van Binsbergen, 1978). Malian policies have maintained the non-capitalist mode of production in a way that, it has been argued, permits the capitalist institutions to pay extremely low wages and to avoid assuming the associated social and economic costs of reproducing, socializing, and sustaining the labor force (Gunder Frank, 1979; Kahn, 1978; Meillassoux, 1975; 1978:327). An examination of regional patterns of migration, as assessed in the 1976 population census, reveals that regions closest to coastal areas of employment still exhibit the highest levels of migration (Fieloux, 1978: Table 8).

Mali's population was estimated at around 4 million in 1960, 5 million in 1970, and 6.5 million in 1980. It was growing at over 2.5 percent per year (U.N., 1976). The proportion urban in 1980 was estimated at about 15 percent compared to 10 percent two decades earlier. Density is low but the median age is young (18 years in 1980), and about 55 percent of the population is under 20 years of age. The crude death rate remains high at 23 per 1,000 and life expectancy for males at birth is 40 years. Crude birth rates have been close to 50 per 1000 for three decades and total fertility is estimated at 6.7 children per woman. More than 80 percent of Mali's population is illiterate. Only 20 percent of the school age population were enrolled in primary schools and only 2 percent were enrolled in secondary schools in 1970 (World Bank, 1976; Camara, 1971). Most of Mali's population are Moslem; about 30 percent are animists.

About 85 percent of the population lives in rural areas, most of them in villages of 100-600 people. Most of the rural population is engaged in agricultural activities which are primarily dependent on adequate rainfall. Irrigated agriculture is not common in Mali. Since much of northern Mali is desert, only 50 million of Mali's 124 million hectares are arable. Only 3.5 percent of the arable land is actively cultivated, while an additional 19 percent lies fallow. Most of the remaining arable land is used as pasture. In economic terms, Mali has few mineral resources. Agricultural production is generally characterized by the use of crude methods of production, though the government is introducing new methods of agricultural practices.

A very significant majority of Mali's adult male population is engaged in agricultural activities. Overall, more than 80 percent are engaged in farming. Farming/gardening and skilled craftsworking are the only important, definable, secondary or supplementary activities. While some non-agricultural primary and secondary activities occur, they do not characterize a large part of activities in any of the regions. While agriculture remains the predominant sector of economic activity, the relative share of Mali's Gross National Product attributed to the agricultural sector is declining slowly (World Bank, 1976). Some growth has occurred in both the industrial and service sectors. Particularly noteworthy is the huge size of the service sector. This is due to the large government bureaucracy inherited at the time of independence. The lack of significant industrial growth has forced the government into the role of "employer in the last resort." Real per capita economic growth declined during the early 1970s.

At the same time that general economic growth was slowing, consumer prices were increasing. Commensurate with this, the urban minimum wage nearly doubled. The balance of payments situation was improving until the drought of the early 1970s occurred. This drought exacerbated the already precarious financial situation in the Sahel. The Sahel's main agricultural exports--notably cotton and groundnuts--were almost everywhere either declining or rising very slowly beginning in the mid-1960s (Berg, 1975:53). The drought produced additional problems by diminishing agricultural and animal production and, therefore, diminishing exports. Increasing imports of foods and increasing transport and related charges for moving heavy food grains from distant ports resulted (Berg, 1975).

The basic theme concerning imbalances or inequalities in access to productive resources is also important for understanding migration in such ecologically sensitive areas as Mali. Because such regions do not have the resources and infrastructure to easily withstand such climatic shocks as droughts, nor the socioeconomic structures to diffuse, share, and soften their effects, catastrophes have implications for the population's welfare and distribution.

Observation of Malian society, then, indicates a situation favorable to out-migration. Most of Mali's population is located in the southern and western area serviced by the Niger and Senegal rivers, near Ghana, the Ivory Coast, and Senegal. Mali's rate of growth between 1965-75 averaged 1.8 percent annually, while its rate of natural increase was estimated at 2.4 percent annually (Zachariah and Conde, 1979:30). These rates suggest substantial emigration. Additionally, increasing rates of urban growth imply rural to urban migration to the capital city (Bamaka, with a population of 409,000 in 1976 and growing at 11 percent annually) and to other urban centers, as well as a small amount of traditional migration (trading, pastoralism, and fishing). The 1976 census registered approximately 400,000 absentees (international emigrants). An even larger number of Malian emigrants may be deduced when censuses of neighboring countries are examined. These migrants sent $44.6 million in recorded remittances during 1970-1974 (Zachariah and Conde, 1979:133). Migration from rural areas, both internal and international, represents a significant social process in present day Mali.

In most of rural Africa, it is the household, not the individual, that operates as a decision-making unit. Decisions concern its maintenance (economic organization) and continuous reproduction (social welfare) by generating and disposing of a collective income (Adepoju, 1977; Byerlee, 1974; Gugler, 1969: 143; Gugler and Flanagan, 1978: 118; Godelier, 1978: 118; Meillassoux, 1970; Wood, 1980: 10). Migration is a deliberate strategy undertaken by the household because the decision involved is major, despite the fact that it is not necessarily a "once and for all" decision. Migration may be seen as a flexible means for a household to realize its goals and interests (Abu-Lughod, 1975: 202; Gugler, 1968: 463; Wood, 1980: 13). Rather than assuming mechanical push-pull forces, it is important to consider the people who are the actors (DuToit, 1975). Of concern here are the demographic, social, and economic roles of persons in the household, as well as their personal characteristics and goals (Gugler and Flanagan, 1978: 55). This framework is simultaneously applied to understanding the non-mobility of rural populations (Adepoju, 1977; Gregory and Piche, 1979: 40).

The basic institution responsible for the production and distribution of food in village Mali is the lu, or family compound (Jones, 1970: 283; 1976: 279-280). It may be thought of as a household. It typically consists of a man, his wife or wives, their children, his sons' wives and offspring, and dependent older relatives. An alternative form of lu organization extends this household to include brothers of the male head of household, or compound, and the wives, children, and other dependents of these brothers. Descent is patrilineal and inheritance of the role of principal decision maker for the family compound is passed to the next oldest brother; only if no brothers are in the compound is inheritance passed to the oldest male in the next generation (Jones, 1970: 284; 1976: 280).

The major clans are too large for farming, eating, and tax purposes. Still, a lu ranges in size from over one hundred people to one small nuclear family. The average lu size is about ten persons and is becoming smaller in size over time (Jones, 1976: 279). Raynaut (1980: 16) associates the decline in the size of lu and the subdivision of the production unit into nuclear households with three interrelated social processes: the weakening of traditional power and decision-making structures; the growth of markets for land and labor; and the increasing individual control of agricultural plots by women and younger males. The security of the household is dependent on retaining the farming labor of the maximum number of members; to do so, the descent groups control two elements crucial to the "success" of an adult male: land and bridewealth (Lewis, 1979). In societies with a low level of technology, retaining control over available labor is more important than merely controlling land or the margin of agricultural surplus per se. Niang (1980) argues that the increasing individual control of fields reflects an increase in the number of decision makers in the household. By decentralizing decision-making, household heads increasingly allocate resources

217

rather than redistributing agricultural produce and its associated income. Increasing individual control of agricultural plots may be necessary in order to keep household members from migrating to obtain needed cash. The relationships among household wealth, individual control of fields, and migration will be one focus of our empirical analysis.

Some additional sources of farming labor need to be considered, particularly because of their implications for migration. While each able household member is required to work on the family's main plot (foroba), women and young men sometimes cultivate small individual plots (dyomforo), the produce of which is used for their subsistence/cash needs (Jones, 1976: 281). Women produce the ingredients for meal sauces and items for sale in local markets; young men grow crops for sale to buy things for their personal needs and wants (Jones, 1970: 284; Koenig, 1976:26). Whether or not one has an individual plot, villagers often join work groups ("associations"). The "ton", for young males, is the basic institution of labor "hiring-in" in Malian villages. Though women's work groups also exist, such work is usually paid cash.

The ability to employ a work group may greatly affect the land a household can cultivate, particularly in overcoming labor bottlenecks (Jones, 1976: 284). At the village level, however, the contribution of work groups is not significant. As a result, there is differentiation among lu such that some operate near the subsistence level and others are quite wealthy (Jones, 1970: 298; Ernst, 1976). There is a tendency to use the work group to replace labor "lost" through the migration of young men (Jones, 1976: 238, 246, 282-283), which in turn increases differentiation as some households gain control over the labor, and indirectly the production, of others (Lewis, 1979: 202, 281-283; Raynaut, 1980: 2, 9).

Analytic Themes

The complexity of out-migration from rural areas of underdeveloped countries focuses attention on appropriate decision-making units. Whether they be families, extended families, or other social groups, they are functional "households" in terms of production and consumption. Households have available to them certain resources, primarily the potential labor and skills of the members of the unit, plus access to land, existing capital, credit, technical knowledge, and social contacts. The problem faced by households is how best to allocate those social and economic resources among the various opportunities known and available to the unit. The observed patterns of labor allocation are assumed to represent the decision-making strategy of households. Decision-making strategies are assumed primarily to assure subsistence production (risk minimization and diversification) and secondarily to increase household wealth. In the West African context, these decisions frequently involve labor migration--of short or long duration--as part of the "solution" or "strategy". The socioeconomic circumstances and socio-demographic structure of a household define the existing structure of opportunities and constraints. These are the principal dimensions which will be examined as determinants of decision-making strategies involving labor allocation and migration.

Household patterns of labor allocation are viewed within the context of four general types of economic activity: on-farm productive work, rural non-agricultural cash-earning work, the exchange or hiring-out of labor to others' farms, and labor migration. It follows that the greater the shortage of material resources vis-a-vis the quantity and skills of a household's human resources, the more likely that some form of migration will be an appropriate response; non-agricultural work can be seen as an "intervening opportunity".

In determining who are the individual migrants, it is necessary to consider the complexity of the social organization of the farm household: land use rights, labor obligations, priorities for work in relation to family status, and roles in decision-making at the household level. In particular, the importance of marginality of an individual's status within the household affects participation in decision-making and in sharing the benefits of productive activity. Those in the most marginal social positions in the household, having fulfilled traditional labor obligations, would have the least to lose by migration. Among males, those who are younger and/or more distantly related to the household head are more likely to be migrants. Such individuals may migrate to obtain cash income for themselves and their family as well as to escape traditional onerous work exactions while still contributing to household material welfare.

Our central hypothesis is that both the socioeconomic circumstances (social class position) of a household and its socio-demographic structure significantly affect its pattern of labor allocation and migration. In particular, "resource-poor" households are expected to be labor sellers both locally and to other rural regions through seasonal and permanent migration. On the other hand, "resource-rich" households should be labor

219

buyers, particularly at the peak period. While it is possible to observe households with poor quality land, landlessness does not exist. Capital-based technology operates as an easily definable and differentiating "resource".

Across regions, several factors affect rural labor markets. Regions and villages which have conditions more favorable to successful agricultural production, in both agricultural and market terms, should have less need for migration. Drier northern areas have a more pronounced seasonal labor peak and a longer slack period for seasonal migration. It is important to examine the extent to which local dry season labor activities reduce the need for seasonal and permanent migration.

Research Design and Operationalization

The data used to assess household labor allocation strategies were collected in Mali in 1978 and 1979 by three agricultural economists (Stan Cohen, 1979, 1980, in the Dogon area; Allen Fleming, 1979, 1980, in the Kita area; and Tom Whitney, 1979, 1980, in the Sikasso area). Overall, the purpose of the Malian research project was to gain policy-relevant insights about the operation of farming systems. The three study areas represent different agro-ecological conditions and various degrees of involvement in commercial agricultural production. While some market sale of crops occurs in all three study areas, the Sikasso area has the highest degree of commercial orientation in agriculture; the Dogon area has the lowest. The two villages in each of the Dogon and Kita areas were selected to represent different ecological zones, reflecting principally variation in rainfall. The four villages in the Sikasso area were selected because of available flood plain land in each village; the villages vary with respect to the level of modernization of agricultural technology. Selected characteristics of these villages will be presented in a subsequent section (See Table 4.10).

The types of agricultural production vary greatly among the areas of study in Mali. In the Dogon area (Cohen, 1979,1980), two different zones were studied: the plateau and the Seno plain in the east. The Dogon farmers have an international market for their dry-season onion gardening. The second is of the millet/peanut economy, typical of the Kayes Region, in two villages near Kita (Fleming, 1979, 1980). Near Sikasso (Whitney, 1979, 1980) the focus is on how a flood plain fits into local agriculture. There, farmers produce millet, rice, citrus, bananas, and Irish and sweet potatoes; their market may be in Mali, in

Upper Volta, or the Ivory Coast.

Data were initially collected by interviewing the male heads of households about the characteristics and economic activities of all household members; when the male head of household could not be interviewed, the eldest male in the household was interviewed. The initial demographic census was used to derive the sample of households which were intensively studied. Households were selected through quota sampling with the intention of sufficiently representing variation in family size (household structure) and/or different degrees of modernization of household agricultural production involving the use of relatively modern equipment and modern inputs. In the Kita area, modernization of agricultural production was the criterion employed; in the Dogon area, family size was used for this purpose (because there was so little evidence of modern equipment usage in the Dogon villages studied); in the Sikasso area, both sets of criteria were used to select the sample of households.

There were 148 sample households with a total population of 1,965. Approximately 10 percent of the people were classified as migrants. In the villages in the Dogon region, data were recorded from October 1979 to September 1980. Comparable dates in the Kita region were May 1978 to February 1979. In villages in the Sikasso region, censuses were taken in September 1978 to September 1979. Since the rainy season generally extends from September to January, minor variations in the timing of data collection are not expected to have produced any systematic bias regarding the classification of household members as either migrants or residents. In contrast to most migration studies which are based on a single visit to a rural study population, these data encompass a year's agricultural cycle.

The sample households were visited twice weekly; information was gathered about each day's activities. This data gathering procedure was undertaken to provide detailed and reliable measures of farm labor times, non-farm work (some of which is cash-earning but most of which involves household maintenance activities), and household revenues and expenditues.[1]

----

[1] Data from the revenue and expenditure questionnaires are known to be less reliable and unpredictably underestimated (Koenig, 1979) and were not available for this study. Norman

The data for agricultural and non-agricultural labor activities will be used to assess seasonal labor migration of household members, since the information on migration in the "Demographic Census" only measured the duration of absence of those who were migrants at the time of census. It should be noted, however, that these data will permit assessment of seasonal migration during the agricultural season but will be of limited value for analysis of migration during the dry season, since the continuous data gathering was normally terminated soon after harvest. To the extent that young men migrate after the weeding period and before threshing, it may be possible to identify those who can be expected to be away for a period of approximately six months until the next agricultural season begins.

Patterns of labor allocation of those defined as part of the household, rather than migration per se, was the focus of the survey. The out-migration of entire households prior to the time of the survey cannot be studied in the present research, since such households were not in the sampling frame. A different type of survey methodology is required to obtain information about such migrants (Goldstein and Goldstein, 1981). The goal of this research is to determine whether criteria of stratification yield significant information about various household strategies of labor allocation, in general, and about migration, in particular. Our secondary analysis of these data focuses on the analytic study of relationships, rather than a statistical description of a study (sample) population in relation to Mali's population as a whole.

Village or community level data can be used to assess the nature and extent to which characteristics of the community have independent effects on individual and household behavior (Freedman, 1974). One aspect of these effects is the manner by which households compare their own socioeconomic status and behavior to those of households in other social classes. Moreover, an increased awareness of a new range of possibilities or alternatives affects household decision-making and therefore behavior, particularly migration.

A number of village level variables will be examined for their effects on aggregate patterns of migration as well as their influence on group- or class-specific patterns of migration.

(1977) and Kearl (1976) discuss some of the problems involved in collecting useful revenue and expenditure data in studies of rural populations.

However, given the small number of villages, we shall be able to assess each of these factors separately but not simultaneously. Two types of village level variables are available for this analysis: measures which characterize the structural position of the village and measures derived from aggregates of individual characteristics. Structural measures at the village level include distance to the nearest market center where the produce of the local area can be sold regularly and employment obtained, and the available modes of transport to larger population centers. Aggregate measures at the village level include: 1) the level of modernization of agricultural technology; 2) the extent to which villagers are engaged in the commercial sale of agricultural produce; 3) inequality of landholdings; and 4) the importance of off-farm employment. These four variables, in addition to the transportation variables, permit an analysis of village level characteristics on the structure of village economic activities, kinship (mutual-aid), and exchange-labor arrangements, and, in particular, on migration. To the extent that ethnic groups have independent effects on migration not explained by these socioeconomic factors, their influence will also be assessed.

These village level structural factors will also be used to examine their influence as contextual reference points for household strategies involving labor allocation. These structural factors affect the nature and availability of local economic opportunities, with potential differences existing for households in each socioeconomic class. Therefore, the analysis of household labor allocation and migration patterns will include not only socioeconomic class but also structural characteristics and the interaction between them as important explanatory factors.

At the individual level of analysis a number of factors will be analyzed for their independent and joint influence on a person's migration status. These include: sex, age, relation to household head, education, ethnic group, field "rights", village, and region. At the household level, these include: the socioeconomic position of the household (comprised of indices of fields and equipment), household size, household socio-demographic structure, village, and region.

Some key concepts require operationalization before we proceed with the analysis.

Household. A household is defined as a residential unit of kin and non-kin who share food communally and spend some time working on common fields. This includes those related to the head of household who have lived in the household but are currently

223

migrants. Household heads defined the membership of the household. To the extent possible, these were checked against local tax lists. This definition included those who ate together and worked together on common fields (though family members may spend time working on individual fields, as well). In essence, a household is characterized by a set of rights and obligations among members, primarily regarding the common production and sharing in a portion of the household's food.

Absent persons were regarded as part of the immediate household if they were so regarded by the household head (Caldwell, 1969:13). It can be assumed that this includes those born to household heads, those reared by them in the household, and those who usually lived there but were temporarily absent at the time of the survey. Female migrants in the study population were almost exclusively gone for marriage-related reasons. As these were not reported consistently, and not likely to contribute to the household's welfare, they were exclued from the household's defined population.

A question may be raised whether 'nuclear households' split off from an extended family. In villages where extended families are the norm, people are likely to include migrants, while villages where nuclear families are the norm are less likely to do so (Connell et al., 1976: 162). This is important in the context of Mali, particularly in distinguishing the Dogon (principally nuclear-type households) from the Kita and Sikasso regions. Caldwell (1969: 76) concludes that married men are almost as likely as single males to plan long-term migration; that is, they would take the whole family for a long or indefinite period. Connell et al. (1976: 79) found that nuclear families moved permanently to plantations or to cities (as absentee landlords) to have access to better education for their children, and seasonally, as agricultural laboring households. It seems more likely that such households would either be represented in the household demographic census or, in the case of the absentee landlords, leave no relatives behind. While this problem of defining membership in households does not appear very serious, it will be taken into account when comparing the Dogon, Kita, and Sikasso regions.

Household Status. Relationships to the head of household among males were categorized as head of household, elder males (fathers or brothers), brothers of cousins, sons, other relatives, and non-relatives.

Migration is defined as residence outside of one's village for a minimum period of one month. Migration destinations are considered cities in Mali, rural areas in Mali, or outside Mali. Reasons attributed to absence are work (either alone or with dependents of one's immediate family), attending school, moving to accompany a working adult male migrant, and a general category of "other" reasons.

Labor Allocation is operationalized from two sources of data: the demographic census and the recording of labor activities over the course of the agricultural year. Categories for these two variables are as follows: farming and primary or domestic activities (vegetable gardening, herding of livestock, fishing, or household maintenance), farming and agricultural labor (on others' farms), farming and non-agricultural cash-earning activities, some rural activities combined with short-term labor migration (labor migration of one year or less), and long-term labor migration (labor migration of more than one year, or less than one year but no activities recorded during the year). It should be noted that this definition differs from the conventional approach which distinguishes seasonal (less than one year), short-term (2-5 years), and long-term or permanent (more than 5 years) types of labor migration (Byerlee, 1974).

Age Groups. The adult population is classified into five age groups: 14-19 years, 20-24 years, 25-34 years, 35-44 years, and 45 years and over.

Education. It is possible to identify two groups with different experiences in formal education; those with at least a primary level education and those with less or no formal schooling.

Ethnic Groups. Five principal ethnic groups in Mali are the Bambara, the Malinke, the Fulani-Peuhl, the Dogon, and the Senoufo.

Household Demographic Aspects. The demographic aspects of a household are assessed by several different criteria: 1) "household size", i.e., the total number of persons listed as household members. 2) "Household socio-demographic structure", which consists of the following measures: the household age-depenedency ratio (defined as the ratio of the number of children and the number of inactive adult members to the number of active adult members), the ratio of consumption/production person-units, the type of household structure (whether or not one or more

225

brothers of the household head live in the household), the educational level, and the ethnic group of the household head.

Social Class Position. The social class position of a household is measured by the households' fields (number of cash crop fields per adult), the modern agricultural equipment owned by the household, and the use of modern inputs (chemical fertilizers).

Migration Patterns: An Overview

About one-fourth of the adult male population of Mali were migrants, and four-fifths of these were labor migrants (Table 4.1). Most migration was for work-related reasons; thus, focusing on labor migration captures most of the out-migration from villages. Migration destinations were more likely to be in Mali than outside, although 44 percent were to areas outside the country. Within Mali, urban destinations were only slightly more common than rural ones. Given the objective of examining the context of labor migration from villages, we will not examine the various destinations of the migrants. More than half of the migrants had been absent for more than one year.

Two sources of information were available to operationalize the broad concept of labor allocation. Both were derived from data on occupations and migration. The first was based on the data contained in the demographic census; the second was based on the recording of labor activities over the course of the agricultural year. There are few differences between these data sources. We will present data using only the labor time observation materials since they had more details on work activities; these data were verified, in part, by cross-checking with the demographic census. From these data it is clear that most adult males are involved in farming and domestic activities, contributing to the basic maintenance of the household. This is followed by migration for more than one year duration, farming and agricultural cash-earning activities, and some rural work and labor mobility. For brevity, we shall refer to the combination of some rural work and labor mobility as "short-term migration." The combination of farming and non-agricultural cash-earning activities will be referred to as "non-agricultural work", though farming is generally the major activity.

Our focus is on the patterns of labor allocation and migration among adult males. Data not shown in tabular form indicate that males have much higher levels of total and labor

TABLE 4.1

PERCENT DISTRIBUTION OF DIFFERENT CATEGORIES OF MIGRATION VARIABLES
(FOR MIGRANTS ONLY) AND LABOR ALLOCATION VARIABLES, BY HOUSEHOLD
STATUS, ADULT MALES

		Total	House-hold Head	Brother or Cousin	Son	Other Rela-tives	Non-Rela-tives	F-ratio
TOTAL POPULATION	N=	584	148	117	201	89	25	
% migrants		23.6	1.4	27.4	28.4	47.2	20.0	20.15*
% labor migrants		18.9	1.4	24.8	21.4	36.0	16.0	13.59*
MIGRANTS ONLY, BY PERCENT	N=	138		33	57	42	5	
REASON ABSENT								
Work, move alone		61.6		50.0	66.7	59.5		1.12
Work, bring family		18.1		40.6	8.8	16.7		4.33*
Attend school		9.4			12.3	14.3		1.45
Other		8.0		9.4	12.3	2.4		.97
Follow male worker		2.9				7.1		2.77*
PLACE ABSENT								
City in Mali		28.3		15.6	28.1	35.7		1.76
Rural Mali		22.5		18.8	29.8	19.0		1.08
Outside Mali		44.2		56.3	36.8	42.9		1.44
Unknown		5.1		9.4	5.3	2.4		.55
TIME ABSENT								
1-12 months		39.1		21.9	49.1	33.3		2.76*
1-2 years		14.5		9.4	15.8	16.7		.94
2-5 years		14.5		25.0	12.3	9.5		1.09
5-10 years		19.6		21.9	8.8	35.7		3.46*
10+ years		7.2		15.6	8.8			1.88
Unknown		5.1		6.3	5.3	4.8		.12
LABOR ALLOCATION, BY PERCENT (FROM LABOR TIME OBSERVATION) N=		584	148	117	201	89	25	
Farming & Domestic Activities (Household maintenance)		53.8	56.1	53.0	56.2	41.6	72.0	2.19*
Farming & Agricultural Labor (On others' farms)		13.0	16.9	17.1	10.4	9.0	4.0	1.69
Farming & Non-agricultural Cash-earning activities		5.3	18.2	0.9	0.5	2.2		14.84*
Some rural work & migration (One year or less)		7.0	3.4	2.6	13.4	6.7	0.0	4.40*
Long-term Migration (More than one year)		14.0	0.7	22.2	11.9	30.3	16.0	10.69*
None recorded		6.8	4.7	4.3	7.5	10.1	8.0	3.17*

* Significant at .05 level.

227

migration than females. Only about one percent of adult females are labor migrants and most move to accompany a male labor migrant. Most adult females do not have any labor activities recorded in the demographic census, but the labor observation data show that labor allocation is mainly in farming and domestic activities.

The adult male population is predominantely young, uneducated, without individual field rights, and comes from a variety of ethnic groups and regions of the country. How do these characteristics relate to labor allocation and migration? How much can these factors account for the level of short and long term migration? These are the questions we address in the next section.

Household Status

Attention turns first to the relationship between household status and migration rates and the reasons for movement of the various categories of household members (Table 4.1). Statistically significant differences exist for both the total and work-related migration rates among the various groups. The highest level (47 percent) of migration is observed for other relatives (those less directly related to household heads than sons and brothers or cousins). Lower, yet significant, rates of migration (approximately 28 percent) are observed for sons and brothers or cousins. A somewhat lower rate of migration is observed among the small number of non-relatives. About three-fourths of migrants in this group moved to work; some also migrated to attend school.

Short-term migration (duration of less than one year) is most common among non-relatives. About one-half of sons, but only about one-third of other relatives and one-fifth of brothers or cousins, are short-term migrants. Short-term migration appears as a means of compensating for an insecure long-term position vis-a-vis agricultural production in the household. Alternatively, those in insecure positions may be more likely to be omitted as household members when they are long-term migrants. Therefore, migration in these groups may be recorded as predominantly short-term in nature, i.e., they may have less to gain by retaining strong ties to the household. The almost negligible rates of migration observed among household heads and elder males reinforce the expectation that the role of household heads and elder males in managing agricultural and non-agricultural resources and activities is crucial year round and effectively precludes migration.

Migration can now be viewed within the broader context of labor allocation. The relative allocation to each of the categories of laboring activity varies significantly among those with different relations to head of household. The only exceptions to this are those engaged in farming and agricultural labor (i.e., there are no statistically significant differences for participation rates in agricultural labor on others' farms). Household heads are primarily engaged in farming and domestic activities. Farming combined with non-agricultural cash-earning activities represents another important type of labor allocation among household heads as does farming and agricultural labor (on others's farm). Among brothers or cousins, the most important types of labor allocation are farming combined with either domestic activities or labor migration for more than one year ("long-term migration"); farming and agricultural labor is also important. Among sons, farming and either domestic activities or agricultural labor are important, as was the case for brothers or cousins. Noteworthy, though, is the fact that short- and long-term migration are significant and occur with relatively similar frequency. When other relatives are considered, the important types of labor allocation are the same as for sons. However, long-term migration is more frequently observed for other relatives than for any other group. Farming and domestic activities stand out as the most frequently observed type of labor allocation for non-relatives; long-term migration is the only other significant type of labor allocation.

In sum, household heads (and elder males) have very low migration rates as expected by their positions in the management of domestic economic activities and social relations. While brothers or cousins are engaged principally in farming and domestic activities, they also have a high rate of long-term migration. This indicates a limit to effectively utilizing their labor time and skills (considered from either an individual or a household perspective) in the predominantly agricultural domestic economy; in a related manner; it indicates the need/ability to diversify sources of income for the household and its constituent members. In other words, households with a complex socio-demographic structure, denoted by the presence of brothers or cousins, appear to exist for reasons other than higher productivity in agriculture. The labor allocation of sons is similar to brothers or cousins, except that short-term migration is more important. Other relatives had the highest migration rate, probably because they were not assured of a long-range position in the domestic economy; they would likely remain in a subordinate position as laborers. Most non-relatives are in household maintenance activities while their moderate rate of short-term migration is probably due to the limitations of economic security which they confront in the domestic economy. Migrants in this group may be less likely to be recorded as household members.

Age

Migration rates show a curvilinear relationship with age at the time of the survey (Table 4.2).[2] Rates of out-migration are moderately high for those aged 14-19, highest for those aged 20-24, and then decline linearly for those over 25 years of age. The vast majority of migrants of all ages moved to work. Moving to attend school is only important for those aged 14-19; yet, almost half of this age group moved for work-related reasons. Those aged 20 and over are more likely to have moved to places outside Mali than within Mali. The tendency for migration to be short-term (i.e., less than one year) decreases with age. There is a tendency for the entire distribution of duration of absence to shift in favor of longer times absent with increasing age.

The age pattern of migration coincides with probable variations in social and economic roles associated with age. Those aged 14-19 are less likely than adults to migrate because their labor is still valuable to the household directly in agricultural activities and they are not yet suited for most types of employment in the wage labor market. Males in the early adult years (20-24) are the most likely to migrate. Most probably are not yet married.[3] Migration toward the cash economy may be an indication of their ability to profitably engage in cash-earning

----

[2] The approximate ages at the time of migration do not indicate a very narrow set of ages during which most current migration occurs.

[3] While marital status of all adult males was not recorded in the survey, there is information on whether migrants were accompanied by a wife and/or children. Of those aged 20-24 who migrated to work, 93 percent were not accompanied by a wife and/or children. Of those aged 25-34 who migrated to work, 78 percent were not accompanied by a wife and/or children. The analogous proportion for those aged 35-44 is only 39 percent.

TABLE 4.2

PERCENT DISTRIBUTION OF DIFFERENT CATEGORIES OF MIGRATION VARIABLES
(FOR MIGRANTS ONLY) AND LABOR ALLOCATION VARIABLES, BY CURRENT AGE,
ADULT MALES

		14-19 years	20-24 years	25-34 years	35-44 years	45+ years	F-ratio
TOTAL POPULATION	N=	153	80	142	79	130	
% migrants		27.5	36.2	30.3	24.1	3.8	10.64*
% labor migrants		13.1	33.8	28.1	22.8	3.8	11.50
MIGRANTS ONLY, BY PERCENT	N=	42	29	43	19	5	
REASON ABSENT							
Work, move alone		45.2	86.2	72.1	36.8		5.34*
Work, bring family		2.4	6.9	20.9	57.9		9.87*
Attend school		28.6	3.4				7.80*
Other		16.7		7.0	5.3		1.92
Follow male worker		7.1	3.4				1.18
PLACE ABSENT							
City in Mali		33.4	20.6	32.6	21.0		.59
Rural Mali		38.1	24.1	9.3	15.8		2.80*
Outside Mali		21.4	55.1	51.1	57.9		3.47*
Unknown		7.1		7.0	5.3		.62
TIME ABSENT							
1-12 months		57.1	48.3	27.9	10.5		4.22*
1-2 years		11.9	17.2	18.6	10.5		.51
2-5 years		11.9	13.8	16.3	15.8		.12
5-10 years		11.9	20.7	23.3	26.3		.62
10+ years				7.0	31.6		6.82*
Unknown		7.1		7.0	5.3		.62
LABOR ALLOCATION, BY PERCENT (FROM LABOR TIME OBSERVATION) N=		153	80	142	79	130	
Farming & domestic activities (Household maintenance)		57.5	50.0	53.5	50.6	53.8	.41
Farming & Agricultural Labor (On others' farms)		12.4	10.0	13.4	15.2	13.8	.28
Farming & non-agricultural Cash-earning activities				2.1	5.1	18.5	16.79*
Some rural work & migration (One Year or Less)		10.5	16.3	4.2	5.1	1.5	5.50*
Long-term Migration (More than one year)		5.9	21.3	24.6	21.5	3.1	11.14*
None recorded		13.7	2.5	2.1	2.5	9.2	5.71*

* Significant at .05 level.

economic activities. They may be attempting to earn capital needed by the household and for their eventual return to the rural economy to establish their own families and domestic economics. They may "play" the wage labor market to decide whether it is more lucrative to remain in the place of migration or to return to the village of origin. Older adult males (those aged 25-44) are more likely to be married and integrated into domestic agricultural and non-agricultural production. Few of those aged 45 and over were migrants, reflecting their central roles in supervision of the domestic economy. Unfortunately, nothing is known about their previous migration history during earlier stages of the family life cycle. Because data are not available on the migrants' long-term intentions, it is not possible to draw further implications at this point.[4]

Farming and domestic activities and long-term migration are the most important types of labor allocation for those aged 20-44. For those aged 14-19, short-term migration is more important than long-term migration. For those aged 45 and over, farming and domestic activities and non-agricultural cash-earning activities are the most important types of labor allocation; very little migration, either short- or long-term, is observed. As age increases, there is a decreasing level of short-term migration and an increasing level of non-agricultural cash-earning activities. Since the data are cross-sectional, and the differential proportions

----

[4] One possible source of bias in dealing with age data is that those in the oldest age group, i.e., those aged 45 years and over, would least likely be reported as household members if they had migrated for long periods. However, of the few migrants aged 45 and over, most are, in fact, outside the country and have been gone 5 years or more. Therefore, the possible age-related omission bias does not appear to exist here. Another possible source of bias in age reporting is a tendency to differentially inflate the reported age of young male migrants relative to non-migrants. The principal cause of concern here is the reporting of ages 20-24, or differential "age-heaping" of migrants at age 20. An examination of the age structure of adult male migrants and non-migrants by single years of age shows that no serious differential age-heaping occurs for either migrants or non-migrants specifically at ages 20 and 25 or, more generally, for the age groups 14-19 and 20-24.

are not very large, this result cannot be interpreted unambiguously to mean that men replace short-term migration with local non-agricultural cash-earning activities; still, there is plausibility to such an interpretation.

Education

Education appears to be significantly related to migration (Table 4.3). Those with at least a primary level education have a much higher migration rate than those with less or no formal schooling. However, when only work-related migration is considered, the difference between migration rates by educational level is greatly reduced and is not statistically significant. This is because over 40 percent of those with formal schooling moved to continue their education. Further, they were more likely to move inside Mali, and to cities in particular. Education is not strongly related to patterns of labor allocation except for its influence on migration. Among those with at least a primary level education, long-term migration occurs more frequently and short-term migration occurs less frequently.

Ethnic Groups

Migration rates among adult males vary by ethnic group (Table 4.4). The overall rates can be considered in two groups: those with migration rates of 30-35 percent and those with much lower rates. In the first group are the Senoufo, the Bambara, the Fulani, and the category labeled "other". In the second group are the Malinke and the Dogon. The distinction between these two sets of migration rates remains when only work-related migration is considered. Moving to attend school is important only for the Bambara and Fulani. Given the supposed similarities in familial structure among the Bambara, Senoufo, and Malinke, the divergence in the migration rate for the Malinke appears, at first, confusing. We shall subsequently examine region of the country and familial structure (individuals' relations to household heads) for the various ethnic groups to clarify these patterns. Destinations outside Mali are significantly preferred by the Dogon, the Senoufo, and those in the "other" category. For migrants with destinations inside Mali, the Bambara, Senoufo, and "others" favor urban destinations; the Dogon favor rural areas when they migrate but remain in Mali. The Malinke, Senoufo, and "others" have a the relatively low percentage of migrants who have been absent for one year or less.

TABLE 4.3

PERCENT DISTRIBUTION OF DIFFERENT CATEGORIES OF
MIGRATION VARIABLES (FOR MIGRANTS ONLY) AND
LABOR ALLOCATION VARIABLES, BY EDUCATION, ADULT MALES

	NO FORMAL SCHOOL	PRIMARY OR MORE EDUC.	F-ratio
TOTAL POPULATION N =	534	50	
% migrants	21.7	48.0	18.50*
% labor migrants	18.1	26.0	1.84
MIGRANTS ONLY, BY PERCENT N =	116	24	
REASON ABSENT			
Work, move alone	66.7	37.5	7.41*
Work, bring family	18.4	16.7	.04
Attend school	2.6	41.7	46.93*
Other	9.7		2.53
Follow male worker	2.6	4.2	.16
PLACE ABSENT			
City in Mali	19.3	70.8	31.53*
Rural Mali	23.7	16.7	.56
Outside Mali	51.8	8.3	16.78*
Unknown	5.3	4.2	.05
TIME ABSENT			
1-12 months	34.2	62.5	6.90*
1-2 years	14.0	16.7	.11
2-5 years	14.9	12.5	.09
5-10 years	22.8	4.2	4.46*
10+ years	7.9	4.2	.41
Unknown	6.1		1.55
LABOR ALLOCATION, BY PERCENT (FROM LABOR TIME OBSERVATION) N =	534	50	
Farming & domestic activities (Household maintenance)	55.2	38.0	5.50*
Farming & agricultural labor (On others' farms)	13.1	12.0	.05
Farming & non-agricultural cash-earning activities	5.4	4.0	.19
Some rural work & migration (One year or less)	7.1	6.0	.09
Long-term migration (More than one year)	13.5	20.0	1.61
None recorded	5.6	20.0	15.16*

* Significant at .05 level.

TABLE 4.4

PERCENT DISTRIBUTION OF DIFFERENT CATEGORIES OF MIGRATION VARIABLES
(FOR MIGRANTS ONLY) AND LABOR ALLOCATION VARIABLES, BY ETHNIC GROUP,
ADULT MALES

		MA-LINKE	BAM-BARA	FULANI-PEUHL	DO-GON	SE-NOUFO	OTHERS	F-ratio
TOTAL POPULATION	N=	102	90	155	138	53	46	
% migrants		15.7	31.1	31.0	10.1	34.0	30.4*	6.09*
% labor migrants		14.7	20.0	23.9	9.4	28.3	26.0	3.36*
MIGRANTS ONLY, BY PERCENT	N=	16	28	48	14	18	14	
REASON ABSENT								
Work, move alone		93.8	39.3	60.4	92.9	61.1	42.9	4.68*
Work, bring family			25.0	16.7		22.2	42.9	2.88*
Attend school			17.9	14.6			7.1	1.82
Other		6.3	14.3	6.3	7.1	5.6	7.1	.38
Follow male worker			3.6	2.1		11.1		1.16
PLACE ABSENT								
City in Mali		31.3	42.9	27.1	14.3	22.2	21.4	1.00
Rural Mali		37.5	17.9	31.3	28.6	5.6		2.48*
Outside Mali		31.3	32.1	35.5	57.1	66.7	71.4	2.77*
Unknown			7.1	6.3		5.6	7.1	.41
TIME ABSENT								
1-12 months		25.0	39.3	43.8	85.7	22.2	14.3	4.56*
1-2 years		31.3	14.3	18.8	7.1		7.1	1.76
2-5 years		18.8	17.9	12.5	7.1	11.1	21.4	.38
5-10 years		18.8	10.7	16.7		61.1	14.3	5.86*
10+ years		6.3	7.1	4.2			35.7	4.50*
Unknown			10.7	4.2		5.6	7.1	.72
LABOR ALLOCATION, BY PERCENT (FROM LABOR TIME OBSERVATION)	N=	102	90	155	138	53	46	
Farming & Domestic Activities (Household Maintenance)		67.6	46.7	39.4	73.2	34.0	50.0	11.36*
Farming & Agricultural labor (on others' farms)		6.9	18.9	20.6	0.0	28.3	10.9	9.86*
Farming & non-agricultural cash-earning activities		6.9	4.4	3.2	9.4	0.0	4.3	1.94
Some rural work & migration (One year or less)		2.0	1.1	7.7	15.9	3.8	4.3	5.63*
Long-term Migration (More than one year)		12.7	18.9	16.8	0.7	26.4	23.9	7.05*
None recorded		3.9	10.0	12.3	0.7	7.5	6.5	3.69*

* Significant at .05 level.

When patterns of labor allocation are considered for the various ethnic groups, significant differences exist for nearly all types, except short-term migration. The principal types of labor allocation for the Malinke are farming and domestic activities and long-term migration; they are not oriented to non-agricultural cash-earning activities or short-term migration. The Bambara are engaged in farming and domestic activities with some long-term migration; only agricultural labor is additionally important. The Fulani are principally involved in farming and domestic activities with some short- and long-term migration; again, only agricultural labor is of additional importance. Among the Dogon, farming and domestic activities is the most important type of labor allocation. Short-term migration and non-agricultural cash-earning activities are of some importance in labor allocation for the Dogon. The lack of long-term migration among the Dogon may be related to their nuclear household formation which substitutes for migration. Among the Senoufo, farming and domestic activities is the most important type of labor allocation; long-term migration and agricultural labor are also very important. In the group labeled "others", farming and domestic activities and long-term migration are the most important types of labor allocation.

In sum, some significant differences in total and work-related migration rates are observed among ethnic groups. Our original expectation was that ethnic differences in migration and labor allocation patterns could be explained by considering other factors. A multivariate analysis of these differences helps explain the extent to which underlying differences in familial structure, age structure, education, and region contribute to the observed differentials in migration rates among ethnic groups.

Caste and Field Rights

Caste differentials in migration exist, particularly between freeman and blacksmiths. Over 90 percent of the sample were in the former caste, so details are not presented in tabular form. Those in the blacksmith caste have higher migration rates, are more likely to move for education-related reasons, and are much more likely to move within Mali, favoring urban destinations. Those in the blacksmith caste are much less involved in farming and domestic activities and more involved in farming and agricultural labor than those in the freeman caste. Blacksmiths seem to be more characterized by long-term migration than freemen, but the differences are not statistically significant. In all, these findings indicate the ability or need to engage in direct cash-earning activities in all locations.

The association between the number of fields cultivated and migration is very clear: those with no fields have a much higher rate of migration. Data not shown in tabular form show that among those with no fields, 37 percent were migrants compared to 2 percent among those with one or more fields. Those with no fields are much more likely to be long-term migrants, while those with some fields are likely to combine farming with agricultural labor or cash-earning activities.

Region

Region of the country significantly affects migration. For both total migration and for work-related reasons, the Sikasso area has the highest rates; the Dogon area has the lowest rates, and the migration rates for the Kita area are near the overall average (Table 4.5). The process of forming small nuclear households among the Dogon may again help explain their observed low migration rates. Migration to attend school is most common in the Kita area; the Sikasso and Dogon areas are characterized by little or no migration of this type. Migration destinations outside Mali are heavily favored in the Sikasso area and nearly as much in the Dogon area. Those in the Kita area do not have easy access to the expanding labor market in the Ivory Coast and Upper Volta as those in the Sikasso and Dogon areas. Their migration destinations are mostly within Mali and more likely to be cities than rural areas. Differences in duration of absence also show regional patterns. Migrants from the Sikasso area are the most likely to be absent for more than one year and those from the Dogon area are the most likely to be absent for one year or less; again, the Kita area is near the average, with about half of its migrants absent for one year or less.

Region also affects patterns of labor allocation. Those in the Dogon area are predominantly engaged in farming and domestic activities. There is also some non-agricultural cash-earning activities and short-term migration. In the Kita area, fewer are involved in farming and domestic activities than in the Dogon area and there are substantially higher rates of long-term migration. The Sikasso area is distinctive by the much higher rates of long-term migration. Almost all statistically significant differences obtained among regions are also found among villages. Significant inter-regional and inter-village differences exist among adult males in terms of relation to head of household, education, ethnic group, caste, and field rights (for the entire population and for non-

TABLE 4.5

PERCENT DISTRIBUTION OF DIFFERENT CATEGORIES OF MIGRATION VARIABLES
(FOR MIGRANTS ONLY) AND LABOR ALLOCATION VARIABLES, BY REGION,
ADULT MALES

		DOGON	KITA	SIKASSO	F-ratio (Region)	F-ratio (Village)
TOTAL POPULATION	N=	143	269	172		
% migrants		9.8	24.5	33.7	13.00*	5.09*
% labor migrants		9.1	18.2	27.9	9.35*	3.45*
MIGRANTS ONLY, BY PERCENT	N=	14	66	58		
REASON ABSENT						
Work, move alone		92.9	65.2	50.0	4.95*	2.37*
Work, bring family			9.1	32.8	8.30*	2.53*
Attend school			16.7	3.4	4.12*	2.15*
Other		7.1	6.1	10.3	.39	.51
Follow male worker			3.0	3.4	.24	.80
PLACE ABSENT						
City in Mali		14.3	43.9	13.8	8.44*	3.33*
Rural Mali		28.6	34.8	6.9	7.73*	2.63*
Outside Mali		57.1	18.2	70.7	23.44*	7.96*
Unknown			3.0	8.6	1.42	.75
TIME ABSENT						
1-12 months		85.7	51.5	13.8	20.91*	9.02*
1-2 years		7.1	19.7	10.3	1.43	1.14
2-5 years		7.1	15.2	15.5	.34	1.60
5-10 years			7.6	37.9	12.71*	5.69*
10+ years			4.5	12.1	1.92	1.84
Unknown			1.5	10.3	2.98*	.94
LABOR ALLOCATION, BY PERCENT (FROM LABOR TIME OBSERVATION)	N=	143	269	172		
Farming & domestic activities (Household maintenance)		73.4	48.3	45.9	15.56*	11.73*
Farming & agricultural labor (On others' farms)		0.0	17.1	17.4	14.82*	8.04*
Farming & non-agricultural cash-earning activities		9.8	5.9	0.6	6.92*	3.39*
Some rural work & migration (One year or less)		15.4	5.6	2.3	11.37	7.40*
Long-term Migration (More than one year)		0.7	12.6	27.3	25.24*	7.77*
None recorded		0.7	10.4	6.4	7.07*	3.15*

* Significant at .05 level.

migrants in particular). The significance of these differences will be discussed in the context of multivariate analyses in which region and village are used as independent, control, and interaction factors with respect to the other variables.

Multivariate Analysis: Individual Level Characteristics

In order to examine the simultaneous influence of age, household status, education, ethnic group, and caste on migration patterns, a multivariate analysis was carried out. This permits an assessment of the relationship between a particular independent variable and each dependent variable. The independent variable may be considered separately, while controlling for the influence of another independent variable, or considered for its interaction with another independent variable. The F-Ratio from the analysis of variance indicates how well the values of the dependent variable can be understood by knowing the category of the independent variable. The R-squared value indicates the proportion of the observed variance in the depenedent variable that is explained by considering the set of independent and control variables.

Household status is significantly related to patterns of labor migration, as can be seen in Table 4.6. This is true for short-term and long-term labor migration. For long-term labor migration, age is not an important factor when it is considered first (as a covariate in the analysis of variance) and household status is therefore assessed when controlling for the effects of age. It is important to recall that age was not a significant predictor of long-term labor migration. The effects of age as a control factor are significant when age is considered simultaneously with household status; in this case, the effects of each are assessed while controlling for the other. Education is not a significant factor in understanding patterns of long-term labor migration when the effects of age are first considered nor is education significant as a control variable with household status.

Household status is significantly related to patterns of short-term labor migration. Age, as a control factor, is generally important when considered first (as a covariate in ANOVA). Both household status and age are moderately significant when considered simultaneously. Education, however, is not significantly related to patterns of short-term labor migration.

Total labor migration represents a composite of short-term and long-term labor migration. Household status is always

Table 4.6

THE EFFECTS OF HOUSEHOLD STATUS ON SHORT-TERM, LONG-TERM AND TOTAL LABOR MIGRATION CONTROLLING FOR THE EFFECTS OF AGE AND EDUCATION (ANOVA)

VARIABLES	SHORT-TERM			LONG-TERM			TOTAL		
	F-Ratio	R^2	Overall F-Ratio	F-ratio	R^2	Overall F-Ratio	F-ratio	R^2	Overall F-ratio
Household Status	2.89*	.04	5.03*	19.32*	.12	15.47*	15.80*	.11	13.57*
(c) Age	13.58*			.04			4.63*		
Household Status	2.91*	.06	2.04*	11.94*	.14	4.96*	9.94*	.13	4.44*
Age	2.89*			9.75*			7.62*		
Interaction	.83			1.03			.76		
Education	1.74	.03	7.58*	1.54	.00	.78	.67	.01	2.43
(c) Age	13.42*			.03			4.20*		
Household Status	5.70*	.04	4.58*	12.83*	.09	10.60*	13.14*	.09	10.90*
(c) Education	.10			1.67			1.91		
Household Status	3.04*	.05	3.26*	19.65*	.12	8.33*	15.99*	.11	7.45*
Education	2.34			2.92			1.33		
(c) Age	13.63*			.04			4.64*		
Interaction	1.25			.74			1.29		

Note: (c) = this variable was entered first as a control variable (covariate)

* = significant at .05 level

N = 580

significant, as was particularly evident for long-term labor migration. Age is always a significant factor, as was observed for short-term labor migration. Education is never significant.

In sum, household status affects long-term labor migration. Neither age nor education has an important controlling influence. Short-term labor migration, on the other hand, is related to household status and also to age. Both household status and age are significant predictors of total labor migration. The findings underscore the theoretical importance given to social, economic, and demographic roles within the household.

Ethnic group is significantly related to patterns of long-term labor migration even when the individual effects of age, household status, and education are taken into account (Table 4.7). When all these factors and region are considered, ethnic group is no longer related to patterns of long-term labor migration; household status, education, and region are significant factors. Ethnic group is significantly related to patterns of short-term labor migration when controlling for the effects of age, household status, and education. Of these latter factors, only age is significant. When all these factors and region are considered, ethnic group is not significant; region and age are significant.

An examination of total labor migration finds that age is moderately significant throughout all equations. Ethnic group is significant when controlling only for age and education; education itself is not significant. Ethnic group is not, however, significant when either household status or region is considered. When household status and region are considered simultaneously, only household status is significant.

When village is substituted for region in this analysis, the results for long-term and total migration are similar to those for region (Table 4.7). The results for short-term labor migration are similar with respect to the importance of age as a control factor. By refining the analysis to the village level, ethnic group never appears to affect migration independently of village location.

In sum, long-term and total labor migration are more adequately predicted by the variables introduced than is short-term labor migration. For the former, household status and region (or village) are the most important predictors. Long-term labor migration is best understood by household status. Ethnic group is also significant as a predictor of long-term labor migration until region or village is considered; that is, the influence of ethnic group on long-term labor migration is a reflection of differences in regional and village characteristics. The moderate interaction between ethnic group and region or village further attests to the

TABLE 4.7

THE EFFECTS OF ETHNIC GROUP ON SHORT-TERM, LONG-TERM AND TOTAL LABOR
MIGRATION, CONTROLLING FOR THE EFFECTS OF AGE, HOUSEHOLD STATUS,
EDUCATION, AND REGION AND VILLAGE (ANOVA)

VARIABLES	SHORT-TERM			LONG-TERM			TOTAL		
	F-Ratio	R^2	Overall F-Ratio	F-Ratio	R^2	Overall F-Ratio	F-Ratio	R^2	Overall F-Ratio
Ethnic Group	6.24*	.07	7.53*	7.09*	.06	5.92*	3.16*	.04	3.35*
(c) Age	14.01*			.04			4.28*		
Ethnic Group	5.38*	.08	2.97*	4.93*	.15	5.05*	1.82	.12	3.67*
Household Status	1.78			16.61*			14.01*		
(c) Age	14.37*			.04			4.71*		
Interaction	1.65*			1.92*			1.36		
Ethnic Group	6.04*	.07	4.65*	6.82*	.06	3.81*	3.02*	.03	2.25*
Education	.77			.19			.02		
(c) Age	14.03*			.03			4.27*		
Interaction	1.29			1.54			1.17		
Ethnic Group	1.54	.08	4.28*	.39	.09	5.93*	.88	.05	3.11*
Region	.95			8.51*			3.77*		
(c) Age	13.94*			.04			4.34*		
Interaction	.06			3.74*			2.09		
Ethnic Group	1.41	.09	4.57*	.61	.18	10.16*	.57	.13	6.86*
Household status	1.87			15.81*			13.05*		
Region	1.21			7.82*			2.33		
(c) Age	14.09*			.04			4.68*		
NA									
Ethnic Group	1.57	.09	4.39*	.87	.19	9.85*	.58	.13	6.47*
Household status	2.12			16.66*			13.33*		
Region	1.64			9.72*			2.92		
Education	2.12			5.23*			1.69*		
(c) Age	14.12*			.04			4.69*		
Ethnic Group	.93	.11	3.32*	.89	.09	3.72*	1.10	.06	2.15*
Village	3.66*			3.26*			1.89		
(c) Age	14.28*			.04			4.36*		
Interaction	.15			2.41*			1.53		
Ethnic Group	.98	.13	4.71*	.95	.19	7.64*	.93	.13	5.13*
Household status	1.74			16.20*			12.78*		
Village	3.70*			3.30*			1.38		
(c) Age	14.55*			.04			4.68*		
NA									
Ethnic Group	.91	.13	4.57*	1.00	.19	7.52*	.97	.14	4.93*
Household status	1.98			16.97*			13.02*		
Village	3.81*			3.77*			1.51		
Education	2.06			4.66*			1.43		
(c) Age	14.58*			.04			4.69*		

Note: (c) = this variable was entered first as a control variable (covariate).
* = significant at .05 level.
N = 580

242

underlying importance of regional and village differences. Age is the only consistently significant predictor of short-term labor migration. The consideration of region and village generally eliminates the influence of ethnic group. Finally, total labor migration is best understood through the consideration of age and household status; ethnic group, region, and village are not important. Differentials in migration patterns among the ethnic groups are not primarily due to underlying differences in household composition, age structure, or education. Rather, the location of the ethnic group in various regions or villages accounts for these differences.

Data not presented in tabular form show that caste (differences between freemen and blacksmiths) does not have a significant effect on labor migration independent of age and education.

Region of the country is significantly related to patterns of labor migration when considering the simultaneous effects of age, household status, and education (Table 4.8). Consistent with the previous analysis, age is significant as a control variable for short-term but not for long-term labor migration. Household status is significant only for long-term and total labor migration. However, there is a significant interaction between region and household status for all types of migration. Education is generally not significant as a simultaneous influence. When village is substituted for region, all the same relationships emerge (bottom Table 4.8).

The final statistical assessment incorporates the simultaneous consideration of all the major factors. The statistical method of Multiple Classification Analysis (MCA) was selected so that we could deal with independent variables with categorical values. This permits a comparison of the values before and after taking into account the influence of all other factors (unadjusted and adjusted). The MCA data indicate the mean value of the dependent variable for each category of an independent variable in its simple (bivariate) form as well as after controlling for the simultaneous influences of other independent or control variables. The specific values represent deviations (+ or -) from the overall mean value of the dependent variable for each category of the independent variable.

For short-term migration most of the variables are little affected by controlling for others (Table 4.9). The only noteworthy finding is that the consideration of all factors decreases the short-term migration rate in the Dogon region and increases the rate in the Kita region. Both villages in each of the Dogon and Kita

TABLE 4.8

THE EFFECTS OF REGION AND VILLAGE ON SHORT-TERM, LONG-TERM AND
TOTAL LABOR MIGRATION, CONTROLLING FOR THE EFFECTS OF AGE,
HOUSEHOLD STATUS AND EDUCATION (ANOVA)

VARIABLES	SHORT-TERM			LONG-TERM			TOTAL		
	F-Ratio	R^2	Overall F-Ratio	F-Ratio	R^2	Overall F-Ratio	F-Ratio	R^2	Overall F-Ratio
Region	12.61*	.06	13.05*	25.75*	.08	17.18*	9.54*	.04	7.80*
Age	13.94*			.04			4.32*		
Region	11.22*	.08	5.88*	20.01*	.17	13.60*	5.73*	.12	9.40*
Household status	2.13			16.80*			14.33*		
(c) Age	14.56*			.04			4.69*		
Interaction	4.50*			8.10*			6.34*		
Region	12.09*	.07	6.96*	25.88*	.09	9.45*	9.53*	.04	4.13*
Education	.78			1.75			.72		
(c) Age	13.93*			.04			4.31*		
Interaction	.92			1.63			.37		
Region	10.29*	.08	6.13*	19.14*	.18	15.49*	5.60*	.13	10.19*
Household status	2.19			16.22*			13.81*		
Education	1.33			3.95*			1.68		
(c) Age	14.05*			.04			4.71*		

Village	7.65*	.11	8.50*	7.78*	.09	6.81*	3.38*	.05	3.49*
Age	14.48*			.04			4.32*		4.08*
Village	7.03*	.12	3.30*	6.57*	.18	5.89*	2.10*	.13	
Household Status	1.74			17.36*			13.72*		
(c) Age	14.84*			.04			4.91*		
Interaction	1.54			2.87*			2.31*		
Village	7.58*	.11	5.24*	7.81*	.09	4.58*	3.31*	.05	2.34*
Education	1.46			1.61			.31		
(c) Age	14.47*			.04			4.31*		
Interaction	.79			1.54			.92		
Village	6.89*	.12	5.98*	6.38*	.19	10.03*	1.99*	.13	6.46*
Household Status	1.94			17.00*			13.32*		
Education	2.38			4.46*			1.26		
(c) Age	14.59*			.04			4.69*		

Note:

(c) = this variable was entered first as a control variable (covariate).

* = significant at .05 level.

N = 580.

245

TABLE 4.9

MULTIPLE CLASSIFICATION ANALYSIS OF MIGRATION BY HOUSEHOLD STATUS,
EDUCATION, ETHNIC GROUP, REGION AND VILLAGE CONTROLLING FOR THE
EFFECTS OF AGE, FOR ADULT MALES

VARIABLES	N	SHORT-TERM			LONG-TERM			TOTAL		
		UN	Adj (Region)	Adj (Village)	UN	Adj (Region)	Adj (Village)	UN	Adj (Region)	Adj (Village)
TOTAL	580	.07			.14			.19		
Household Status										
Household head	148	-.04	-.01	.00	-.13	-.24	-.24	-.18	-.26	-.26
Brother or cousin	117	-.05	-.03	-.03	.08	.06	.05	.06	.04	.04
Son	201	.06	.04	.03	-.02	.04	.05	.02	.08	.08
Other relative	89	.00	-.01	-.02	.16	.19	.20	.17	.19	.20
Non-relative	25	-.07	-.08	-.08	.02	.10	.10	-.03	.03	.02
Education										
No formal school	530	.00	.01	.00	-.01	-.01	-.01	-.01	-.01	-.01
Primary or more	50	-.01	-.05	-.05	.06	.11	.10	.07	.07	.07
Ethnic Group										
Malinke	102	-.05	-.09	-.09	-.01	.06	.06	-.04	-.02	-.02
Bambara	88	-.06	-.05	-.05	.05	-.05	-.05	.01	-.07	-.06
Fulani-Peuhl	155	.01	-.02	-.01	.03	.01	.03	.05	.00	.05
Dogon	137	.09	.13	.09	-.13	.00	-.01	-.09	.06	.04
Senoufo	53	-.03	-.02	.02	.12	-.05	-.11	.09	-.04	-.10
Others	45	-.03	.00	.03	.10	.02	.00	.08	.03	.01
Region										
Dogon	142	.08	-.05		-.13	-.08		-.10	-.12	
Kita	269	-.01	.04		-.01	-.05		-.01	-.01	
Sikasso	169	-.05	-.02		.14	.15		.09	.11	
Village										
1	61	-.04		-.13	-.12		-.04	-.14		-.09
2	81	.18		.07	-.14		-.11	-.07		-.09
3	109	-.04		.03	-.01		-.06	-.03		-.01
4	160	.00		.03	-.02		-.07	.01		-.05
5	32	-.04		-.02	.08		.13	.03		.08
6	38	-.04		-.02	.20		.26	.15		.22
7	54	-.05		-.08	.15		.20	.13		.16
8	45	-.05		-.03	.10		.09	.05		.02

Age is entered as a control variable (covariate).

regions correspond to this pattern of change. Regional differences in education account for the slightly decreased values for those with at least primary education.

When long-term migration is considered, migration rates increase for sons, other relatives, and non-relatives and decrease for household heads and brothers and cousins. In other words, those who are further removed from positions of decision-making authority in households are more likely to migrate, all other things being equal. Migration rates would also increase in the Dogon region and in the villages in the Sikasso region. Changes in the values for ethnic groups probably reflect the influence of region and village more than any other factors, since the others did not alter the significance of ethnic group.

Taken together, the multivariate analyses suggest that long-term labor migration is significantly determined by household status and regional or village location. Further, there is a significant interaction between household status and regional or village location. Where agriculture is not strong commercially, and alternative cash-earning opportunities are virtually non-existent, sons become seasonal migrants. Where agriculture is commercially quite strong, only long-term migration is evidenced, and only among those with less immediate responsibilities and rewards in the agricultural enterprise. Long-term labor migration is the most completely predicted of the types of labor migration when its key variables (household status and region or village) are considered. Short-term labor migration is not predicted as well by its key variable (age) or the less consistent influences of regional or village location or of household status. Total labor migration is predicted better than short-term labor migration and almost as well as long-term labor migration. The major factors of importance are age, household status, and regional or village location.

Several key findings emerge, therefore, from the multivariate analyses. The first is that the separation of labor migration into short-term and long-term types is essential. Substantively, some variables continue to have independent effects on migration patterns after the influence of other factors is controlled. In particular both age and household status are important to consider. Unfortunately, adequate attention cannot be given to either of these factors in targeting specific groups at the household level; the relatively small number of adult males and households in particular render such an analysis impossible. Attention will be given, instead, to household structure. It is significant that education, ethnic group, and caste did not generally appear as signifiant predictors when other variables were also considered. Finally, the consideration of region and village characteristics proved to be central in this analysis.

Village Level Analysis

The focus of the analysis has been on individual level determinants of out-migration. Emerging from that analysis and from our theoretical framework is the need to focus on labor allocation and migration at the village and household levels. The structural and aggregate characteristics of villages in social, economic, demographic, and geographic terms may affect actual and perceived alternative opportunities and, therefore, individual and household decision-making. The influence of village characteristics may supercede or interact with particular characteristics of individuals and households regarding labor allocation and migration.

Two sets of relationships are expected. Adult male labor migration from villages is expected to be lower in villages which are further from any important towns, where non-agricultural commercial activities are observed, where agriculture is characterized by the use of modern techniques, and where cash cropping is prevalent. While distance is a negative factor discouraging migration, the other factors are positive incentives to remain in rural areas; they inhibit migration by providing greater overall levels of productive activities in the village. On the other hand, inequality of landholdings is expected to restrict widespread income-earnings opportunities in agriculture; the common occurrence of labor exchange, either between households or through participation in the various work associations, is expected to provide labor to compensate for that foregone by households' migrants. These relationships are assessed via simple bivariate correlation analysis since there are only eight villages. Given this significant limitation, the observed associations are not intended to be generalized other than to suggest future data collection and analysis priorities at the village level.

A variety of social, economic, demographic, and geographic characteristics of the study villages are presented in Table 4.10. With the exception of the distance from each village to a town, they represent the average characteristics of the sample households. No variable was introduced about modes of transportation and road conditions linking the villages to towns, since all villages had similar characteristics; during the rainy season, the roads are impassable for motorized vehicles. The data show wide variation among villages in migration patterns, agricultural-economic activities, distance to towns, agricultural modernization, inequality, and household size.

Data in Table 4.11, lines 1 and 2, show that commercial activities are more important in villages where short-term labor migration is also relatively more important. Conversely, non-agricultural commercial activities are less important where long-term labor migration is important. The relationships between the non-agricultural commercial activities variables (in effect, part-time employment) reflecting the dry, wet, and harvest seasons considered here and the various types of migration generally do not meet the criteria of statistical significance. The general pattern is that migration is higher where seasonal non-agricultural employment is higher in the dry season and at harvest and lower in the wet season. Short-term labor migration is not related to the seasonal measures of non-agricultural employment.

It thus appears that non-agricultural commercial activities complement short-term labor migration and conflict with long-term labor migration. It cannot be determined here whether non-agricultural employment permits short-term migration and prohibits long-term labor migration. Similarly, it is plausible that short-term labor migration encourages non-agricultural employment by providing needed cash remittances and serves as a way to transport raw materials to the village and finished products from the village.

Migration is expected to diminish as distance to a town increases because of the time and expense involved in traveling. When distance from each village to a sizeable town, either for the sale of produce or employment, is considered, the overall relationship is one of decreasing migration rates as distance increases (Table 4.11, line 3). This is, however, entirely a function of long-term labor migration. Short-term labor migration increases as distance between village and town increases. This latter result appears to contradict the conventional wisdom regarding the relationship between distance and short-term labor migration; proximity usually underlies short-term labor migration and circulation. This pattern reflects the relationship between non-agricultural employment and migration. Migration is less important where non-agricultural employment is greater; short-term labor migration is an exception to this rule. Overall, non-agricultural employment is higher in villages which are further from towns. This is consistent with the findings about non-agricultural employment and distance in relation to migration

TABLE 4.10

SOCIAL, ECONOMIC, DEMOGRAPHIC AND GEOGRAPHIC CHARACTERISTICS OF STUDY VILLAGES

	V1	V2	V3	V4	V5	V6	V7	V8	TOTAL
MIGRATION									
% migrants	3.9	10.7	16.4	14.7	13.7	30.7	22.4	16.1	13.8
% labor migrants	3.9	10.7	14.4	11.7	9.3	14.3	12.5	10.6	10.4
% short-term labor migrants	2.8	26.7	1.6	6.3	3.3	2.0	0.7	1.4	6.7
% long-term labor migrants	1.1	0.0	14.8	8.3	13.7	30.7	21.7	16.1	10.0
SEASONAL MIGRATION									
% with 2+ weeks in labor migration									
- dry season	0.0	21.9	0.0	0.0	22.8	0.0	1.9	2.2	4.8
- wet season	0.0	8.5	0.9	0.0	20.0	15.8	0.0	2.2	3.8
- harvest	0.0	3.6	0.0	0.0	0.0	0.0	1.9	2.2	1.0
NON-AGRICULTURAL COMMERCIAL ACTIVITIES									
% in farming & non-agricultural comm. act.	5.0	17.8	7.8	10.9	1.0	0.0	0.0	0.0	5.3
% with 2+ weeks in commercial activities									
- dry season	6.6	22.0	37.6	18.8	42.9	34.2	14.8	17.8	23.5
- wet season	72.1	26.9	2.7	10.6	37.1	36.9	18.5	46.7	24.6
- harvest	1.6	9.8	6.4	26.9	25.8	18.4	11.2	6.6	14.3
DISTANCE TO TOWN									
Approximate # Km. to major town	67	105	45	32	28	28	25	25	-

COMMERCIALIZATION OF AGRICULTURE

% of all fields that are cash cropped	13.3	0.0	35.6	58.0	55.6	54.3	69.3	56.3	43.8
% of households with 1+ cash crop fields per adult	0.0	0.0	19.2	27.6	30.0	40.0	50.0	30.0	18.9

LABOR EXCHANGE AND HIRING

% in farming & working as agric. laborers	0.0	0.0	5.5	25.0	17.1	15.8	22.2	13.3	13.0
% of households w/5+% of labor as hired-in	33.3	0.0	88.5	96.6	100.0	100.0	100.0	80.0	66.9
% of households w/20+% of labor as hired-in	0.0	0.0	38.5	58.7	40.0	70.0	40.0	30.0	30.4

AGRICULTURAL MODERNIZATION

% of households w/chemical fertilizer	46.7	43.5	80.8	55.1	40.0	90.0	90.0	100.0	62.9
% of households w/modern equipment & chemical fertilizer	0.0	0.0	30.8	37.9	30.0	50.0	80.0	80.00	29.1

AGRICULTURAL INEQUALITY

GINI index of inequality									
- # fields per person	.26	.30	.34	.26	.25	.16	.44	.27	—
- # food-crop fields per person	.26	.30	.36	.38	.39	.22	.52	.33	—
- # cash-crop fields per person	.26	NA*	.34	.29	.30	.14	.39	.21	—

HOUSEHOLD SIZE

Average household size (relatives only)	5.3	8.1	15.8	17.2	13.0	10.0	22.0	16.6	12.6

Note: GINI is adjusted for the number of categories and therefore ranges between 0 and 1.
*There were NO cash fields recorded in this village.

TABLE 4.11

CORRELATION BETWEEN SELECTED VARIABLES AND LABOR
MIGRATION AMONG ADULT MALES: VILLAGE LEVEL

| | | LABOR MIGRATION | | |
		ALL	SHORT-TERM	LONG-TERM
1.	% in farming and non-agricultural commercial activities	.03	.85*	-.73*
2.	% with 2+ weeks in non-agricultural commercial activities			
	– dry season	.53	-.08	.42
	– wet season	-.80*	-.11	-.22
	– harvest	.30	-.02	.25
3.	Approx. Km to town	-.35	.86*	-.75*
4.	% of all fields cash cropped	.45	-.83*	.75*
5.	% HH with chemical fertilizer	.58	-.49	.75*
6.	% HH with modern equipment and chemical fertilizer	.49	-.57	.74*
7.	GINI of number of (Per person in HH)			
	a. total fields	.12	.00	-.11
	b. food crop fields	.22	-.21	.11
	c. cash crop fields	.17	-.78	.26
8.	% in farming and working as agricultural workers	.42	-.45	.57
9.	% of households			
	a. with 5+% hired-in labor	.52	-.78*	.77*
	b. with 20+% hired-in labor	.69*	.52	.80*
11.	Household size	.33	-.71*	.45

Note: All are labor time observation
*Significant at .05 level.

patterns.

When we note that villages which are closer to towns have greater proportions of their fields engaged in producing cash crops, the picture becomes clearer. Commercial agriculture is more pervasive when the village is located closer to a town, a marketplace for its produce. Villages which have a greater commercial orientation in agriculture are also more likely to have migrants, particularly long-term labor migrants (Table 4.11, lines 4-5). Short-term labor migration follows the reverse pattern. It thus seems that villages which have a relatively well-developed orientation toward commercial agriculture do not need to rely on non-agricultural employment to obtain cash and can afford long-term labor migration. The term "afford" is used cautiously, since data are not available to analyze remittances from long-term labor migrants which could offset "losses" incurred by the families of such migrants. In villages without a commercial agricultural orientation, non-agricultural employment and short-term labor migration are needed to compensate for the lack of profit generated by agricultural activities. Non-agricultural employment, it should be noted, is more important in villages further from town.

Finally, the inverse relationship between commercial agricultural orientation and non-agricultural employment indicates that commercial non-agricultural activities, for which short-term labor migration is probably necessary, are greatest where commercial agriculture is not viable due to the distance between the village and a town.

Thus, distance has a negative impact on the viability of commercial agriculture. The latter, in turn, diminishes the need for both non-agricultural commercial activities and short-term labor migration, while permitting long-term labor migration. In subsequent analysis, attention will, therefore, focus on the more substantively interesting variable of the relative commercial orientation of agricultural production than on distance per se.

The development of commercial agricultural production is expected to increase the use of labor exchanges. Although it is theoretically important to separate traditional labor exchange practices which involve some form of cash payment, the distinction is difficult to maintain in this study. Labor exchange was not recorded to any significant degree in the Dogon villages (Villages 1 and 2), while in the Kita villages (Villages 3 and 4), no distinction was made regarding method of payment. In the Sikasso villages (Villages 5, 6, 7, and 8), several methods of payment were distinguished. Direct reciprocity of labor time between households was predominant, with only very small proportions being paid in-kind or in cash, either individually or as part of a village work association. In short, cash payments for labor exchanged or hired between households is not an important feature (or, perhaps, people are reluctant to indicate when or how they were working for someone else for cash) in any of the villages in the study. Using three variables which do not reflect the distinction between paid and unpaid labor exchange practices, then, it appears that villages with a greater commercial agricultural orientation are consistently those where labor exchange is more important.

Implicitly, the modernization of agricultural techniques and socioeconomic stratification generate the expectation that greater commercial agricultural production leads to increasing reliance on labor exchange. Specifically, agricultural commercialization favors the modernization of agricultural techniques and stratification of landholdings; both modernization and stratification, in turn, are likely to produce an increased emphasis on hiring-in of others' labor.

The data indicate that modern agricultural techniques are more widely used in villages where commercial agriculture is more important. Labor exchange is a more prevalent feature in such villages as well. The modernization of agricultural techniques, like the commercialization of agriculture, favors long-term labor migration while inhibiting short-term labor migration (Table 4.11, line 6). Thus, the commercial agricultural orientation of villages underlies the importance of modern agricultural techniques and its influence on patterns of labor migration.

Stratification, as measured by inequality of landholdings,[5] also occurs to a greater extent in villages where commercial agriculture is more important. Stratification is only weakly related to the modernization of agricultural techniques; stratification is weakly, and inconsistently, related to the rate of labor exchange. In particular, where households tend to rely on labor exchange for more than 20 percent of their agricultural labor

----

[5] GINI is calculated as $(\sum_{i=1}^{n} X_i Y_{i+1}) - (\sum_{i=1}^{n} X_{i+1} Y_i)$ where X_i and Y_i are the cumulative proportions of population and landholdings, respectively, where each household is weighted equally. The GINI varies between 0 and $1-(1/n)$; each "crude" GINI was multiplied by $n/(n-1)$ to standardize for the different numbers of groups in each village.

input, inequality among both food and cash crop fields is relatively low. Most of the measures of stratification show no significant relationship to patterns of migration (Table 4.11, lines 7a,b,c,). The exception is that inequality of cash crop fields appears to diminish short-term labor migration. This pattern of migration is generally consistent with those found for the commercialization of agriculture and the modernization of agricultural techniques.

The final variable at the village level is average household size which appears to be negatively related to short-term labor migration and very weakly but positively related to long-term labor migration (Table 4.11, line 11). Smaller households find short-term labor migration to be an important activity. Larger households, on the other hand, have either a greater ability or need to have members absent for long durations.

In sum, short-term labor migration tends to occur at higher rates in villages where distance to town and non-agricultural commercial activities is greater, agriculture is less commercialized, modern agricultural techniques are less widely used, stratification of landholdings is less pronounced, and labor exchange is less important. Conversely, long-term labor migration tends to occur at higher rates where in villages distance to towns is shorter, non-agricultural employment is not too important and agriculture is more commercialized, modern agricultural techniques are more widely used, stratification of landholdings is more pronounced, and labor exchange is more important.

The results of the correlation analysis at the village level present consistent evidence regarding both the interrelationships among the explanatory factors and the explanation of patterns of short- and long-term labor migration. Reliance on these findings must be qualified, however. Only 8 villages are involved in the present study. With such a small number of villages, the calculation of the correlation coefficients can be greatly biased by an extreme value for any of the variables considered. This may be especially true in the measurement of short-term labor migration. In scattergrams not presented here, the correlations and associated regression lines were representative of the distribution of village characteristics and migration rates in the case of long-term but not short-term labor migration. The "fit" for most of the interrelationships among the explanatory variables is quite good.

Two findings at the village level require emphasis. The first is that short- and long-term labor migration need to be considered separately. Their different relationships with each of the explanatory variables argue strongly for such separate treatment.

Second, it is important to distinguish among the villages in the household level of analysis. Given the observed consistency among the explanatory variables and the desire to parsimoniously compare the role of village location in understanding migration and labor allocation at the household level, we selected one variable--the commercialization of agricultural production--because of its substantive meaning and central role in explaining all the other variables.

Household Level Analysis

Migration rates are expected to be higher among households from the wealthiest and the poorest households, among larger households--those with a demographic "surplus", among those which are more heavily involved in labor exchange practices, and among those which do not have non-agricultural cash-earning activities and where dependent males do not have field rights. Since we treat migration within the context of household labor allocation, we examine four dependent variables--short-term migration, long-term labor migration, those engaged principally in farming and agricultural laboring, and those in farming and non-agricultural commercial activities.

The major independent variables at the household level are: 1) household socioeconomic class (agricultural technology and agricultural field use); 2) household socio-demographic structure (size, family structure, and demographic dependency--the ratio of children to adults and the ratio of consumption to production units); 3) household labor force characteristics (number of adult male non-relatives, labor exchange including hired-in and hired-out labor hours).

Socioeconomic Class and Labor Allocation

We begin the analysis of the household level with the socioeconomic class of the household. The expectation is that migration rates are highest for households in the nascent agricultural entrepreneurial (upper) class and the subsistence farming (lower) class. Marginal cash cropping (middle class) households are expected to have lower rates of migration among adult males. The two major variables used to measure socioeconomic class are the level of agricultural technology in the household and the number of cash crop fields per adult household member. The term socioeconomic class, or simply class, will be used throughout, despite the lack of precise correspondence to the

256

usage of the term in conventional sociological analysis.

The MCA results show (Table 4.12) that short-term migration is the highest among those with traditional agricultural technology, while lower rates are observed for those using chemical fertilizer and those using modern equipment. A similar pattern is observed if socioeconomic class is measured by the number of cash crop fields per adult or per household production unit, as well as the number of total fields per adult in the household, i.e., those with a greater number of total or cash crop fields per adult have lower short-term migration rates.[6] It is impossible to discern causally whether the inability to cash crop successfully (for reasons of inadequate land or capital) encouraged short-term migration or whether migration meant foregoing the probable lesser economic rewards of cash cropping. Furthermore, it seems that short-term migration rates are negatively related to the proportion of dependent adult males who have any fields. It should be recalled that most of the fields of dependent adult males are for cash cropping, since the food crop fields are the responsibility of the household head; every household member, of course, is required to work on the communal food crop fields.

When long-term labor migration is considered, the pattern is very different. Long-term migration is highest among those with modern equipment and lowest among traditional farming households. It is lowest among those with the lowest number of cash crop fields per adult or per production unit. This indicates that higher socioeconomic class is generally supportive of long-term migration and implies that "better off" households are able to bear the cost of long-term migrants' foregone labor.

The variables representing socioeconomic class appear to have some influence on the importance of agricultural laboring and non-agricultural work. A greater proportion of adult males are farmers and agricultural laborers in households where cash cropping is more prevalent, where modern equipment is used, and where a larger proportion of adults have field nights. These results suggest that where cash cropping is more prevalent there is also a greater tendency to be working on others' farms as well. This seems contradictory, since there is generally no recorded cash

----

[6] It is important to note this measure weights each field equally; size measurements of all fields cultivated by the sample households could not be obtained.

257

TABLE 4.12

LABOR ALLOCATION BY SOCIO-ECONOMIC CLASS AND VILLAGE: ANOVA AND MCA

Independent Variables	SHORT-TERM MIGRATION F-ratio	LONG-TERM MIGRATION F-ratio	AGRICULTURAL LABORING F-ratio	NON-AGRIC WORK F-ratio
Agricultural Technology	3.31*	.87	2.36	.79
Village	7.36*	4.71*	9.90*	1.58
Interaction	1.95*	2.17*	1.95*	.97
R^2	.30	.23	.32	.10
Overall	4.27*	3.46*	4.58*	1.32

	N	SHORT-TERM MIGRATION UN	Adj	LONG-TERM MIGRATION UN	Adj	AGRICULTURAL LABORING UN	Adj	NON-AGRIC WORK UN	Adj
Agricultural Technology									
Traditional	55	5.29	3.05	-2.49	1.44	-0.92	1.33	1.38	0.07
Chemical Fertilizer	50	-3.09	-4.16	-3.54	-2.60	-1.15	4.57	2.92	2.61
Modern Equipment	43	-3.16	0.94	7.30	1.17	2.51	-7.01	-5.17	-3.12
Village									
1	30	-3.95	-3.64	-8.89	-8.45	-14.08	-16.92	-2.36	-3.62
2	23	19.94	20.02	-10.01	-9.69	-14.08	-16.82	10.46	9.29
3	26	-5.15	-3.95	4.77	5.43	-3.44	-3.82	0.47	0.11
4	29	-0.39	-1.40	-1.67	-2.32	26.58	27.85	3.53	4.24
5	10	-3.40	-5.09	3.66	2.70	0.75	1.60	-6.36	-5.73
6	10	-4.73	-3.84	20.71	21.02	0.92	2.46	-7.36	-6.85
7	10	-6.02	-6.66	11.68	10.86	5.74	10.76	-7.36	-5.13
8	10	-5.30	-5.22	6.11	5.69	-0.89	-3.81	-7.36	-5.39

258

	N	UN	ADJ	F-ratio	UN	ADJ	F-ratio	UN	Adj	F-ratio	UN	Adj	F-ratio
# Cash fields per adult													
Village				.09			3.99*			1.66			.09
Interaction				3.22*			5.77*			5.79*			1.10
				.15			2.93*			2.75*			.30
R^2				.27			.28			.32			.09
Overall				2.61*			4.52*			5.11*			.86
# Cash fields per adult													
0.0 - .25	36	11.23	-0.67		-7.69	7.77		-14.08	-4.64		6.80	2.60	
.26- .50	36	-3.85	-0.86		-1.26	4.56		-3.31	-3.16		-1.30	-0.72	
.51-1.00	48	-4.01	0.23		7.11	-2.62		4.07	0.03		-2.22	-0.61	
1.01+	28	-2.62	1.59		-0.68	-11.36		15.38	9.96		-3.28	-1.37	
Village													
1	30	-3.95	-3.16		-8.89	-14.63		-14.08	-10.38		-2.36	-2.86	
2	23	19.94	20.61		-10.01	-17.77		-14.08	-9.45		10.46	7.87	
3	26	-5.15	-5.32		4.77	6.61		-3.44	-4.29		0.47	1.00	
4	29	-0.39	-0.66		-1.67	1.13		26.58	24.79		3.53	4.39	
5	10	-3.40	-3.92		3.66	8.18		0.75	-1.94		-6.36	-5.51	
6	10	-4.73	-5.50		20.71	26.82		0.92	-3.09		-7.36	-6.45	
7	10	-6.02	-6.92		11.68	18.67		5.74	0.74		-7.36	-6.37	
8	10	-5.30	-5.83		6.11	10.63		-0.89	-3.58		-7.36	-6.51	
TOTAL**	148	6.73	—		10.01	—		14.08	—		7.36	—	

* Significant at .05 level.
**This total characterizes all subsequent MCA tables.

259

payment for such labor "exchanged" and the labor requirements of producing one's own cash crops would conflict with laboring on others' fields.

One factor which may be involved is village location. ANOVA results considering village, along with the two principal socioeconomic class variables, are presented in Table 4.12. When village is considered, the low short-term and high long-term migration rates in households with modern equipment are eliminated. This suggests that village determines migration patterns through its influence on the existence of modern equipment. Patterns of short-term migration by village are unaffected by the consideration of agricultural technology; only Village 2 is characterized by high rates. Likewise, patterns of long-term migration by village are unaffected by the additional consideration of agricultural technology; rates remain high in Villages 3, 5, 6, 7, and 8. Agricultural laboring by household agricultural technology is greatly affected by the consideration of village; in particular, participating in agricultural laboring is highest among those using only chemical fertilizer and lowest among those with modern equipment. In the sense that modern equipment is labor saving, households have less need to engage in labor exchange practices. When cash cropping and village are considered, the most important findings are that once village location is taken into account, cash cropping discourages long-term migration and favors agricultural laboring. Yet, overall village location exerts the more important influence and clarifies the relationship between class and labor allocation.

Detailed cross-tabulations not presented in tabular form show that the only village with significant short-term migration is Village 2, in which only traditional farming households have a high rate. As for long-term migration, rates are higher for traditional households and those with modern equipment in the two Kita villages, Villages 3 and 4, where cash cropping is moderately important. In other words, long-term migration occurs more frequently in the poorest and richest households. In the Sikasso villages, on the other hand, where cash cropping is more important, long-term migration occurs in middle and upper class households. No clear pattern emerges for agricultural laboring or non-agricultural work. When labor allocation rates are cross-classified by cash cropping and village, there is no new pattern of short-term and long-term migration. The only significant finding is that agricultural laboring rates increase with cash cropping in the Sikasso villages.

In sum, short- and long-term labor migration are differently

260

affected by socioeconomic class. The modernization of agricultural technology is associated with lower rates of short-term but higher rates of long-term migration. The same association is observed when the number of cash crop fields per adult or per production unit is considered. Cash cropping, then, appears to substitute for short-term labor migration and support long-term labor migration. Higher socioeconomic class is associated with higher rates of farming and working as agricultural laborers. This finding is consistent with the results of the village level analysis; those who are cash cropping may have increased labor needs. The only way to obtain sufficient labor for one's own fields in rural Malian society may be to work at least some time on others' farms as well; the relationship may be unequal while meeting the formal criteria of labor exchange. The non-agricultural work component of the labor allocation framework was not explained by the consideration of socioeconomic class. The additional consideration of village location dominated the influence of agricultural technology on short-term and long-term labor migration. Households with modern equipment engage less in labor exchange practices. Finally, cash cropping tends to eliminate the need for long-term labor migration, but village location overrides the role of cash cropping. Village location thus appears to have predominant background influence on relationships at the household level.

Socio-Demographic Structure and Labor Allocation

Higher rates of migration are expected in households which are large and which have a complex structure in which several brothers of the household head are present. Data in Table 4.13 show that short-term migration is significantly related to household size but not complexity (number of brothers and cousins): short-term migration rates are highest among the smallest families and those with the simplest structure, i.e., no brothers (Table 4.13, lower panel). The factors contributing to long-term labor migration, again, are altogether different. Long-term migration is highest when household size is larger and where household structure is characterized by a large number of brothers. Agricultural laboring, on the other hand, is inversely related to household size and complexity. When non-agricultural work is considered, only household size is a significant predictor. However, the general relationship is not linear. Non-agricultural work is more prevalent among average sized households (6-9 members) but much lower among larger households. If the average value of the smallest households (1-5 members) is treated

261

TABLE 4.13

LABOR ALLOCATION BY SOCIO-DEMOGRAPHIC STRUCTURE AND VILLAGE: ANOVA AND MCA

Independent Variables	SHORT-TERM MIGRATION F-ratio	LONG-TERM MIGRATION F-ratio	AGRICULTURAL LABORING F-ratio	NON-AGRIC WORK F-ratio
# Household members	3.11*	2.93*	2.94*	3.12*
Village	9.13*	4.70*	9.75*	1.93
Interaction	2.10*	2.43*	.97	.70
R^2	.31	.26	.34	.15
Overall	3.93*	3.66*	3.23*	1.32

	N	SHORT-TERM MIGRATION UN	SHORT-TERM MIGRATION Adj	LONG-TERM MIGRATION UN	LONG-TERM MIGRATION Adj	AGRICULTURAL LABORING UN	AGRICULTURAL LABORING Adj	NON-AGRIC WORK UN	NON-AGRIC WORK Adj
# Household Members									
1-5	36	4.84	4.04	-7.23	-3.52	1.19	9.19	-0.88	-0.63
6-9	43	-2.51	-4.38	-4.04	-3.66	-4.63	0.26	7.44	7.52
10-15	36	-1.26	-1.81	3.75	0.92	2.18	-0.34	-3.98	-3.78
16+	33	-0.64	3.27	9.05	7.60	2.35	-10.00	-4.40	-4.99
Village									
1	30	-3.95	-4.71	-8.89	-5.47	-14.08	-19.68	-2.36	-4.62
2	23	19.94	21.08	-10.01	-7.58	-14.08	-16.90	10.46	8.37
3	26	-5.15	-5.15	4.77	2.67	-3.44	-0.26	0.47	1.86
4	29	-0.39	-1.46	-1.67	-3.65	26.58	28.84	3.53	5.21
5	10	-3.40	-1.83	3.66	2.78	0.75	2.84	-6.36	-5.73
6	10	-4.73	-2.48	20.71	22.06	0.92	0.06	-7.36	-8.42
7	10	-6.02	-6.82	11.68	8.78	5.74	9.83	-7.36	-5.55
8	10	-5.30	-5.60	6.11	3.87	-0.89	2.24	-7.36	-5.67

	F-ratio	F-ratio	F-ratio	F-ratio
# Brothers and cousins	1.18	3.57*	1.14	.85
Village	7.39*	5.21*	8.08*	1.80
Interaction	.89	2.11*	.12	.31
R^2	.28	.26	.31	.10
Overall	2.88*	3.59*	2.54*	.83

	N	UN	Adj	UN	Adj	UN	Adj	UN	Adj
# Brothers									
0	92	1.13	0.73	-4.01	-2.76	0.28	1.41	1.76	1.20
1	26	-3.49	-4.26	4.34	3.25	-2.21	2.13	-1.30	0.74
2+	30	-0.43	1.46	8.53	5.66	1.07	-6.18	-4.28	-4.33
Village									
1	30	-3.95	-3.73	-8.89	-7.89	-14.08	-15.13	-2.36	-3.10
2	23	19.94	20.23	-10.01	-9.28	-14.08	-14.99	10.46	9.84
3	26	-5.15	-5.88	4.77	5.03	-3.44	-2.84	0.47	0.77
4	29	-0.39	-1.20	-1.67	-2.02	26.58	27.76	3.53	4.26
5	10	-3.40	-2.28	3.66	2.34	0.75	0.57	-6.36	-6.27
6	10	-4.73	-4.26	20.71	18.30	0.92	2.32	-7.36	-6.21
7	10	-6.02	-4.90	11.68	10.36	5.74	5.56	-7.36	-7.27
8	10	-5.30	-5.11	6.11	6.82	-0.89	-1.69	-7.36	-7.92

*Significant at .05 level.

263

as a special case of rather unique circumstances (e.g., very young or very old household heads), the general relationship between household size and non-agricultural work is negative. Similar results, though not reflecting statistically significant differences, are found for the number of brothers. Thus, agricultural laboring and non-agricultural work seem less important in larger and more complexly structured households. Long-term migration and working on their own farms are the principal activities.

Data not presented show that when labor allocation rates are cross-classified by household size and village, short-term migration characterizes only the smallest households in Village 2. The only other significant finding is that the tendency for long-term migration to be positively associated with household size is due exclusively to the pattern in the Sikasso villages, Villages 5, 6, 7, and 8. Similar results are found when village and the number of brothers or cousins are considered.

In sum, long-term labor migration is more prevalent among large households and those with a more complex structure. Conversely, the opposite results tend to characterize short-term labor migration. Migration for short periods may be the only type acceptable under such circumstances; these households also have higher rates of agricultural laboring. Viewed in broader perspective, it appears that migration is an important component of a household's labor allocation strategy. Those with a more substantial demographic and economic base (i.e., labor force) are better able to diversify their sources of income. For those with a smaller demographic base, there is greater reliance on agricultural laboring and non-farm income sources and on short-term labor migration.

Socioeconomic Class, Socio-Demographic Structure, and Labor Allocation

Having considered the influence of socioeconomic class and household socio-demographic structure separately on patterns of labor allocation, it is appropriate to consider their joint, simultaneous impact. When agricultural technology is used as the measure of socioeconomic class, short-term migration is consistently predicted in the same manner as was observed when socioeconomic class and socio-demographic structure were considered separately. In other words, socioeconomic class and socio-demographic structure do not affect the relationship of the other to short-term migration. Thus, short-term migration exists primarily among the poorer agricultural class (Table 4.14). In addition, households with a low age-dependency ratio are involved in short-term migration.

As for long-term labor migration, class and household structure affect the relationship of the other. Generally, similar results are found when agricultural technology is considered with either household size, the number of brothers, or the number of consumption and production units. All the patterns are the same before and after adjustment in the MCA data, but the role of agricultural technology is reduced in explaining long-term migration. Thus, household socio-demographic structure appears as the dominant influence for long-term migration, though socioeconomic class still is important. The simultaneous consideration of class and household structure on both agricultural laboring and non-agricultural work produces no differences than when each was considered separately.

When the number of cash crop fields per adult (referred to as "cash cropping") replaces agricultural technology as the measure of class, some important differences may be noted (Table 4.15). For short-term labor migration, lack of cash cropping is a significant predictor and is unaffected by controlling for household structure, regardless of the measure used. However, household size appears as a significant predictor of short-term migration because of its significant interaction with cash cropping. It should be recalled that socio-demographic characteristics were not significant predictors either when considered separately or when considered jointly with agricultural technology. The MCA is of limited value when interaction is present, yet it does reveal that migration rates are generally highest for the smallest and largest households when cash cropping is taken into account. In other words, higher rates of short-term migration among these households exist regardless of the level of cash cropping.

When long-term migration is examined, household size and structure remain significant predictors, as when they were previously considered separately and when controlling for level of agricultural technology. Class, as measured by cash cropping, generally remains a significant predictor that is unaffected by the demographic variables. There is no significant interaction between the socioeconomic and socio-demographic variables.

None of the socio-demographic variables significantly predicts agricultural laboring; at the same time, class is a significant predictor, regardless of the socio-demographic variable considered. The strong, positive relationship between cash cropping and agricultural laboring is unaffected by any of the socio-demographic variables. Non-agricultural work is not

TABLE 4.14

MULTIPLE CLASSIFICATION ANALYSIS OF LABOR ALLOCATION BY SOCIO-ECONOMIC CLASS AND SOCIO-DEMOGRAPHIC STRUCTURE

Independent Variable Categories	N	SHORT-TERM MIGRATION		LONG-TERM MIGRATION		AGRICULTURAL LABORING		NON-AGRICULTURAL WORK	
		U	A	U	A	U	A	U	A
# Household Members									
1-5	36	4.84	3.33	-7.23	-6.30	1.19	1.74	-0.88	-2.04
6-9	43	-2.51	-2.85	-4.04	-3.24	-4.63	-4.27	7.44	6.55
10-15	36	-1.26	-2.08	3.75	3.43	2.18	2.15	-3.98	-3.72
16+	33	-0.64	2.35	9.05	7.36	2.35	1.32	-4.40	-2.25
Agricultural Technology									
Traditional	55	5.29	5.57	-2.49	-0.63	-0.92	-0.91	1.38	1.30
Chemical fertilizer	50	-3.09	-2.93	-3.54	-1.80	-1.15	-0.36	2.92	1.62
Modern equipment	43	-3.16	-3.72	7.30	2.90	2.51	1.59	-5.17	-3.54
# Brothers and Cousins									
0	92	1.13	0.76	-4.01	-3.43	0.28	0.54	1.76	1.30
1	26	-3.49	-3.93	4.34	4.46	-2.21	-2.14	-1.30	-1.37
2+	30	-0.43	1.08	8.53	6.64	1.07	0.22	-4.28	-2.81
Agricultural Technology									
Traditional	55	5.29	5.43	-2.49	-1.74	-0.92	-8.88	1.38	1.06
Chemical fertilizer	50	-3.09	-3.15	-3.54	-2.99	-1.15	-1.21	2.92	2.71
Modern equipment	43	-3.16	-3.28	7.30	5.70	2.51	2.53	-5.17	-4.51
# Household Consumption Units									
0-4	37	1.83	0.33	-7.30	-6.11	3.48	4.69	1.65	0.35
5-7	42	-2.17	-2.71	-3.18	-2.45	-6.07	-5.42	4.54	3.76
8-12	35	4.08	3.68	3.67	3.28	3.26	3.09	-2.83	-2.44
13+	34	-3.51	-0.80	8.10	6.29	0.34	-1.59	-4.49	-2.51

266

Agricultural Technology

	N								
Traditional	55	5.29	5.08	-2.49	-0.59	-0.92	-1.63	1.38	0.78
Chemical fertilizer	50	-3.09	-2.68	-3.54	-2.24	-1.15	-0.94	2.92	2.25
Modern equipment	43	-3.16	-3.37	7.30	3.36	2.51	3.18	-5.17	-3.62

Household Production Units

	N								
0-4	28	2.20	-0.29	-10.01	-8.65	8.14	9.24	3.75	2.33
5-7	35	-1.02	-1.62	-0.48	0.59	-7.60	-7.01	1.43	0.40
8-12	38	0.99	0.98	-0.27	0.11	-2.11	-1.96	0.71	0.35
13+	47	-1.35	0.59	6.54	4.62	2.85	1.64	-3.83	-1.93

Agricultural Technology

	N								
Traditional	55	5.29	5.49	-2.49	-0.52	-0.92	-1.47	1.38	0.74
Chemical fertilizer	50	-3.09	-2.92	-3.54	-2.87	-1.15	-0.46	2.92	2.57
Modern equipment	43	-3.16	-3.63	7.30	4.00	2.51	2.42	-5.17	-3.93

Age-Dependency Ratio

	N								
0.0 - .33	36	6.24	5.03	-2.02	-0.42	-6.18	-5.57	1.67	0.72
.34- .67	38	-1.05	0.20	-0.44	-1.17	-5.51	-5.82	0.75	1.14
.68- .99	33	0.95	1.01	-2.28	-3.85	-0.99	-1.53	-3.37	-2.37
1.00+	41	-5.27	-5.41	4.02	4.55	11.33	11.52	0.55	0.22

Agricultural Technology

	N								
Traditional	55	5.29	4.87	-2.49	-2.65	-0.92	-1.16	1.38	1.42
Chemical fertilizer	50	-3.09	-2.88	-3.54	-3.90	-1.15	-1.19	2.92	2.65
Modern equipment	43	-3.16	-2.88	7.30	7.92	2.51	2.87	-5.17	-4.90

Ratio Consumption/Production Units

	N								
0.0 - .85	70	3.02	2.62	-1.15	-0.25	-6.88	-6.84	0.39	-0.28
.86- .95	61	-1.59	-1.16	-0.16	-1.02	7.04	7.00	-3.31	-2.69
.96-1.05	16	-6.73	-6.31	6.27	5.44	4.15	4.12	11.39	12.00
1.06+	1	-6.73	-11.71	-10.01	-7.65	-14.08	-14.36	-7.36	-8.89

Agricultural Technology

	N								
Traditional	55	5.29	5.04	-2.49	-2.35	-0.92	0.28	1.38	1.53
Chemical fertilizer	50	-3.09	-3.38	-3.54	-3.57	-1.15	-0.67	2.92	2.89
Modern equipment	43	-3.16	-2.52	7.30	7.17	2.51	0.42	-5.17	-5.32

TABLE 4.15

MULTIPLE CLASSIFICATION ANALYSIS OF LABOR ALLOCATION BY
SOCIO-ECONOMIC CLASS AND SOCIO-DEMOGRAPHIC STRUCTURE

Independent Variable Categories	N	SHORT-TERM MIGRATION U	A	LONG-TERM MIGRATION U	A	AGRICULTURAL LABORING U	A	NON-AGRICULTURAL WORK U	A
# Household Production Units									
0-4	27	2.53	6.93	-10.01	-11.51	8.14	11.02	3.75	6.23
5-7	36	-1.18	-6.10	-0.75	2.30	-7.60	-4.19	1.43	-1.09
8-12	38	0.99	-1.44	-0.27	0.98	-2.11	-3.48	0.71	-0.49
13+	47	-1.35	1.86	6.54	4.06	2.85	-0.31	-3.83	-2.34
# Cash Crop Fields per Adult									
0.0 - .25	36	11.23	14.26	-7.69	-8.89	-14.08	-11.32	6.80	7.38
.26 - .50	36	-3.85	-6.96	-1.26	2.89	-3.31	-7.95	-1.30	-3.51
.51 - 1.00	48	-4.01	-3.79	7.11	4.89	4.07	5.48	-2.22	-0.98
1.01+	28	-2.62	-2.90	-0.68	-0.65	15.38	15.38	-3.28	-3.29
Age Dependency Ratio									
0.0 - .33	36	6.24	3.03	-2.02	0.75	-6.18	-0.59	1.67	-1.04
.34 - .67	38	-1.05	-1.32	-0.44	-0.24	-5.51	-5.18	0.75	0.56
.68 - .99	33	0.95	2.32	-2.28	-3.74	-0.99	-1.93	-3.37	-2.60
1.00+	41	-5.27	-3.31	4.02	2.58	11.33	6.86	0.55	2.49
# Cash Crop Fields per Adult									
0.0 - .25	36	11.23	10.04	-7.69	-7.69	-14.08	-12.66	6.80	7.32
.26 - .50	36	-3.85	-4.03	-1.26	-1.09	-3.31	-3.10	-1.30	-1.15
.51 -1.00	48	-4.01	-3.76	7.11	7.34	4.07	3.87	-2.22	-2.23
1.01+	28	-2.62	-1.26	-0.68	-1.29	15.38	13.63	-3.28	-4.13
Ratio Consumption/ Production Units									
0.0 - .85	70	3.02	0.68	-1.15	0.89	-6.88	-2.83	0.39	-1.56
.86- .95	61	-1.59	0.61	-0.16	-2.03	7.04	3.08	-3.31	-1.46
.96- 1.05	16	-6.73	-5.09	6.27	4.42	4.15	1.34	11.39	12.79
1.06+	1	-6.73	-2.81	-10.01	-8.89	-14.08	-11.36	-7.36	-6.53
# Cash Crop Fields per Adult									
0.0 - .25	36	11.23	10.89	-7.69	-8.37	-14.08	-12.31	6.80	7.55
.26- .50	36	-3.85	-3.93	-1.26	-1.11	-3.31	-2.72	-1.30	-0.83
.51- 1.00	48	-4.01	-3.81	7.11	7.16	4.07	3.34	-2.22	-2.80
1.01+	28	-2.62	-2.42	-0.68	-0.09	15.38	13.61	-3.28	-3.84

(Continued)

TABLE 4.15 (cont'd)

Independent Variable Categories	N	SHORT-TERM MIGRATION		LONG-TERM MIGRATION		AGRICULTURAL LABORING		NON-AGRICULTURAL WORK	
		U	A	U	A	U	A	U	A
# Household Members									
1-5	36	4.84	5.63	-7.23	-6.28	1.19	4.76	-0.88	-1.33
6-9	43	-2.51	-6.84	-4.04	-2.50	-4.63	-1.79	7.44	6.37
10-15	36	-1.26	-0.72	3.75	2.86	2.18	0.11	-3.98	-3.58
16+	33	-0.64	3.56	9.05	6.97	2.35	-2.97	-4.40	-2.95
# Cash Crop Fields per Adult									
0.0 - .25	36	11.23	13.77	-7.69	-5.29	-14.08	-14.30	6.80	4.29
.26- .50	36	-3.85	-6.75	-1.26	0.39	-3.31	-4.97	-1.30	-0.15
.51- 1.00	48	-4.01	-3.80	7.11	4.59	4.07	5.20	-2.22	-1.29
1.01+	28	-2.62	-2.50	-0.68	-1.55	15.38	15.87	-3.28	-3.13
# Brothers and Cousins									
0	92	1.13	1.18	-4.01	-3.67	0.28	0.40	1.76	1.85
1	26	-3.49	-5.73	4.34	5.52	-2.21	0.11	-1.30	-2.58
2+	30	-0.43	1.35	8.53	6.45	1.07	-1.31	-4.28	-3.44
# Cash Crop Fields per Adult									
0.0 - .25	36	11.23	11.95	-7.69	-7.70	-14.08	-14.21	6.80	6.77
.26- .50	36	-3.85	-4.29	-1.26	-0.02	-3.31	-3.43	-1.30	-1.92
.51- 1.00	48	-4.01	-4.09	7.11	5.87	4.07	4.29	-2.22	-1.57
1.01+	28	-2.62	-2.84	-0.68	-0.13	15.38	15.33	-3.28	-3.55
# Household Consumption Units									
0-4	37	1.83	2.99	-7.30	-6.93	3.48	5.64	1.65	2.36
5-7	42	-2.17	-6.87	-3.18	-1.03	-6.07	-1.84	4.54	2.69
8-12	35	4.08	4.21	3.67	3.21	3.26	0.88	-2.83	-2.86
13+	34	-3.51	0.90	8.10	5.50	0.34	-4.77	-4.49	-2.95
# Cash Crop Fields per Adult									
0.0 - .25	36	11.23	13.72	-7.69	-6.46	-14.08	-14.30	6.80	5.41
.26 - .50	36	-3.85	-5.11	-1.26	1.24	-3.31	-5.20	-1.30	-2.09
.51 - 1.00	48	-4.01	-4.52	7.11	4.50	4.07	5.70	-2.22	-0.80
1.01+	28	-2.62	-3.32	-0.68	-1.02	15.38	15.31	-3.28	-2.89

predicted by either set of variables.

In sum, short-term migration is higher among the lower classes, regardless of which measure of class is used or which socio-demographic variable is considered simultaneously. Long-term migration is higher in larger and more complexly structured households. The higher rates of long-term migration among the upper class households are slightly reduced, yet still important, when agricultural technology is used as a measure of class. Cash cropping, as a measure of class, generally does not predict long-term migration but indicates the greater likelihood of being engaged in agricultural labor. Finally, there is no interaction between the socioeconomic and socio-demographic variables. This implies that households with a given set of socio-demographic characteristics allocate their labor in particular patterns regardless of the level of cash-earning resources.

A detailed examination of interactions among the variables suggests that among smaller households, higher long-term labor migration rates are observed only for those with traditional agricultural technology. In general, small household size and traditional agricultural technology are associated with low rates of long-term labor migration. Similarly, among larger households, higher rates of long-term labor migration are observed among households using chemical fertilizer or modern equipment. As one increases the levels of agricultural technology, medium-sized households work more as agricultural laborers, while large households work less as agricultural laborers. It seems that only the larger households are able to satisfy the increased labor requirements associated with improved agricultural technology without engaging in labor exchange relations.

Labor Exchange and Labor Allocation

It is expected that households which rely on exchange or hired-in labor will exhibit higher rates of migration. This substitution of labor from an outside source for that foregone through the migrants' absence is expected to occur regardless of socioeconomic class.

The key variable in this analysis is the percentage of a household's agricultural labor time that is exchanged or hired-in (hired-in labor time). Hired-in labor time exhibits a pattern favoring long-term migration and agricultural laboring, while reducing short-term migration and non-agricultural work (Table 4.16). The presence of navetanes, semi-permanent agricultural laborers, has the same relationship with the labor allocation variables. The pattern of relationships between hired-in labor time and the labor allocation variables persists even when controlling for agricultural technology as a measure of socioeconomic class.

Because there is rarely a financial gain involved in hiring-out one's labor, and only somewhat less rarely in in-kind payment, households which hire-out relatively greater amounts of their labor are expected to be those which also send out proportionately more migrants. Households which hire-out relatively more of their labor have lower short-term migration rates, higher long-term migration rates, a higher proportion of their adult males working as farmers and agricultural laborers, and a lower proportion as farmers and non-agricultural workers. Again, social class does not influence these relationships. When hired-in labor time is also considered, the pattern of relationships remains but the level of statistical significance is diminished; this change is due to the positive correlation between lived-in labor time and hiring-out. Both are associated with a household having a higher proportion engaged as agricultural laborers.

In short, households which are heavily involved in the process of labor exchange (whether hiring-in, hiring-out, or both) exhibit higher rates of long-term migration and lower rates of short-term labor migration. This occurs regardless of the class position of the household. We noted earlier that cash cropping required the participation of some household members in labor exchange. It is likely that better-off households are especially able to obtain the labor needed for successful cash cropping while also benefiting from the migration of a household member.

Non-agricultural Work and Labor Allocation

Households which have a greater proportion of their adult males engaged in farming and non-agricultural commercial activities are expected to have lower rates of migration. Non-agricultural commercial activities should produce enough income to substitute for migration. This relationship is expected regardless of socioeconomic class. Data not presented in tabular form show that there is a weak direct relationship between non-agricultural work in a household and higher rates of short-term and lower rates of long-term migration. This is true whether it is considered separately or with agricultural technology as a measure of socioeconomic class. There is also a clear inverse relationship between non-agricultural activities and agricultural laboring on others' fields. The relationships between non-agricultural work

TABLE 4.16

MULTIPLE CLASSIFICATION ANALYSIS OF LABOR ALLOCATION BY
LABOR EXCHANGE AND HIRING-IN AND HIRING-OUT

Independent Variable Categories	N	SHORT-TERM MIGRATION		LONG-TERM MIGRATION		AGRICULTURAL LABORING		NON-AGRICULTURAL WORK	
		UN	ADJ	UN	ADJ	UN	ADJ	UN	ADJ
Navatanes									
0	118	1.14	0.70	-0.58	0.61	-0.62	-0.33	1.65	1.16
1+	30	-4.47	-2.74	2.27	-2.39	2.45	1.29	-6.50	-4.58
Agricultural Technology									
Traditional	55	5.29	4.78	-2.49	-2.93	-0.92	-0.68	1.38	0.53
Chemical fertilizer	50	-3.09	-3.38	-3.54	-3.79	-1.15	-1.02	2.92	2.45
Modern equipment	43	-3.16	-2.18	7.30	8.15	2.15	2.05	-5.17	-3.53
% of Agric. Hours Hired-In									
0-5	49	6.76	6.20	-7.20	-5.53	-13.74	-15.45	5.38	4.32
6-19	54	-3.70	-3.31	4.21	3.59	-1.16	-0.45	-1.85	-1.48
20+	45	-2.91	-2.78	2.79	1.71	16.36	17.37	-3.64	-2.93

Agricultural Technology								
Traditional	55	5.29	3.80	-2.49	-1.16	-0.92	2.69	1.38	0.36
Chemical fertilizer	50	-3.09	-3.72	-3.54	-3.04	-1.15	1.03	2.92	2.43
Modern equipment	43	-3.16	-0.54	7.30	5.01	2.51	-4.63	-5.17	-3.28
Ratio Hired-Out/Hired-In Hours								
0	55	6.38	4.30	-8.96	-8.86	-14.08	-7.11	4.34	1.13
.01 - .99	49	-3.34	-2.23	0.24	0.34	6.79	0.10	-2.00	0.31
1.00 - 1.99	44	-4.25	-2.89	10.94	10.71	10.04	8.77	-3.19	-1.76
% of Agric. Labor Hired-In								
0-5	49	6.76	3.31	-7.20	-0.31	-13.74	-8.23	5.38	4.52
6-19	54	-3.70	-2.49	4.21	0.75	-1.16	-3.97	-1.85	-1.33
20+	45	-2.91	-0.62	2.79	-0.57	16.36	13.72	-3.64	-3.32

Note: (c) means this variable was entered first as a control variable (covariate).

and short-term migration (positive) and between non-agricultural work and long-term migration (negative) at the village level are also evident at the household level. Thus, the relationship between non-agricultural activities and forms of labor allocation operates both directly and indirectly through lower levels of agricultural laboring.

The expectation that migration rates would be lower in households where a greater proportion of dependent males have field rights is upheld for short-term migration, but the relationship is not statistically significant (data not presented in tabular form). In the case of long-term migration, the pattern does not correspond to the expectation. Therefore, whether dependent males have field rights bears no relationship to overall patterns of labor allocation. For individuals, we should recall, field rights clearly substitute for migration.

Ethnic Group, Region-Village, and Labor Allocation

Ethnic group does not serve as an important predictor of either short-term migration, long-term migration, or non-agricultural work. Region, however, is important in understanding long-term migration, agricultural laboring, and non-agricultural work. The MCA data in Table 4.17 indicate that long-term migration is highest in Sikasso, average in Kita, and lowest in the Dogon area. This relationship is unaffected by the consideration of ethnic group or the socio-demographic control variables. Region is also important in understanding non-agricultural work but the reverse pattern emerges, i.e., it is highest among the Dogon and lowest in Sikasso. Again, this relationship holds regardless of the influences of the other variables (Table 4.17, lower panel). Therefore, long-term migration appears as the preferred non-agricultural means of obtaining cash. Those in the Sikasso region generally have the easiest access to well-paying jobs through migration to the Ivory Coast. In the Dogon region, and to a lesser extent in the Kita region, long-term migration entails greater costs; hence, non-agricultural work is developed as a substitute method of generating cash income.

In the case of agricultural laboring, however, ethnic group and region are important factors. Agricultural laboring is highest in the Kita region and lowest in the Dogon region. Adding in ethnic group has little impact. Ethnic group, however, has an independent effect on agricultural laboring. When regional influence is taken into account, the rates for the Malinke and

TABLE 4.17

MULTIPLE CLASSIFICATION ANALYSIS OF LABOR ALLOCATION BY
ETHNIC GROUP AND REGION CONTROLLING FOR HOUSEHOLD
SOCIO-DEMOGRAPHIC STRUCTURE

	N	SHORT-TERM MIGRATION		LONG-TERM MIGRATION		AGRICULTURAL LABORING		NON-AGRICULTURAL WORK	
		U	A	U	A	U	A	U	A
Ethnic Group									
Malinke	25	-5.66	-8.81	2.21	2.50	-3.02	-20.39	2.78	13.73
Bambara	22	-5.97	-6.50	3.61	-8.55	0.67	1.82	-5.36	13.89
Fulani-Peuhl	27	-0.01	-2.69	4.57	2.61	23.94	9.92	-0.62	11.83
Dogon	51	6.93	10.15	-9.35	1.62	-14.08	-0.03	1.66	-25.62
Senoufo	9	-3.72	-3.66	10.39	-4.54	17.39	22.66	-7.36	13.73
Others	14	-3.33	-3.51	8.94	0.97	-1.70	-0.03	3.35	15.36
Region									
Dogon	53	6.41	-3.22	-9.38	-10.97	-14.08	-14.05	3.20	27.28
Kita	55	-2.64	3.15	1.37	-0.29	12.39	17.38	2.08	-10.95
Sikasso	40	-4.86	-0.06	10.54	14.93	1.63	-5.27	-7.11	-21.09
Ethnic Group									
Malinke	25	-5.66	-8.96	2.21	2.49	-3.02	-20.20	2.78	13.74
Bambara	22	-5.97	-7.65	3.61	-8.61	0.67	3.25	-5.36	13.96
Fulani-Peuhl	27	-0.01	-2.59	4.57	2.61	23.94	9.79	-0.62	11.82
Dogon	51	6.93	10.95	-9.35	1.66	-14.08	-1.03	1.66	-25.67
Senoufo	9	-3.72	-4.01	10.39	-4.56	17.39	23.10	-7.36	13.75
Others	14	-3.33	-4.32	8.94	0.93	-1.70	0.98	3.35	15.41
Region									
Dogon	53	6.41	-5.03	-9.38	-11.06	-14.08	-11.79	3.20	27.40
Kita	55	-2.64	3.98	1.37	-0.24	12.39	16.34	2.08	-11.00
Sikasso	40	-4.86	1.19	10.54	15.00	1.63	-6.84	-7.11	-21.17
(c) Age-Dependency Ratio									
Ethnic Group									
Malinke	25	-5.66	-7.71	2.21	2.85	-3.02	-21.42	2.78	12.54
Bambara	22	-5.97	-6.69	3.61	-8.62	0.67	2.00	-5.36	14.09
Fulani-Peuhl	27	-0.01	-1.87	4.57	2.87	23.94	9.16	-0.62	10.94
Dogon	51	6.93	9.22	-9.35	1.32	-14.08	0.84	1.66	-24.61
Senoufo	9	-3.72	-2.54	10.39	-4.18	17.39	21.61	-7.36	12.51
Others	14	-3.33	-4.06	8.94	0.79	-1.70	0.49	3.35	15.96
Region									
Dogon	53	6.41	-3.11	-9.38	-10.94	-14.08	-14.16	3.20	27.15
Kita	55	-2.64	2.85	1.37	-0.38	12.39	17.65	2.08	-10.63
Sikasso	40	-4.86	0.19	10.54	15.01	1.63	-5.51	-7.11	-21.36

(c) Ratio Consumption/
Production Units

(Continued)

TABLE 4.17 (Cont'd)

	N	SHORT-TERM MIGRATION		LONG-TERM MIGRATION		AGRICULTURAL LABORING		NON-AGRICULTURAL WORK	
		U	A	U	A	U	A	U	A
Ethnic Group									
Malinke	25	-5.66	-9.21	2.21	1.49	-3.02	-18.28	2.78	14.32
Bambara	22	-5.97	-6.62	3.61	-8.85	0.67	2.43	-5.36	14.06
Fulani-Peuhl	27	-0.01	-3.17	4.57	1.38	23.94	12.47	-0.62	12.53
Dogon	51	6.93	10.72	-9.35	3.04	-14.08	-3.00	1.66	-26.44
Senoufo	9	-3.72	-4.18	10.39	-5.86	17.39	25.42	-7.36	14.49
Others	14	-3.33	-3.39	8.94	1.26	-1.70	-0.64	3.35	15.19
Region									
Dogon	53	6.41	-2.77	-9.38	-9.84	-14.08	-16.42	3.20	26.62
Kita	55	-2.64	2.95	1.37	-0.79	12.39	-18.44	2.08	-10.66
Sikasso	40	-4.86	-0.38	10.54	14.13	1.63	-3.59	-7.11	-20.62

(c) # Household Members

	N	SHORT-TERM MIGRATION		LONG-TERM MIGRATION		AGRICULTURAL LABORING		NON-AGRICULTURAL WORK	
		U	A	U	A	U	A	U	A
Ethnic Group									
Malinke	25	-5.66	-8.81	2.21	2.36	-3.02	-20.29	2.78	13.81
Bambara	22	-5.97	-6.53	3.61	-9.80	0.67	2.74	-5.36	14.62
Fulani-Peuhl	27	-0.01	-2.71	4.57	1.71	23.94	10.58	-0.62	12.35
Dogon	51	6.93	10.20	-9.35	3.53	-14.08	-1.45	1.66	26.75
Senoufo	9	-3.72	-3.72	10.39	-7.18	17.39	24.62	-7.36	15.28
Others	14	-3.33	-3.54	8.94	-0.36	-1.70	0.96	3.35	16.14
Region									
Dogon	53	6.41	-3.24	-9.38	-11.68	-14.08	-13.53	3.20	27.70
Kita	55	-2.64	3.15	1.37	-0.04	12.39	17.20	2.08	-11.09
Sikasso	40	-4.86	-0.04	10.54	15.53	1.63	-5.72	-7.11	-21.44

(c) # Brothers & Cousins

	N	SHORT-TERM MIGRATION		LONG-TERM MIGRATION		AGRICULTURAL LABORING		NON-AGRICULTURAL WORK	
		U	A	U	A	U	A	U	A
Ethnic Group									
Malinke	25	-5.66	-8.38	2.21	7.31	-3.02	-16.04	2.78	-1.96
Bambara	22	-5.97	-6.12	3.61	-4.25	0.67	5.71	-5.36	-0.14
Fulani-Peuhl	27	-0.01	-2.31	4.57	6.91	23.94	13.81	-0.62	-2.20
Dogon	51	6.93	9.41	-9.35	-6.81	-14.08	-7.66	1.66	1.87
Senoufo	9	-3.72	-3.28	10.39	-0.24	17.39	26.55	-7.36	-0.30
Others	14	-3.33	-3.13	8.94	5.27	-1.70	3.87	3.35	1.33
Region									
Dogon	53	6.41	-2.51	-9.38	-2.80	-14.08	-6.66	3.20	0.63
Kita	55	-2.64	2.75	1.37	-4.84	12.39	13.25	2.08	3.92
Sikasso	40	-4.86	-0.46	10.54	10.37	1.63	-9.40	-7.11	-6.22

(c) Education of Head

Note: (c) means this variable was entered first as a control variable (covariable).

276

Fulani-Peuhl are significantly lowered. It appears that agricultural laboring is common among the Fulani-Peuhl, nomadic herdsmen who may need to obtain agricultural surplus food as payment for laboring on others' farms. The Senoufo are in a minority position in Sikasso and therefore more readily become agricultural laborers.

When ethnic group is considered along with village, it emerges as a significant factor only for non-agricultural work. Village, however, is important in short-term migration, long-term migration, and non-agricultural work. The high rates of short-term migration are due to the extreme values in the two Dogon villages. (These data are not presented in tabular form.) The villages where there are higher rates of long-term migration are those which are most developed in terms of commercial agriculture. Conversely, non-agricultural work is most important in the villages which have the lowest levels of commercial orientation in agricultural production. The importance of ethnic group relates to the very low rate of non-agricultural work among the Dogon (who engage in dry season vegetable production for cash earnings) and the very high rate among the Malinke, who exhibit the lowest rate of agricultural laboring.

In sum, ethnic group generally is not an important predictor of labor allocation. More particularly, it does not help explain short-term or long-term migration and is not consistently related to agricultural laboring and non-agricultural work. Region, however, emerges as significant since long-term migration is highest from the most commercially oriented region in agricultural terms; non-agricultural work is highest in the region which is the least developed agriculturally. This pattern is replicated when villages are considered.

Some Concluding Observations

It has been essential to examine Mali's social, economic, political, and demographic history in order to understand the role of labor migration in the contemporary context. Malian society has been subject to colonial and neo-colonial policies which have resulted in Mali becoming a "labor reserve" for the more profitable commercial agricultural and industrial developments of coastal West Africa. Agro-ecological conditions, contemporary developmental policies, types of colonial economic and labor recruitment policies, the mix of subsistence and commercial agricultural production, the incomplete processes of class formation, and the extent and types of migration found in Mali are similar to those which exist, in varying combinations, throughout the developing world.

Viewing Mali's rural population in relation to development in West Africa generally and vis-a-vis the urban-based political and bureaucratic structure gave overall meaning to the consideration of population processes in relation to agricultural development. Within its overall disadvantaged structural position, some definite degree of stratification exists within the agricultural sector; it is this degree of stratification which structures differential opportunities and constraints regarding the ability to engage productively in economic activities. The consideration of stratified social relations of production, both those within households and those resulting from modernization and commercialization of agricultural production, influence patterns of labor allocation and migration at the individual, household, and village levels.

The household level of analysis focused on a set of factors usually omitted from migration research. The household operates as a producing and consuming unit in the rural areas of less developed nations. As such, the productive capacity of household members, whether as villagers or as migrants, is of concern to the household's survival and prosperity.

The central finding of this analysis is that short- and long-term labor migration are quite distinct processes. The factors associated with short- and long-term labor migration are different at both the village and household levels of analysis. At the village level, the commercial orientation of agricultural production emerged as a major factor, dependent on proximity to a town for the easy marketing of its produce. While agricultural produce is, in fact, marketed over great distances in West Africa, proximity to town remains an important differentiation among villages. Commercialization of agricultural production, in turn, favors class differentiation in terms of agricultural technology and stratification of landholdings. In such villages, there is greater use of labor exchange practices and non-agricultural work is less important. Finally, this type of village is characterized by higher rates of long-term labor migration and lower rates of short-term labor migration. The small number of villages in this study and their generally low rates of short-term labor migration limit the strength of this interpretation. Nevertheless, the consistency between the village level analysis and the individual and household levels of analysis adds greater confidence to these interpretations.

At the household level, short-term and long-term labor

migration, agricultural laboring (exchange labor), and non-agricultural work were treated as aspects of a household's pattern of labor allocation. Socioeconomic class emerged as an important determinant of higher rates of long-term, and lower rates of short-term, migration. Wealthier households can afford the long-term absence of household members, while poorer households can afford only the short-term migration of members. Village location, however, determines whether or not such wealthier households exist. In this context, cash cropping was seen to diminish long-term labor migration.

The problem of the inclusion of persons as household members must be considered. It seems plausible to argue that long-term migrants are more likely to be considered household members in upper class households. Migrants from such households may be contributing to the household's welfare through remittances and there may be no strong incentive to drop them from the household tax list. This possible bias may also exist in the more commercially-oriented villages, where long-term migration rates were higher. On the other hand, those in poorer households and villages may be forced to remove non-contributing migrants from the tax lists.

Participation in agricultural laboring is also highest among those with more commercially oriented agricultural systems. Members of these households are working more hours on the fields of others as well as their own. The labor requirements of cash cropping are higher than those of food laboring; hiring-in and hiring-out of agricultural labor are mutually coincident, though most likely on unequal terms. These results suggest that commercial agricultural production does not effectively substitute for migration but supports it.

Larger and more complex households are characterized by higher rates of long-term migration. There are some limitations on the availability of, or ability to organize successfully, agricultural resources in such types of households. It may also be that they can best "afford" the "risk" involved in migration. These households have lower rates of short-term migration, agricultural laboring, and non-agricultural work.

If households are larger and more complex because they disproportionately retain long-term migrants as household members, the issue of inclusion/omission again needs to be underscored. However, if such households are viewed as relieving demographic and economic pressure on household resouces by encouraging migration, they would be most likely to eliminate long-term migrants from the household list. In this case, the issue of inclusion and omission of household members becomes much less important. What emerges is that the issue of household membership is important and deserves greater attention in future research.

When a household's socioeconomic class and socio-demographic structure are simultaneously considered, each remains important in understanding patterns of labor allocation and migration. They do not eliminate the effects of each other on these patterns and little interaction is observed.

Households which are more involved in labor exchange (either hiring-in or hiring-out) are characterized by higher rates of long-term labor migration and lower rates of short-term labor migration. Labor exchange may exhaust the time available for the short-term migration upon which other households rely. This is consistent with the fact that higher rates of long-term migration characterize upper class households and labor exchange practices are more prevalent in villages where commercial agriculture is more developed. It is also noteworthy that non-agricultural work is less prevalent in households and villages with these characteristics.

In short, the consideration of village and household factors, particularly those dealing with the socioeconomic class and socio-demographic structure of households is useful in understanding patterns of labor allocation. The focus on short- and long-term labor migration, combined with agricultural laboring and non-agricultural work, is essential in a comprehensive view of the economic activities of households.

The analysis of labor allocation and migration in rural Mali has been exploratory. Limitations of the data which were designed and collected for other purposes have restricted the more detailed measurement and in-depth analysis of dependent and independent variables. There is no doubt that the household levels of analysis merit more attention in labor migration research than has been the case to date. Issues associated with household structure and the meaning of various types of households, social and economic roles within the households, the processes of labor exchanges, and the measurement of stratification and class formation at the household level are important areas for continuing research.

Traditional sources of stratification within and between households as well as class patterns resulting from modernization and commercial orientation in agricultural production definitely influence the allocation of labor. Increasingly profitable economic opportunities in agriculture substitute for short-term labor migration by permitting or requiring greater involvement in agricultural work and labor exchange practices while stimulating long-term labor migration. Yet, village characteristics accounted for most of the explanatory power of this concept at the household level. This suggests that the existence of wealthier households, at least in terms of agricultural production, is fundamentally affected by agro-ecological conditions and the village's accessibility to an important town for the sale of agricultural produce. Key elements in future research on this issue should focus on the system of land tenure and land use as well as cooperative and competitive labor arrangements. The analysis of the means of production and the social relations of production within and between households are important areas of research.

Understanding decision-making associated with the maintenance and improvement of household welfare, in the context of Sahelian Africa, has focused on labor allocation. However, other aspects of economic decision-making are equally important in the long run. How households invest scarce resources can have significant consequences for the household's future welfare either by materially increasing their productive capacity, by diversifying sources of income, or by investing in human capital, i.e., education.

Policies which attempt to foster the development of commerical agriculture must give particular attention to the characteristics of villages where such changes take place. Principal among these is the establishment of reliable, efficient transportation systems which effectively permit widespread participation in the market for sellers of agricultural produce.

The recent course of agricultural development in Mali has simulated migration as well as increased socioeconomic class stratification based on agricultural wealth and laboring activities. The recent aims in modernizing and commercializing agricultural production may produce additional surplus for the government, while simultaneously improving the position of select households. However, the overall effect on the welfare of the rural population, which is neither benefiting from increased commercialization of agricultural production nor from the remitted income of long-term migrants, is less easily discernible. As villages become increasingly incorporated into the cash economy, changes in land tenure and use, labor exchange practices, modification of family size and structure, and the importance of household versus individual decision-making will affect the total change in the material welfare of those in rural Malian society.

References

Abu-Lughod, Janet. 1975. "The End of the Age of Innocence in Migration Theory." In *Migration and Urbanization*. Eds. Brian M. DuToit and Helen I. Safa. The Hague: Mouton Publishers.

Adepoju, Aderanti. 1977. "Migration and Development in Tropical Africa: Some Research Priorities." *African Affairs* 76 (303):210-225.

Amin, Samir. 1972. "Underdevelopment and Dependence in Black Africa- Origins and Contemporary Forms." *Journal of Modern African Studies* 10(4):503-524.

_____, ed. 1974. *Modern Migrations in West Africa*. Oxford: Oxford University Press.

Berg, Elliot. 1975. *The Recent Economic Evolution of the Sahel*. University of Michigan, Center for Research on Economic Development.

Byerlee, Derek. 1974. "Rural-Urban Migration in Africa: Theory, Policy and Research Implications." *International Migration Review* 8(4):543-566.

_____ et al. 1976. *Rural-Urban Migration in Sierra Leone: Determinants and Policy Implications*. Africa Rural Economy Paper No. 13. East Lansing: Michigan State University.

Caldwell, John. 1969. *African Rural-Urban Migration: The Movement to Ghana's Towns*. New York: Columbia University Press.

Camara, Adama. 1971. "Problems du Developement Economique et Social du Mali." No. 3033, Institute International d'Etudes Sociales, Geneva.

Clifffe, Lionel. 1976. "Rural Political Economy of Africa." In *The Political Economy of Contemporary Africa*. Eds. P. Gutkind and I. Wallerstein. Beverly Hills: Sage Publications.

Cohen, Stan. 1979. "Dogon Agriculture--A Socioeconomic Study:

A Preliminary Report." Paper prepared for the Workshop in Sahelian Agriculture, Department of Agricultural Economics, Purdue University, February.

_____. 1980. "The Pattern of Labor Use in a Dogon Village." Paper presented for the Workshop on Sahelian Agriculture, Department of Agricultural Economics, Purdue University, May.

Connell, John et al. 1976. *Migration from Rural Areas: The Evidence from Village Studies.* Delhi: Oxford University Press.

Crowder, Michael. 1968. *West Africa Under Colonial Rule.* Evanston: Northwestern University Press.

DuBois, Victor. 1975. *Food Supply in Mali.* American Universities Field Staff Reports, West African Series, Vol. XVI, No. 1.

DuToit, Brian. 1975. "A Decision-Making Model for the Study of Migration." In *Migration and Urbanization: Models and Adaptive Strategies.* Eds. Brian DuToit and Helen Safa. The Hague: Mouton Publishing Co., pp. 49-75.

Diop, Majhemout. 1977a. "Tactical Problems of the Socialist Option in Mali." In *African Social Studies- A Radical Reader.* Eds. P. Gutkind and P. Waterman. New York: Monthly Review Press, pp. 405-411.

_____. 1977b. "Workers in Mali." In *African Social Studies- A Radical Reader.* Eds. P. Gutkind and P. Waterman. New York: Monthly Review Press, pp. 263-267.

Ernst, Klaus. 1976. *Tradition and Progress in the African Village: Non-Capitalist Transformation in Rural Communities in Mali.* New York: St. Martin's Press.

Fieloux, Michele. 1978. *Mali: Internal and International Migration.* World Bank--OECD.

Fleming, Allen. 1979. "Farm Management in Kita, Mali: A Preliminary Report." Paper prepared for the Workshop on

283

Sahelian Agriculture, Department of Agricultural Economics, Purdue University, February.

_____. 1980. "The Use of Labour and Choice of Technology in Agricultural Production in the Kita Zone, Mali." Paper prepared for the Workshop on Sahelian Agriculture, Department of Agricultural Economics, Purdue University, May.

Foster-Carter, Aidan. 1978. "The Modes of Production Controversy." *New Left Review* 107:47-77.

Freedman, Ronald. 1974. "Community Level Data in Fertility Surveys." London: World Fertility Survey, Occasional Papers No. 8.

Fuller, Theodore. 1979. "Rural-to-Urban Population Redistribution." In *Population Redistribution: Patterns, Policies and Prospects.* Eds. L.A.P. Gosling and L.Y.C. Lim. New York: UNFPA.

Gerald-Scheepers, Terese and Wim M.J. Van Binsbergen. 1978. "Marxist and Non-Marxist Approaches to Migration in Tropical Africa." *African Perspectives* 1:21-35. Leiden: Afrika-Studiecentrum.

Godelier, Maurice. 1978. "The Object and Method of Economic Anthropology." In *Relations of Production-Marxist Approaches to Economic Anthropology.* Ed. D. Seddon. London: Frank Cass.

Goldstein, Sidney. 1976. "Facets of Redistribution: Research Challenges and Opportunities." *Demography* 13(4):423-434.

Goldstein, Sidney and Alice Goldstein. 1981. "The Use of the Multiplicity Survey to Identify Migrants." *Demography* 18(1):67-83.

Gregory, Joel and Victor Piche. 1978. "African Migration and Peripheral Capitalism." *African Perspectives* 1:37-50.

_____. 1979. "The Demographic Regime of

Peripheral Capitalism Illustrated with African Examples."
Unpublished paper. Montreal: Universite de Montreal,
Department de Demographie.

Gugler, Josef. 1968. "The Impact of Labour Migration on Society
and Economy in Sub-Saharan Africa: Empirical Findings
and Theoretical Considerations." *African Social Research*
6:463-486.

_____. 1969. "On the Theory of Rural-Urban
Migration: The Case of Sub-Saharan Africa." In
Migration. Ed. J.A. Jackson. Cambridge Univ. Press.

Gugler, Josef and William Flanagan. 1978. *Urbanization and
Social Change in West Africa*. Cambridge University
Press.

Gunder Frank, Andre. 1979. *Dependent Accumulation and
Underdevelopment*. New York: Monthly Review Press.

Hance, William. 1970. *Population, Migration and Urbanization in
Africa*. New York: Columbia University Press.

Hopkins, Anthony. 1973. *An Economic History of West Africa*.
London: Longman.

Hoyt, Michael. 1962. "Migratory Labor in West Africa."
Northwestern University and Department of State:
Foreign Service Institute.

Imperato, Pascal. 1977. *Historical Dictionary of Mali*. Metuchen,
N.J.: The Scarecrow Press.

Jones, William. 1970. "The Food Economy of Ba Dugu Djoliba,
Mali." In *African Food Production Systems--Cases and
Theory*. Ed. P.F. McLoughlin. Baltimore: The Johns
Hopkins University Press, pp. 265-306.

_____. 1972. "The Rise and Demise of Socialist
Institutions in Rural Mali." *Geneve-Afrique* 11(2):19-44.

_____. 1976. *Planning and Economic Policy:
Socialist Mali and Her Neighbors*. Washington, D.C.:
Three Continents Press.

285

Kahn, Joel. 1978. "Marxist Anthropology and Peasant Economics: A Study of the Social Structures of Underdevelopment." In *The New Economic Anthropology.* Ed. J. Clammer. New York: St. Martin's Press, pp. 110-137.

Kearl, Bryant, ed. 1976. *Field Data Collection in the Social Sciences: Experiences in Africa and the Middle East.* New York: Agricultural Development Council.

Koenig, Dolores. 1979. "The Socioeconomics of Farming in the Kita Region, Mali: Analysis of the Results of an Agricultural Census." Paper presented at the Annual Meetings of the American Anthropological Association.

Lewis, John van Dusen. 1979. "Descendents and Crops: Two Poles of Production in a Malian Peasant Village." Unpublished Ph.D. dissertation, Yale University.

Lipton, Michael. 1977. *Why Poor People Stay Poor: Urban Bias in World Development.* Cambridge: Harvard University Press.

Mabogunje, Akin. 1975. "Migration and Urbanization." In *Population Growth and Socioeconomic Change in West Africa.* Eds. J.C. Caldwell et al. New York: Population Council and Columbia University Press.

Matlon, Peter. 1977. "Farm-Level Data Collection in Northern Nigeria--Problems and Guidelines for Questionnaire Design." Draft.

Meillassoux, Claude. 1970a. "A Class Analysis of the Bureaucratic Process in Mali." *Journal of Development Studies* 66(2):97-110.

_____. 1970b. "From Reproduction to Production- A Marxist Approach to Economic Anthropology." *Economy and Society* 1(1):93-105.

_____. 1975. *Femmes, Greniers et Capitaux.* Paris: Maspero.

_____. 1978. "Kinship Relations and Relations of Production." In *Relations of Production- Marxist Approaches to Economic Anthropology*. Ed. D. Seddon. London: Frank Cass, pp. 289-330.

Niang, Abdoulaye. 1980. "L.P. Modelling of African Farms, the Sahel Farm Model: Case Studies--Mali and Senegal." Paper presented for the Workshop on Sahelian Agriculture, Department of Agricultural Economics, Purdue University, May.

Norman, David. 1977. "Problems Associated with the Gathering of Technical, Economic and Social Data at the Farm Level in West Africa." Paper presented at the International Conference on the Economic Development of Sahelian Countries, Centre de Recherche en Developement Economique, Universite de Montreal, October 13-14.

Raynaut, Claude. 1980. "The Contribution of the Anthropologist in the Study of Agricultural Production Systems (The Case of Maradi in Niger)." Paper presented for the Workshop on Sahelian Agriculture, Department of Agricultural Economics, Purdue University, May.

Riddell, J. Barry. 1978. "The Migration to the Cities of West Africa: Some Policy Considerations." *Journal of Modern African Studies* 16(2):241-260.

Shaw, R. Paul. 1975. *Migration, Theory and Fact*. Philadelphia: Regional Science Research Institute.

Standing, Guy. 1979. "Migration and Modes of Exploitation: The Social Origins of Immobility and Mobility." International Labour Organization, Population and Employment ProgrammeWorking Paper No. 72.

United Nations. 1976. *World Population Prospects as Assessed in 1973*. Sales No. 76.XIII.4.

_____. 1978. *Concise Report on Monitoring of Population Policies*. E/CN.9/338. 22 December. United Nations Economic and Social Council, Population Commission, Twentieth Session.

_____. 1979. *World Population Trends and Policies. 1977 Monitoring Report.* Volume II. New York: United Nations.

United Nations Fund for Population Activities. 1978. *Mali--Report of Mission on Needs Assessment for Population Assistance.* Report No. 8.

Van Binsbergen, Wim M.J. and Henk A. Meilink, eds. 1978. *Migration and the Transformation of Modern African Society--African Perspectives 1978/1.* Leiden: Afrika-Studiecentrum.

Van de Walle, Etienne. 1975. "Population Development." In *Population Growth and Socioeconomic Change in West Africa.* Eds. J.C. Caldwell et al. New York: Population Council and Columbia University Press.

Whitney, Thomas. 1979. "Dryland and Bas Fond Farming Near Sikasso, Mali: A Preliminary Repot." Paper prepared for the Workshop on Sahelian Agriculture, Department of Agricultural Economics, Purdue University, February.

_____. 1980. "Labor Utilization of Small Farms in the Bas-Fons Area of Eastern Mali." Paper presented for the Workshop on Sahelian Agriculture, Department of Agricultural Economics, Purdue University, May.

Wolpin, Miles. 1975. "Dependency and Conservative Militarism in Mali." *Journal of Modern African Studies* 13(4):585-620.

Wood, Charles. 1980. "Structural Change and Household Strategies: An Integrated Approach to Rural Migration in Latin America." Population Association of America, Denver, CO, April 10-12.

World Bank. 1976. *World Tables.* Baltimore: The Johns Hopkins University Press.

Zachariah, K.C. and Julien Conde. 1979. *Migration in West Africa: Demographic Aspects.* Paris: World Bank-OECD.

5
Comparative Perspectives on Rural Migration and Development

Calvin Goldscheider

Out-migration from rural areas to industrial cities characterized the historical experience of more developed nations and transformed their social, demographic, economic, political, and cultural patterns. Rural population movements are conspicuous features of contemporary Third World countries. Not all of these migrations have been toward urban places nor have all the movements been permanent. Indeed, there is a wide range of migration patterns which characterizes developing nations and these are only in part similar to the past experiences of industrialized nations. Systematic research on the determinants and consequences of rural out-migration in less developed nations has helped to isolate the unique features of these processes and has enhanced comparative and historical generalizations. The extent to which rural movements in Third World nations will be part of the transformation of their societies remains an open question until more comprehensive studies are undertaken.

The research reported in this book has focused on the rural context of out-migration in three countries: Korea, Sri Lanka, and Mali. These studies provide a foundation for the continuing investigation of the determinants and consequences of rural migration. The extensive volume of rural migration in the less developed areas of Asia and Africa, the large reservoir of the rural population who are potential migrants, and the wide range of migration types (from short-term to long-term; from rural-rural, rural-urban, to urban-rural; from temporary, seasonal, and permanent, to international migrations) justify an in-depth comparative analysis of rural migration and social structure.

A major finding of previous comparative research in urban

areas of developing nations was that migrants were not disadvantaged relative to the urban native population (see studies reported in Goldscheider, 1983). To the extent that any disadvantage appears, it was confined to the initial period of settlement, subsequent to arrival in the city. In the context of the rural population, the questions become: What impact does migration have on rural areas? How does the urban experience influence those returning to rural areas? What are the consequences of moving from one rural area to another? Do these consequences vary when migration is sponsored by governments or when it is voluntary? These are some of the major questions posed by the studies of rural migration in Korea, Sri Lanka, and Mali which have been detailed in previous chapters.

It is difficult to compare the results of the three studies, given their different methodologies, their various definitions of migration, their inclusion of a different range of variables, as well as the broader macro- differences among these societies. Cumulative conclusions are problematic when theoretical frameworks, methodologies, and data analysis differ. In the focus on the details of their case studies, broader comparative features were deemphasized. Nevertheless, each made important contributions to the cumulative analysis of rural migration and its relation to development. It is these general patterns which will be reviewed in this chapter.

The Determinants of Rural Migration

We begin with the fundamental premise that migration is not a uniform process, i.e., the causes and effects of migration vary with the type of migration examined. Often the various types of migration are viewed solely in terms of a descriptive taxonomy. Migrants are classified by a measure of time (e.g., short-term, long-term), an element of permanence is added, mixed with direction (urban or rural) and boundaries crossed (e.g., nations, regions, provinces, neighborhoods), and these are subdivided by who moves (e.g., individuals, families, and groups) and by whether it is forced or voluntary. For completeness, migrants are categorized by social-economic-demographic characteristics.

The importance of analyzing migration types goes beyond attempts at descriptive classification. The evidence from the three rural studies, along with the earlier comparative urban samples, points to the very different determinants and consequences of various migration types. Return rural migrants in Korea are different from one-way migrants; short-and long-term migrants in Mali have different social and economic correlates; voluntary and sponsored migrants in rural Sri Lanka differ from each other and from local migrants ("mobile" natives).

What can be learned comparatively from these studies about the determinants of rural out-migration? Our comparative review starts with return migration to rural areas of origin. In Korea, the evidence clearly indicates that rural return migrants are not negatively selected; they are not failures in the city returning to their place of origin. Indeed, rural return migrants are better educated than in-migrants who remain in the urban area. While there appears to be no overall occupational selectivity, return migrants had jobs which were less tied to urban occupational networks. They are more likely to work for themselves and tend to be young, risk-takers compared to those who migrated to the city and remained there. Their urban ties are weaker in other ways. While almost all migrants to the city had relatives in their place of origin, return migrants visited their families more frequently. They are less tied to the city through home ownership or urban organizational affiliation. In short, return migrants have more links to their place of origin, less ties to their place of destination, and are more likely to move back to their rural origins after having attained their educational and income goals in the city. They are drawn back to the areas of origin not by some primordial tie, family obligation, or direct government policy. Rather, they moved to economic opportunities in their rural areas of origin which were opening up for more educated, urban-skilled persons. Taken together, the factors associated with return migration to rural areas in Korea are very similar to the determinants of urbanward migration in many other places.

The key to understanding the return to rural areas in Korea is the changing opportunity structure. As attractive jobs in rural areas expand, people will respond. Those previously resident in rural areas are more likely to know of these opportunities (perhaps through family and friends, or through return visits) and respond to them if they are relatively better than their current job opportunities. Hence, it is not necessarily the lack of success in the city or "imperfect information" about urban opportunities but "location-specific capital" plus economic opportunities at the rural place of origin which are critical in return migration.

How important are these factors when the rural migration is part of direct government policy? When opportunities in agriculture are designed by policy to move landless peasants from a densely settled rural zone to sparsely settled agricultural lands, what role do "ties"--family and administrative--play in determining who moves? In both Korea and Sri Lanka government policies were important factors in migration. Return migration to rural areas in Korea fits in with government policies to "close" the largest urban areas, redirect industries to alternative urban centers, and invest in rural areas to create new opportunities. In Sri Lanka, government investment in peasant agriculture resulted in higher levels of rural-rural migration than rural-urban migration.

A key difference between migrants in Sri Lanka and return migrants in Korea is the education factor. In Korea, many people move from rural areas to the city to obtain an education. Those who return to their place of origin have higher levels of education than those who remain in the city. Return migrants use their urban educational attainment as a means of obtaining good jobs in their places of origin. In contrast, formal education does not have a major place in the agricultural sector of Sri Lanka and the migrant colonists there have the lowest educational levels. Therefore, education is positively associated with return migration in Korea but is unrelated to rural migration in Sri Lanka. These contrasting relationships between education and migration in rural Korea and Sri Lanka do not imply that we cannot generalize. It means that we must specify the context of rural migration so as to understand the role of education in rural development. In particular, education is tied in to exposure to modernity, work skills, and urban networks. Often, some minimum educational level is an important factor in economic mobility, the acquisition of new tastes, and the symbols of modernity. The importance of education in Korean rural migration suggests that migration is associated with differentiation and modernization. The absence of educational differentiation in Sri Lankan migration (and in Mali as well) suggests that some rural migrations are less tied to processes of social and economic development associated with education.

The key set of factors in rural-rural sponsored migration in Sri Lanka revolves around the economic viability of farming and social ties. Most everyone in rural Sri Lanka is a farmer. Migrant colonists were not disproportionately drawn from landless agricultural laborers. Agricultural laborers tended to migrate less, while peasant proprietors were more mobile. No simple relationship, therefore, emerges between social class (i.e., occupation) and migration. Rather, the stratification patterns of rural communities, particularly patron-client relationships, are of

292

primary importance. Laborers are clients who are both more secure and more economically tied in to patron control than are peasant proprietors, who cultivate small plots of land which have low levels of economic productivity. Hence, a disproportion of landowners became migrant colonists. In this sense, rural migration patterns are an integral component of the rural social class structure. Although government policy affected the structure of opportunities and specified some limited criteria (age and marital status, for example) for selectivity, the policy was neither random nor uniform in its attractiveness. The tie of individuals to a powerful system of economic, social, and political relationships was the source of selectivity, as it was the basis of social life generally. Indeed, potential migrants were screened by the local patrons who more likely encouraged peasant proprietors to move than agricultural laborers (clients).

Consistent with this were findings which showed that neither landownership nor its location within the rural area of origin precipitated the response to government agricultural policy. Inequalities in landholdings were greatest among the migrants before their move and most migrants used crops for consumption only. When crops were sold, farmers usually dealt with family relations. In general, all the measures of land show migrants to be less economically viable and less tied to others. Taking together land dimensions, non-land economic factors, socioeconomic and social ties, the Sri Lankan data, as did the Korean data on return migrants, show the powerful influence of social ties in understanding rural-rural migration. In Korea, these social ties stimulated migrants in urban places to consider returning home; ties in rural places of origin conveyed information and provided networks to facilitate the return of former residents. In Sri Lanka, the lower levels of integration of selected segments of the rural communities facilitated their response to new opportunities generated by government policy. Scarcity of land was a fundamental situation at the time of migration, but it did not effectively discriminate between migrants and non-migrants. Levels of integration are related, in turn, to the stratification of rural places, linking family units into communal networks. Indeed, at low levels of structural differentiation, as in rural Sri Lanka, the connections between family and community are strong. The changing opportunity structure and government policies operate in that context.

More generally, the evidence from Korea and Sri Lanka argues for the centrality of the opportunity structure in migration. Yet that factor, whether by government policy or other

293

developments, does not account for variation in the response to the opportunity. Just as differential opportunities are important in rural-urban and return migration, the lack of opportunities generally militates against rural out-migration to other rural areas. The lack of economic differentiation among areas (i.e., low differential opportunities) results in overall stability. Government initiatives, policies, and incentives may change the opportunity structure. In Sri Lanka, such policies have resulted in rural-rural migration. Those who are less integrated in their place of origin are more likely to be responsive to such initiatives, if they meet the specific eligibility criteria defined and implemented at the local level.

Several issues which emerge out of the Korean and Sri Lankan studies are extended in the research in Mali, the least demographically and economically developed of the three countries. Four are central in our context: (1) Levels of analysis of rural migration cannot be limited to individual decision-making units or broad societal level characteristics. Rather, they must focus on the household unit, which links families to communities. (2) Out-migration from rural areas is not necessarily permanent but involves several types. A consideration of moving decisions at the household level requires a focus on the short- and long-term absence of members from the household. (3) Migration is linked fundamentally to economic opportunities. To understand these links requires an analysis of migration in the context of labor allocation at the household level. (4) Opportunities per se are not determinants of migration and access to opportunities varies. Broad categories of access include social class and social demographic factors.

In general, the argument in both Sri Lanka and Mali is that out-migration in rural society does not directly hinge on individual decision-making nor on broad societal transformations. It does focus on the links between the community and the household. This is basically the significance of social ties and integration. Migration represents one strategy of social and economic survival of rural households. Households, not individuals, are more likely to control resources in rural areas. These include labor and skills of household members, land, capital, credit, technical knowledge, social contacts, and networks. The central question then becomes: How do households allocate these resources among opportunities known and accessible to the unit? Part of this decision is labor migration--short- or long-term. Migration, or in this framework the absence of a household member for a period of time, is too important to the survival of the household to be treated casually or left primarily to individual decision-making.

Migration, therefore, is not a marginal feature of the rural society in Mali. As elsewhere in Africa and in other less developed nations, migration occurs for economic reasons and is work-related. Many of the migrants, perhaps a majority, move across national boundaries, working in neighboring countries. The labor-related context of out-migration and the opportunities available outside of Mali result in higher migration rates among the young and among males than females. Of no less importance is the fact that heads of households and elder males do not generally migrate. Only those with marginal economic and administrative roles in the rural community are likely to move. This finding for Mali fits very well with the centrality of social and economic ties in the analysis of Korean return migration and rural-rural movements in Sri Lanka. Similarly, those with no fields to cultivate have higher out-migration rates, while those with some fields combine agricultural labor with some cash-earning activities. The absence of land or possession of non-viable agricultural holdings makes the cash-earning opportunities appear more attractive. Often the opportunities are short-term and not organized for the permanent settlement of families. The household pressure to return to areas of origin is sufficient to result in high rates of short-term labor mobility.

At the individual level several factors in combination emerge as important for out-migration in Mali. Household status, i.e., relationship to the head of the household, is important for both short- and long-term migration. Similar to Sri Lanka, education is not a factor. Ethnic group affiliation has an important relationship to migration beyond age, household status, and education effects but it overlaps, and is almost identical with, region and village. Long-term migration is more predictable than short-term migration. Where agriculture is not strong commercially and alternative cash-earning opportunities are weak, sons become seasonal migrants. In contrast, where agriculture is strong commercially, only long-term migration is evidenced and only for those with less immediate responsibilities to local agriculture.

Going beyond the individual level of analysis, the evidence for Mali shows that non-agricultural activities complement short-term mobility and conflict with long-term mobility. Short-term mobility tends to occur where the distance to towns is greater, where non-agricultural activities in rural areas are greater, where agriculture is less commercialized, where there is less use of modern agricultural equipment, where stratification of

295

landholdings is less pronounced, and where labor exchange is less important. In contrast, long-term migration occurs more frequently when these conditions are reversed. To examine total out-migration, combining short- and long-term movement, is to obscure these contrasting relationships.

Hence, the village analysis in Mali points to two major findings: (1) short- and long-term migration must be treated separately, since they are associated with fundamentally different community conditions; and (2) commercialization of agricultural production appears central in the extent to which migration--short- or long-term--occurs.

Integrating the household level of analysis with village and individual levels adds important insights into the determinants of rural out-migration in less developed nations. Social class factors affect short- and long-term migration in different ways: the modernization of agricultural technology and cash cropping diminishes the need for short-term labor mobility but increases the rates of long-term migration. It can be argued that economic modernization creates opportunities for stability as well as mobility, depending on the community level of development. Moreover, long-term migration is associated with larger and more complex households; short-term migration is associated with smaller and simpler households.

Commercialization of agriculture results in greater social class differentiation and inequalities in landholdings. Higher rates of long-term migration and lower rates of short-term migration characterize areas of greater class differences. The commercialization of agriculture is linked to transportation and market locations of villages. These create conditions which facilitate the stability of labor, except for long-term migration.

The development of agriculture in Mali results in increased migration and increased stratification and inequality. The links between inequality and migration relate to processes of differentiation in the early period of economic development. Links between development, inequality, and migration can be ameliorated by government intervention through the redistribution of land and the investment in agriculture as in Sri Lanka.

The Consequences of Rural Migration

How do migrants to rural areas in less developed nations compare to the rural populations of these places who do not move? How well are they integrated? In previous research on migrant adjustment in places of destination, the evidence, almost without exception, pointed to the positive social and economic adjustment of migrants compared to natives. But that was for migrants to urban destinations (see the studies in Goldscheider, 1983). What does the evidence show when we focus on rural places of destination?

To evaluate the consequences of migration, we need first to separate out the initial effects of the positive selectivity of migrants from the effects of living in urban areas. This allows us to control the "selectivity" effects, so as to focus on the "exposure" effects, and thereby isolate the consequences of the migration experience per se. This was most clearly and directly done in the Korean study. Using the socioeconomic status of the fathers of returnees at the time the returnees first moved from the rural area, the data showed that initial selectivity was significant, with higher socioeconomic status (fathers' education and occupation) characteristic of out-migrants compared to natives. Nevertheless, controlling for the initial selectivity, differences between migrants and non-migrants remain. Hence, migration per se had an independent impact on educational and occupational levels, and, in turn, on the higher income of return migrants and their possession of consumer items.

What specific urban experiences were most important in the socioeconomic levels of return migrants? Obtaining a formal education, at least completing high school in the city, is the most important variable accounting for the relatively higher socioeconomic status level of return migrants. Next in importance are media contacts and economic activity in the city.

Are return migrants agents of change? What roles do they play in the rural community to which they return? The evidence for Korea suggests that in many ways the migrants do not fit neatly back into the community structure of rural areas. On the one hand, only a small proportion had sent back remittances to their area of origin when they were in the city and the amounts were small, mainly for household living expenses. Nor was the flow all one way. On the other hand, larger sums of money were brought back with them when they returned for use in business activities, and these were invested in the community. Return migrants are relatively small in number and tend not to participate in activities of the community. Overall, there is no direct evidence of a significant economic or social impact on their communities.

Nor is the return of the migrants to rural places of origin necessarily permanent. Return migrants tend to be repeat migrants as well. Very high proportions (70 percent of return migrants from Seoul and 47 percent of return migrants from Daegu) intended to move back to the urban place of residence. Indeed, it becomes unclear where their place of origin is; in a dynamic view, return migration may refer either to the return to the place of origin (i.e., birth) or to the place of last residence. The reasons given for wanting to move again relate to economic factors and education of their children. Evaluated by their intentions, return migrants are temporary returnees to places of birth. It is not clear how the migratory behavior will correlate with migratory intentions. Nor is it clear whether respondents referred to their own migration intentions, their childrens', or other members of their household. These distinctions are of course critical in assesing the "integration" of return migrants in their areas of origin and in evaluating their subsequent migration behavior.

Unlike the importance of the educational factor in rural return migration in Korea, education figures less predominately in Sri Lanka. In rural-rural migration in Sri Lanka, the major consequences revolve around land use and cultivation. Since migration was designed to attract people to work new lands, it is not surprising that rural migration resulted in a marked decline in landlessness. Few specific occupational changes occurred as a result of moving, since farming was encouraged. Some individual level and aggregate changes away from farming characterize migrants, but the dominant feature is occupational stability among migrants and non-migrants. It is not clear, however, what would have been the pattern without government intervention and without new agricultural opportunities. Indeed, it may be argued that had there been no rural land policy in Sri Lanka, some shifts out of agriculture, particularly among those at the margins of viability, would have occurred. Hence, stability in the occupational and industrial sectors may be a powerful counterforce to developments in Sri Lankan society.

At the individual level, migrants are more likely to have improved their farming situation by coming to own and cultivate more of their lands as a result of the move to new rural areas. Moreover, as an integral feature of the government allocation policy, a more equitable distribution of land was found among migrant colonists than among any other subpopulation. Nor were improvements restricted to the migrants. Natives in the place of destination improved as well, even moreso than natives in the place of origin, probably because of government investments in the area. Moreover, the data suggest that government policy resulted in the provision of adequate land to the marginally landowning sector rather than in the enhancement of the amount of land owned by those who were already landowners.

Among the major consequences of rural-rural migration are the changes in the organization of agriculture. Overall, as a result of the increase in acreage, the proportion of migrants using only family labor decreased, agricultural production for commercial marketing increased, and new agricultural institutions (particularly cooperatives) developed as a major outlet for surplus produce. General living standards also improved for migrants. Housing quality increased, particularly for migrant colonists.

One feature of the migration to new rural areas, and the resultant change in the mode of agricultural production, is the changing levels of social and economic differentiation. Ties between family and community have become less integrated in the rural area of destination. The growing differentiation and increased commercialization make it inaccurate to describe the economic activity of migrants as "peasant production." The changing modernization of rural areas means an improved standard of living. In interesting ways, the areas of rural destination have become more "modern" than the areas of rural origin. Possession of consumer durables is higher among dry-zone residents of Sri Lanka than among wet-zone natives. Thus, despite their lower educational levels and lower development levels in general, residents of the dry zone have acquired the symbols of modernity.

Again, the comparative evidence from return rural migration in Korea and rural-rural migration in Sri Lanka points to the conclusion that migration improves the standards of living of the migrants. Rural migration is associated with opportunities and results in some forms of structural differentiation and development. For Mali, this has meant greater social inequalities, which does not seem to characterize Sri Lanka. Perhaps these differences reflect government policies about land distribution in Sri Lanka or the character of migration in Mali (rural laborers in neighboring countries). Household level consequences of rural migration were not specifically analyzed and require in-depth research.

Whether the policy is to decentralize industry so as to redirect migrants to areas away from the largest cities and reduce metropolitanization (as in the case of Korea) or to invest in agricultural development in underdeveloped rural areas (as in Sri Lanka), migration seems to result in an improvement among those who migrate and among natives who are in these areas. There is some sketchy but less conclusive evidence that out-migration relieves pressures--economic, social, and demographic--in areas of origin so that the standard of living improves there as well. This is particularly difficult to evaluate fully, since comparisons to what would have been the situation in the area of origin had the migration not taken place are required.

Research and Methodological Issues

The three studies in this volume, as the four studies reported in the previous collection (Goldscheider, 1983), have contributed to the systematic, comparative analysis of migration in less developed nations. In the process of trying to solve complex theoretical, methodological, and empirical puzzles, new problems have emerged. These require continuing research efforts and creative methodological strategies. The seven studies, and other recent research, have brought us to the frontiers of knowledge about migration in less developed countries. We now briefly peer beyond what we know to highlight several research and methodological issues which these studies have raised.

To cover the range of issues involved in understanding rural out-migration, in-depth surveys need to be carried out. Such surveys may be extended by making selected comparisons with relevant census data redesigned to facilitate analytic comparisons or by reanalyzing previously collected data. Supplementing the surveys in the three rural areas of Korea were comparisons with special tabulations from the 1970 Korean census. Data from a survey of migrant adjustment in urban Seoul were also used. In Sri Lanka, the focus was on surveys carried out in the rural wet and dry zones along with observations and some use of limited census data. In Mali, a secondary analysis of data collected for other purposes included detailed demographic data and observations.

One methodological lesson from these studies relates to the need to make comparisons among many different subgroups. Maximizing comparisons from different data sources covers non-migrant populations at origin and destination and allows for the inclusion of a wider range of migration types. These comparisons involve various time periods (before and after migration) and different research designs to obtain data on the determinants and consequences of rural migration.

All the studies reported in the two collections have struggled with the issues associated with capturing the process of migration using a cross-sectional research design. The use of multiple data sources--surveys and censuses--and the reconstruction retrospectively of migration histories and life cycle changes for samples of migrants and non-migrants have been creative strategies. The detailed reconstruction of individual life histories is a complex and challenging task, often with measurable limitations. While it is possible to obtain these histories at a household level, they are usually directed at the micro-level.

At the same time, community level changes are rarely incorporated in the reconstruction of individual life histories. To fully analyze the dynamics of movement between areas with multi-level relationships (individual, household, and community) and rural (and urban) social structure, a prospective dynamic research design is needed. Prospective longitudinal studies have their own limitations but remain ideals. As such, longitudinal, comparative studies of rural and urban communities, focusing on macro- and micro-levels of change over time, should be coordinated. The closer we approach the ideal, the more comprehensive our insights about the relationships between migration and social structure.

It has been repeatedly observed that the dynamics of migration operate at macro- and micro-levels: migration varies with the social, economic, and demographic changes in the society (or community) and with the life cycle and related characteristics of individuals. An additional perspective emerging out of these studies focuses specifically on household dynamics, weaving together community and individual characteristics. In particular, a different set of analytic questions may be addressed when the focus is on household structure: When do children leave the household? How are economic activities in the household managed when family members are absent? Which household members are more likely to move? When are outside laborers brought in to substitute for absent household (or community) laborers? How long can a household remain viable when sons and daughters are absent to earn money and obtain an education? How are ties among migrants and non-migrants maintained at the household level? How do households facilitate the selective movement of household members? These questions address household concerns more than individual or family migrant issues. To the extent that households are the major analytic units in rural societies, these issues are core areas of research.

Once our focus shifts to the level of households, some of the continuing theoretical, methodological, and empirical issues of migration research require reformulation. For example, the definition of migration and who is a migrant has been a continuing

301

problem in research. At the household level the question is, when does someone who has been absent for a period of time become defined as a migrant? When does return migration become repeat migration? How are short-term or circular migrants defined by the household? A fundamental and no less complex issue is how households are defined. Co-residence is one criterion, if "residence" per se can be clearly delineated. Joint economic activities, common meals, and other cooperative patterns among family members are other criteria. Defining migration and households is a problem in all societies and at all levels of analysis. These definitions are complicated in less developed countries and particularly in rural areas where short-term mobility and seasonal movements are common and where household membership and residential units are more amorphous.

A similar problem relates to how social class, status, power, wealth, and access to resources at the household level in rural areas of less developed nations should be measured. While solutions to the measurement problem can be ad hoc and appropriate at the local level, the question of comparability over time and among places is formidable.

An analogous difficulty relates to a focus on decision-making at the household level. Often, notions of individual decision-making and calculations of alternative responses in more developed societies are applied mechanically to rural places in less developed nations. If the household, however defined, is the unit for which the costs and benefits of migration are calculated, then we need to know more about how these decisions are made, who is involved in making them, and what are the relevant household costs and benefits which enter into such calculations. In this context, the costs and benefits for any particular person, including the migrant, may be different than for the household as a whole in terms of what enters into the calculation and what is the relative balance of factors. Individual and collective rationality (economic and social) may not be identical.

A focus on households, as for families, moves us away from looking at the migration of men in search of economic opportunity. We need to include in systematic ways women and children. Our questions have in the past focused primarily on why individual women migrate? How does their migration differ from men? Is it short- or long-term? Do they mainly accompany men in search of jobs? Much attention has centered on the reproductive roles of women and has examined the effects of migration on the fertility of women migrants. While these questions are of importance, they do not address the fundamental linkages between migration

302

and the distribution of roles (economic, family, and cultural) within households. What happens to women who remain in rural areas while their husbands or children work for periods of time elsewhere? Do their economic roles expand? Is their status as workers and producers altered? How are their household obligations and authority (or lack thereof) affected? Do new networks of relationships emerge for wives and daughters--migrants and stayers? The essential thrust of these questions is not toward women as individuals but toward relationships which affect and are affected by their migration and that of other household members. Even the demographic questions may be formulated beyond the individual level impact of migration (e.g., spouse separation or temporary absences) on fertility. The issues relate to the impact of migration on changing roles and statuses of women within the family and household, changing power and control over their lives by others, and, in turn, changing pressures on family formation, reproduction, and the tempo of childbearing.

The recognition of the household as a unit of analysis should not obscure the fact that empirically we obtain information from and about individuals. What the household level of analysis requires is an emphasis on the relationship between individuals and other members of the social and economic network. Placing the individual in this larger context of relationships and settings (families and communities) is the research challenge of future migration studies. Households link individuals to communities and are therefore the most fruitful analytic units to study change and variation.

It may be argued further that the dynamics of migration extend beyond the life cycle of persons and communities to generations. In Sri Lanka, for example, the government distribution of land resulted in migration to rural areas, greater equalities of landholding, and improved living standards. What happens to the children of these sponsored migrants? A division of land among surviving offspring will reduce landholdings. If there is differential fertility or survivorship among migrants, inequalities will emerge. If there is differential inheritance among offspring, some children will be more likely to move than others, either in search of better opportunities or to obtain an education so as to use other means to secure non-agricultural employment. These are, of course, classic demographic problems, which are no less characteristic of less developed countries in the 1980s than of European countries in the 19th century. Their analysis requires a focus on households and generations. The conceptualization of the relationships of migration and rural social structure in this context places the study of rural migration patterns in less developed nations at the very core of demographic theory.

The three studies reported in this volume and the four previous reports on urban areas have sensitized us to the complex selectivities associated with diverse migration streams. These complexities revolve around the range of comparative groups needed to isolate relative selectivity and the difficulties of measuring retrospectively the characteristics of migrants (various types) and non-migrants (in various localities) at the time the migrants initially moved.

The complexities of migrant selectivity need to be disentangled. Migration is selective differently when it is toward urban places than when toward rural areas--not only relative to the current populations at origin and destination but also relative to populations at the time migration took place; not only in the context of one-way permanent moves but also in terms of return, repeat, and temporary migrations.

The studies reported here have reinforced the notion of migrant selectivity at a variety of levels. Comparisons to isolate the characteristics of migrants at the time of the move involve the resolution of three problems: (a) when did the "initial" migration occur; (b) in what ways can social, economic, and cultural information be obtained from non-migrants around the time of this initial migration; and (c) how do you obtain the socioeconomic characteristics of migrants prior to their first permanent job or the completion of their education. Obtaining data on father's occupation and education is one solution; getting at the characteristics of the household of origin before the move would be valuable but difficult. Certainly, more research on this topic is needed before any definitive resolution can be offered. These problems underscore the need to move migration research beyond individual toward family level analysis.

Much can be learned by treating sectors of the society in integrated ways. A focus on rural areas is a step forward from the biases of urban studies. Yet some of the same limitations of the urban bias characterize analyses of rural areas: when examining the part we often lose a perspective of the whole. Rural areas are linked to urban markets and non-rural locations. Indeed, migration is one of the conspicuous mechanisms linking rural and urban places. The social and economic networks which integrate places are related as well to migration patterns. Our research designs need to attempt to capture this aspect of migration. Since return, circular, and temporary migration imply

304

ties among places, we need to study these linkages directly.

Indeed, the results of research on rural return migration in Korea help sharpen our focus on factors related to the positive adjustment of migrants to cities. One tentative explanation offered for the successful economic adjustment of rural migrants in urban areas has been that the urban migrants being studied represented a select residual of all rural-urban migrants. This assumed that migrants who are successful remain in the urban area; the unsuccessful return to the rural area. The methodological bias inherent in examining cross-sectional residuals suggests, for example, that the similarity in employment levels among migrants and life-time urban residents may be the result of return migration among the unemployed. In general, the move from rural to urban areas in search of jobs and opportunities when there are few available and competition is fierce can be accounted for by this "survival of the fittest" argument. The empirical evidence, however, does not fully support this argument. Indeed, return migrants in some areas are successes, economically and educationally, relative to the population at the place of origin (the rural area) and relative to the population at the place of destination (the urban area).

In the examination of the adjustment of rural migrants to urban areas, an obvious issue to be resolved is "adjustment" to what. When urban natives are the standard, the focus is on how urban-like rural migrants become, after what length of time, and along which dimensions. In the adjustment mode of defining problems, issues of competition and conflict are de-emphasized, if not ignored completely. The movement of people from one rural place to another or from urban areas back to rural areas of origin and the short-term movement of laborers does not fit conveniently into the framework of "adjustment". A more fruitful orientation focuses directly on the many layers of competition and conflict among household members or groups, in different places, over time.

Along similar lines, the community dimension has been shown to be an important level of migration analysis. Our sampling strategies need to reflect this. Ethnicity, region, neighborhood, social class, or some other feature often defines the nature of the community. We have not fully taken this into account. One strategy is to neutralize the effects of ethnic group affiliation by sampling procedures, as in the sample used in Sri Lanka. Another is to statistically control for the overlap of ethnicity and village-region as was done in Mali. Recognizing the importance of ethnic affiliation as the basis for community continuity requires careful and systematic analysis as well. In the urban area, it is clear that settlement patterns of migrants are concentrated along ethnic lines. In rural areas, it is also clear that not all ethnic groups are located ecologically or socially in similar proximity to opportunity. Distance and access are clearly related. Nor are all ethnic groups located in the same social structural position--in terms of stratification, landownership, ties to people in areas where opportunities are available, and social networks which convey information and provide support.

Ethnic variation in migration relates as well to policy issues. Often the sources of economic opportunities are government investments. It is unlikely that governments develop projects and distribute opportunities randomly. Given the overlap of ethnicity and residence, on the one hand, and relationships between ethnic affiliation, social class, and power, on the other, it is reasonable to assume that government investments in development projects will reinforce ethnic differences. As a result, it becomes even more important to be explicit about community level effects of migration policies. We need to better understand the links between ethnic community contexts, economic opportunities, and migration. Eliminating community differences through sampling and statistical controls does not adequately deal with the importance of ethnic networks.

The rural out-migration which has been reported in these three studies has been largely movements within countries. In Mali, as in other parts of West Africa, rural out-migration often is to other countries. International labor mobility across national boundaries is at times an artifact of the administrative and political designation of borders, even when they are part of an integrated labor market. It is not clear what specific features differentiate rural out-migration across borders from rural out-migration to urban or rural areas within countries. It is not clear if these differential destinations have different implications for the determinants and consequences of rural out-migration. As the process of labor mobility extends across national boundaries in more and less developed countries, research has addressed questions associated with areas of destination. More research needs to examine the differential impact of international and internal migration on areas of rural origin. In turn, there is a growing need to examine how different types of migration are related to each other. How does labor mobility relate to more permanent migration? How are international and internal migrations linked?

Three case studies are too few to provide a basis for cross-national generalization at the macro-level. Even adding the previous studies to the research cumulating on migration is not adequate. International dependencies, inequalities, economic and demographic growth rates, urbanization levels, and migration types are patterned in fundamental ways. We have examined parts of the puzzle but have not yet fully mapped the complex interrelationships. These macro-patterns require analyses using different methodologies and analytic strategies than have been used in these surveys. Yet, there is much to be learned from the detailed case studies to provide a comparative basis for generalization. There is as well a need to appreciate the complexities involved in studies of migration and development which operate at different levels of analysis. The studies reviewed here, as the earlier research on migrants in urban areas, provide a promising basis for future research in the area. They indicate clearly not only the value of the research completed but provide guidelines and frameworks for future investigations.

References

Goldscheider, Calvin, ed. 1983. *Urban Migrants in Developing Nations*. Boulder, Colorado: Westview Press.

Appendix:
Doctoral Dissertations
within the Scope of the
Comparative Urbanization Project

Completed Dissertations:

Dayalal Abeysekera* (1980)

"Determinants and Consequence of Internal Migration: The Rural Wet Zone to Dry Zone Stream in Sri Lanka"

Melvin R. Brown* (1981)

"Migrant Adjustment in Teheran

Jin Ho Choi* (1981)

"Determinants and Consequence of Urban to Rural Return Migration in Korea, 1970-77"

Robert B. Corno* (1979)

"Migrant Adjustment in Bogota, Colombia: Occupation and Health Care"

Gabriel B. Fosu* (1984)

"Modernization of Health Attitudes and Its Effects on Mortality and Fertility Behavior in Accra"

Sara C. Green (Clark)* (1977)

"Dimensions of Migrant Adjustment in Seoul, Korea"

Mahgoub E. Mahmoud* (1983)

"The Impact of Partial Modernization on the Emigration of Sudanese Professionals and Skilled Workers"

Anthony C. Masi* (1982)
"Socioeconomic and Demographic Consequences of State-Sponsored Industrialization: A Case Study of the Italsider Location at Taranto in Italy's Underdeveloped South"

Laurie McCutcheon* (1977)
"Migrant Adjustment in Surabaya, Indonesia"

Venansio Muludiang* (1983)
"Urbanization, Female Migration, and Labor Utilization in Urban Sudan"

Completed Dissertations Based on Survey Data:

Robert Mazur (1982)
"Migration and Rural Socioeconomic Structure in Tropical Africa: The Case of Mali"

Scott Radloff (1982)
"The Effect of Migration Definition on the Observed Prevalence of Migration and on Migrant-Nonmigrant Socioeconomic Differentials"

Penporn Tirasawat (1977)
"Urbanization and Migrant Adjustment in Thailand"

Ching-Lung Tsay (1980)
"Employment and Earnings of Cityward Migrants: A Study on Individual Outcomes of Migration to Taipei"

In-progress Dissertations:

Josiah Atemie*
Ethnicity and Social Adaptation: A Study of Status Change in Port-Harcourt, Nigeria

Sally Findley

"Community Structure and Family Migration Strategies in Ilocos Notre, Philippines"

Philip Guest*

"Household Labor Allocation and Labor Mobility in Rural Central Java"

Charles Lerman*

"The Determinants and Patterns of Occupational Improvement and Migration in Semerang, Indonesia"

Donna Muncey*

"The Effect of Migration on Social Structure: A Comparative Study of Two Spanish Villages"

*Funded in whole or part by the Ford Foundation Grant or by external support.

Contributors

Dayalal S.D.J. Abeysekera, Demographic Training and Research Unit, University of Colombo, Sri Lanka.

Jin Ho Choi, Korea Research Institute for Human Settlements, Seoul, Korea.

Calvin Goldscheider, Population Studies and Training Center, Brown University; Department of Sociology and Demography, The Hebrew University, Jerusalem, Israel.

Sidney Goldstein, Population Studies and Training Center and Department of Sociology, Brown University, Providence, Rhode Island.

Robert E. Mazur, Department of Sociology, University of Zimbabwe, Harare, Zimbabwe.

313